CONTENTS

DEREK ATTRIDGE

THE WORK OF LITERATURE

OXFORD UNIVERSITY PRESS

Great Clarendon Street, Oxford, OX2 6DP,
United Kingdom

Oxford University Press is a department of the University of Oxford.
It furthers the University's objective of excellence in research, scholarship,
and education by publishing worldwide. Oxford is a registered trade mark of
Oxford University Press in the UK and in certain other countries

First published 2015
First published in paperback 2017

Impression: 2

Published in the United States of America by Oxford University Press
198 Madison Avenue, New York, NY 10016, United States of America

British Library Cataloguing in Publication Data
Data available

Library of Congress Cataloging in Publication Data
Data available

ISBN 978–0–19–873319–5 (Hbk.)
ISBN 978–0–19–879890–3 (Pbk.)

Printed and bound by
CPI Group (UK) Ltd, Croydon, CR0 4YY

ACKNOWLEDGEMENTS

Although this book presents itself as a work by a single author—the only overt conversation is one with myself—it's in reality the outcome of many conversations, and will, I hope, constitute a spur to further conversations. Among the considerable number who have contributed in this way over many years and in many countries I can single out only a few to thank by name: Michael Beaney, Peggy Kamuf, John Bowen, Kate Briggs, Jonathan Culler, Ziad Elmarsafy, Tom Furniss, Ian Hacking, Nicholas Harrison, Martin Hägglund, Julián Heffernan, Peter Lamarque, Jūratė Levina, Paul Muldoon, Henry Staten, Asja Szafraniec, and Aukje van Rooden. I'm grateful too to the colleagues who invited me to give talks that led to a large portion of this book, and the audiences whose questions forced me to sharpen my thinking. A significant number of the questions I put to myself in the 'cross-examination' of Part 1 arose in these interchanges, both private and public.

The book benefited enormously from fellowships in two tranquil and supportive environments in South Africa and Italy, the Stellenbosch Institute for Advanced Study and the Bogliasco Foundation, where the staff were unfailingly efficient and helpful. A month at the Maison Suger of the Fondation Maison des Sciences de l'Homme in Paris was also immensely productive. As always, my three close family members, Suzanne Hall, Laura Attridge, and Eva Attridge, provided loving support, welcome distraction, and much laughter.

I wish to dedicate this book to the memory of Colin Gardner (1934–2013), academic, activist, and politician, whose 'Poetics' seminar in Pietermaritzburg, South Africa, fifty years ago invited me into the never-ending conversation about the meaning and value of literature.

* * *

Some of the material in this book has been reprinted, in revised form, from the following publications:

'Can We Do Justice to Literature?', *PN Review* 182 (2008), 14–20.

'Signature/Countersignature: Derrida's Response to *Ulysses*', in *Derrida and Joyce: Texts and Contexts,* ed. Andrew J. Mitchell and Sam Slote, SUNY Press, 2013, 265–80.

'Context, Idioculture, Invention', copyright © *New Literary History*, The University of Virginia. This article first appeared in *NEW LITERARY HISTORY* Volume 42, Issue 4, Autumn, 2011, 681–99.

'Afterword: Responsible Reading and Cultural Difference', *New Formations* no. 73 (2011), *Reading after Empire,* 117–25.

'Performing Metaphors: The Singularity of Literary Figuration', *The Idea of the Literary,* ed. Nicholas Harrison, Special Issue of *Paragraph,* 28.2 (July 2005), 18–34.

'On Knowing Works of Art', in *Inside Knowledge: (Un)doing Ways of Knowing in the Humanities,* ed. Carolyn Birdsall et al., Cambridge Scholars Press, 2009, 17–34.

'Once More with Feeling: Fiction, Performance and Affect', 'Affects and Performativity', ed. Alex Houen, Special Issue of *Textual Practice,* 25.2 (2011), 329–43.

I am grateful for permission to quote poems as follows:

Emily Dickinson, 'As imperceptibly as Grief', reprinted by permission of the publishers and the Trustees of Amherst College from THE POEMS OF EMILY DICKINSON: VARIORUM EDITION, edited by Ralph W. Franklin, Cambridge, Mass: The Belknap Press of Harvard University Press, Copyright © 1998 by the President and Fellows of Harvard College. Copyright © 1951, 1955, 1979, 1983 by the President and Fellows of Harvard College.

Paul Muldoon, 'The Loaf', in *Moy Sand and Gravel* (Farrar, Straus and Giroux, 2002), by kind permission of Paul Muldoon.

John Wilkinson, 'Mount Disk', in *Blackbox Manifold* Issue 9 (2012), by kind permission of John Wilkinson.

Introduction

In an uncollected story called 'As a Woman Grows Older', J. M. Coetzee's elderly Australian novelist, Elizabeth Costello, disparages her life's work in the following terms:

> The question I find myself asking now is, What good has it done me, all this beauty? Is beauty not just another consumable, like wine? One drinks it in, one drinks it down, it gives one a brief, pleasing, heady feeling, but what does it leave behind? The residue of wine is, excuse the word, piss; what is the residue of beauty? What is the good of it? Does beauty make us better people?

In response, her daughter Helen insists that her writing has 'changed the lives of others, made them better human beings, or slightly better human beings ... Not because what you write contains lessons but because it *is* a lesson'. And she reaches for a word that plays an important part in Coetzee's ethical and aesthetic terminology: 'You teach people how to feel. By dint of grace. The grace of the pen as it follows the movements of thought'.

Costello is unconvinced; perhaps Coetzee is too, though he's clearly willing at least to entertain the idea of a value for the literary that is linked to the idea of grace. In any case, to treat this fictional exchange as *containing* a lesson on aesthetics for its readers would be to go against both Costello and her daughter, and, I'm sure, Coetzee himself. Though works of literature may well offer lessons on living, and this may be an important aspect of their social value, it's not *as literature* that they do so. To treat Coetzee's story as literature is not to look for moral or other truths that can be taken away from it but to experience the verbal sequence as an *event*, an event that may leave the reader a different person from what he was before reading it, but not in any way that could have been predicted or could be presented as a concrete, categorizable effect. It's perhaps in this way that the work of literature, to echo Costello's daughter, *is* a lesson, rather than containing one, and the outcome of that lesson is not a matter of precepts learned or information gained, but a modification of the reader's outlook, or sense of the world, or emotional make-up, or some other aspect of the relation of self and other. This modification may be very slight, and there's no reason to assume that the reader who has had such an experience is fully aware of how it may have altered him or her.

This can't be the whole story, however: while the experience of a powerful literary work does feel like an event, something that happens to the reader, it is also, of course, an act. We have to engage in the willed activity of reading the work, as we do all verbal texts, and if we are to treat it as literature we have to read it in a particular way—not, for instance, for the lessons it may contain. (This is not, I hasten to add, to denigrate the reading of literary works as historical reflection, psychological evidence, moral treatise, stylistic example, or theoretical model. Much of our activity as literary scholars is of this kind, perhaps more than ever today given the material rewards offered to those who undertake projects that follow the protocols laid down by the scientific model of research.) The mode of reading that allows the literary work to be experienced as literature is not easy to describe. As well as the act of interpreting the visual or aural signifiers, as in all reading, there is, in a literary response, an act that I can only describe as *willed passivity*: an opening-up, a loosening of constraining frameworks, a readiness to be surprised and changed.

I'd like to quote from an essay that expresses extremely well this aspect of the response to the artwork, Michel Chaouli's 'Criticism and Style'. Chaouli uses the term 'exposure', glossing it as follows:

> Exposure names that way of being in which I put myself into a position such that I can be affected in ways I cannot fathom. When I lean back in the theater seat before the movie starts or walk back and forth looking for the right spot from which to take in a painting, I am developing techniques of becoming passive in the right ways. This learned passivity, this developed sensitivity is what exposes me to what is 'beyond myself', a region that names the way I remain opaque to myself. I run a risk, for I may or may not be able to grapple with what hits me. But without this exposure my experience remains aesthetically deficient. What is more, without this exposure my experience fails to open to others. For it is precisely by exposing myself to an experience I potentially fail to master that an intensive experience of art radiates beyond the confines of my self to make demands on the attention of others. (333–4)

Because the existing terminology is unsatisfactory, I've found myself using the awkward term 'act–event' to refer to the reader's engagement with the text, an engagement in which the work comes into being as a work of literature.

So, to go back to Costello's jaundiced reflection on her career as a writer, what role does beauty, or, let us say, the 'aesthetic', play in this process? Although most of us no doubt share, to a greater or lesser degree, Costello's scepticism about the idea that beauty can be accorded an instrumental value in making us better people, perhaps fewer would be prepared to say that beauty is *entirely* a mystified, ideological concept. At any rate, most of us would be willing to acknowledge that we have had experiences of deep enjoyment from encounters that seem to involve something like a traditional notion of beauty, even if we would be reluctant to claim any lasting value for these experiences. This isn't enough to account for the unique experience offered by the artwork, however; the beauty we can recall being moved by is as likely to have been natural as artistic. Kant's founding account of the aesthetic in the Third Critique is concerned much more with judgements of beauty in nature than in art. If we want to determine the *specificity* of art's contribution to human good, assuming it makes any, it's not enough to talk of a generalized beauty.

Perhaps Costello's daughter's rephrasing of the issue will help: 'You teach people how to feel. By dint of grace. The grace of the pen as it follows the movements of thought'. 'Grace' is often used to mean something close to 'beauty' (and I'll come back to this meaning), but Helen clearly feels she is doing more than rephrasing her mother's notion of the latter concept; her use of 'grace' points to a different attribute of writing. It's perhaps not reading too much into her comment to point out that 'grace' brings with it a secondary sense of 'unmerited gift'. The term may be derived from theology, but in its secular incarnation it usefully points to a frequently-mentioned feature of the creative process: that the work, or the part of it the artist is engaged on, seems to come from outside, as a kind of blessing. There are countless examples in the history of artistic self-commentary, from the notion of inspiration by the Muses to contemporary guides to creativity. One of the best descriptions of this phenomenon I know comes, again, from Coetzee: David Lurie, in *Disgrace*, is attempting to write a chamber opera,

> and astonishingly, in dribs and drabs, the music comes. Sometimes the contour of a phrase occurs to him before he has a hint of what the words themselves will be; sometimes the words call forth the cadence; sometimes the shade of a melody, having hovered for days on the edge of hearing, unfolds and blessedly reveals itself. As the action begins to unwind, furthermore, it calls up of its own accord modulations and transitions that he feels in his blood even when he has not the musical resources to realize them. (183)

The writer's experience, then, like the reader's, involves passivity; but an *active* passivity that makes a space and a time for the work, or its beginnings, to emerge, an active passivity that is able to welcome the incipient creation when it would be easy to shut it out or not be aware of it in the first place. The paradoxical nature of this active passivity is brought out in Derrida's struggle to articulate a description of unconditional hospitality, a topic we shall return to in the final chapter of this book:

> To be hospitable is to let oneself be overtaken, *to be ready to not be ready*, if such is possible, to let oneself be overtaken, to not even *let* oneself be overtaken, to be surprised, in a fashion almost violent... precisely where one is not ready to receive—and not only *not yet ready* but *not ready, unprepared* in a mode that is not even that of the 'not yet'. ('Hostipitality', *Acts of Religion*, 361)

The theological controversies that hover around the notion of grace—is it possible to achieve by one's own efforts a state of receptiveness that makes the operation of unmerited grace more likely?—have their equivalents here; we have to understand creation or invention as including both the idea of working actively towards a goal and passively allowing oneself to be surprised by what one could not have foreseen.

But what does this question of authorial invention matter to the reader? The finished work, however it came into being, is what concerns him or her. Helen, in Coetzee's short fiction, implies that the value of her mother's work to its readers lies precisely in its grace, and if we are to take this term as meaning more than elegance of expression, we must assume she believes that the writing carries with it something of that sense of the receiving of an unexpected gift, and that the reader who benefits from it does so because of that quality. We've already seen that there's a parallel between creator and receiver. The reader's active passivity in opening him- or herself to the work repeats the writer's strenuously achieved openness to what cannot be compelled into existence, and the literary experience is not simply a response to a beautiful form, as would be the case with a natural object, but of a created entity that in its beauty—if it's perceived as beautiful—bears witness to that original openness. (Twentieth-century art in particular has taught us that beauty is by no means an essential ingredient; the pen blessed by grace in its following of the movements of thought may in fact be tracing shocking ugliness.) Drawing on Levinas and Derrida, I've described this openness elsewhere as a hospitality to the other, on the part of both the artist and the one who responds fully to, who welcomes and does justice to, the work of art. This is not, of course, a matter of psychological equivalence between creator and receiver; the reader gains no access to the private world of the writer. I like Blanchot's way of putting it in *The Space of Literature*:

> Reading draws whoever reads the work into the remembrance of that profound genesis. Not that the reader necessarily perceives afresh the manner in which the work was produced—not that he is in attendance at the real experience of its creation. But he partakes of the work as the unfolding of something in the making. (*The Space of Literature*, 202)

Helen's 'grace' is not her mother's 'beauty', then, and an important aspect of the former concept is the uncertainty associated with it. If it's unmerited, if, finally, there is no way this quality can be actively achieved, if it's always a surprise—to writer and to reader—it always may not manifest itself. The next poem we read or reread, may not take us unawares with its precision or penetration, its richness or shapeliness, its uncanniness or urgency. (All these, and many more qualities, I take to be included in a notion of literary grace.) Cultural history shows clearly the chanciness and changeableness of literary value, and when one reaches a certain age, personal history does too.

So literature *does* make something happen, I'm arguing, and not just if its literary dimension is ignored and it's treated as sermon or history or philosophy. I'm a different person from what I would have been had I never picked up a book or attended a play. A society in which art has flourished is not the same as one in which it has been stifled. But since these literary effects arise from a multiplicity of singular experiences and the changes they produce may not be registered consciously, it's impossible to predict or accurately chart them. And it's important to register that they may be changes for the bad as well as for the good, since the openness to alterity that I'm suggesting lies at the heart of both artistic production and artistic reception means that there is no possibility of knowing in advance what one is opening oneself to. It also means that the value of art can't be instrumentalized;

as soon as a critic—or a regime—seeks to specify in advance the kind of experience the work of art should produce, it is programming what is inherently and constitutively unprogrammable.

How, then, does the work of literature, as an event, produce effects? Let me go back to Helen's description of her mother's accomplishment as a writer: 'The grace of the pen as it follows the movements of thought'; clearly, although she advances this comment as an alternative to the issueless beauty her mother excoriates, some notion of *formal* achievement is implicit here. While the concept of beauty suggests stasis, the grace invoked in this statement is inseparable from movement, and points to a notion of form as something that *happens*. A literary work is a verbal text that, when read in the appropriate manner, gives pleasure through its manipulation, in a temporal medium, of the formal properties of the language—though 'formal properties' must be understood in the widest sense, including not only sounds and shapes, rhythm and syntax, but all the ways in which language engages with meaning, through reference, metaphor, imitation, allusion and so on, and all the ways in which writers either fulfil or thwart generic expectations of narrative, character, voice, point-of-view, stanza, scene, etc. The literary is to be found wherever these properties are exploited in a verbal event—and this includes the historian who builds up narrative tension, the preacher who makes use of regular rhythms, the journalist who employs a telling metaphor.

Elizabeth Costello's achievement, according to her daughter, is to have been able to follow, in her writing, the movements of thought; but Helen has already asserted that what she does is 'teach people how to feel', and I wouldn't want to make too clear a distinction between thinking and feeling in this context. The experience of the powerful literary work, when read as literature and not as something else, is an affective and somatic as well as an intellectual one, and it's not possible to separate these dimensions. The feelings engaged are not simple: pleasure, certainly, but underlying this pleasure, or passing through it, are a range of emotions, in complex and shifting combinations that we lack a language to describe with any precision. And this, again, is an aspect of the formal dimension of the literary work as event. To speak of the moving grace of a poem, play, or novel, is to use 'moving' in a double sense. The didacticism in Helen's statement is, it's true, not easy to accept; but we might read it as an attempt to articulate the way in which the literary work, experienced as an event rather than as an object, alters readers through affect as much as, if not more than, through intellect, through feelings as much as through meanings. To be taught how to feel is not to be put in possession of some content or even instructed in some skill; it's to have one's affective sensibility enlarged or refined through an experience. This, then, is how one might understand Helen's claim that her mother's art has 'changed the lives of others, made them better human beings, or slightly better human beings'.

* * *

What, we now have to ask, is the role of the literary critic, with respect to the moving grace of the literary work? (And I would include in this category the teacher and the reviewer of literature.) T. S. Eliot, in 'The Function of Criticism', famously insisted that 'a critic must have a very highly developed sense of fact', and judged that a fact 'even of the lowest order' is 'a better piece of work than nine-tenths of the most pretentious critical journalism' (*Selected Essays* 19, 21). Indisputably, the critic must get his facts right, and providing pieces of relevant information that the reader may not be in possession of is a useful contribution to an understanding of a work. But if literature has the kind of value I've been suggesting, and if that value can only be realized when the work is approached with a certain openness and readiness to be surprised, the recitation of facts isn't going to get us very far. I recently read some volumes published in a series which aims 'to provide accessible and informative introductions to the most popular, most acclaimed and most influential novels of recent years'. The subjects were novels that had evoked a range of feelings in me from exhilaration to dismay, abhorrence to admiration. These short books do with great proficiency what they are supposed to do: they accessibly inform new readers about the author, the setting, the critical reception, the themes, the adaptations. Plenty of Eliot's facts. But nowhere do they convey to those readers *why* they are among the most acclaimed novels of recent years. Nowhere is there a sense that the critic has been moved—let alone changed—by the work in question. And in this these books are typical of the numerous introductions to literary works and authors pouring from the academic presses.

Now it might be argued that what I've described is not the job of the critic who has been asked to provide an introduction; and presumably the same argument would apply to the teacher with a group of students being introduced to a work or an author. Eliot might have taken this line (though he wouldn't have liked the emphasis in such introductions on 'interpretation'). But doesn't this approach reduce literature to something other than literature in the fullest sense, to mere collections of fictional statements that can be situated and interpreted, logged and examined? What is the value of this activity, other than the accumulation of cultural capital? Not that there is a simple alternative: one can attempt to convey what a work has meant to you, but this can quickly deteriorate into the merely subjective and impressionistic. What is required is testimony to the particularity of the work's power, intellectual and affective, that at the same time points very precisely to the features that have produced this response; and given that the sources of our most profound responses are probably obscure to us, this is a tall order. Most of the assertions claiming that a particular facet of a work produces a particular effect can, without difficulty, be matched with an invented sentence or line that contains the same feature and produces a quite different effect, or none at all.

The critical response can't *prove* anything about a work; but it can affirm and convey a work's singularity for a particular reader. A minimal requirement is careful description and honest testimony. (Although much now seems outdated in the essay that lies behind Eliot's, Matthew Arnold's 'The Function of Criticism at the Present Time', it's worth holding on to his insistence that criticism requires 'inflexible honesty', exercised without putting the critical activity at the service of a political or religious cause). It's very easy to be seduced by the appeal of the ingenious new interpretation, and the need to compete in the academic arena adds to the impetus towards cleverness in multiplying ideas rather than honesty in conveying one's own response. And, as Gérard Genette points out with admirable realism, 'it also sometimes happens that when various factors—conformism, snobbism, ideological interferences—induce us to feign a judgment that is not our own, our judgment can then be affected by what we say, since it's never easy to differentiate between what we feel and what we think we feel, or wish to feel' (*The Aesthetic Relation*, 197).

Furthermore, the critical work is itself a verbal text that can draw on the resources of the literary: although both Eliot and Arnold are in no doubt that criticism is a different, and lesser, activity in comparison with what the former calls 'autotelic' literary creation, there is nothing to prevent the critic from using these resources in registering her response. The value of criticism lies primarily in enhancing the reader's experience of what I term the work's singularity, alterity, and inventiveness, though it may well have intrinsic value itself as a result of its own singularity, alterity and inventiveness. Of course, nothing can guarantee the success of the critical enterprise; the fate of the critical text, like that of the literary work itself, is in the hands of its readers or hearers.

* * *

This book assembles a number of talks and essays in which I have explored these and related issues, with a central focus on the question of the distinctiveness and value of the cultural practice we call 'literature'. My title, apart from its obvious meaning, is intended to suggest that literary practice is indeed work, in both creation and reception, although—in the latter case, at least—it is always pleasurable work. (A literary theorist who has exploited the same ambiguity in a title is Genette: the argument with which *The Work of Art* culminates is most concisely summed up in the jacket copy: 'The work of art is always already the work that art does'). Some of the chapters are revised versions of articles published elsewhere, and my hope is that in bringing them together with new material I've succeeded in providing a fuller account of the richness and complexity of literary writing and reading than I was able to do in my earlier book *The Singularity of Literature*, which was designed to be read without the commitment of a significant amount of time. That book was the product of several decades of engaging with, thinking about, and teaching literary works, and of studying literary theory and philosophical aesthetics. It went through several revisions during the writing, thanks partly to rejections by a number of publishers, and I trust some of the weaknesses in my initial draft were removed in the process; but I was aware that, in aiming to write a book that was both short and as accessible as I could make it, I had to move rather rapidly over a number of complex issues. I've tried not to lose sight of the needs of the reader without specialized knowledge, although this study does delve more fully than the earlier one into existing, and sometimes competing, theoretical accounts of literature and the literary, accessibility and clarity have remained important goals.

There will be frequent references back to *The Singularity of Literature*, for which I apologize; since this book is conceived to some degree as a supplement to that one, I've found repeated self-reference inevitable. Like the various supplements mentioned in Rousseau's writing, this work has a double function: it both adds new topics and arguments to what was covered in the previous study and supplies some of the detail absent from that book. No prior knowledge of the earlier book is assumed, however—nor, in fact, is any familiarity with philosophical traditions or literary theory, as I've tried to make explicit any arguments I'm endorsing, qualifying or resisting. In the first part I've attempted to deal with the most telling criticisms that I've encountered or that I'm able to produce myself when examining my earlier arguments. The best way I have found to do this is to set the chapter out as an interview; this strategy has enabled me to muster counter-arguments as strongly as I can, while providing space for responses that I hope are convincing. I've also used this chapter to clarify or expand upon points that were dealt with quickly in the earlier study; and where a topic merits more attention than the format of the interview allows, I've devoted a separate chapter to it. Each of the chapters may be read on its own (and I've permitted myself a certain amount of repeated exposition of key ideas to make this possible), but they have been planned to make a reading from start to finish a cumulative one. It will quickly become clear that the guiding theoretical figure is Jacques Derrida (whose discussion of the supplement I have just invoked), with Emmanuel Levinas a secondary influence. But it will also be clear that I've drawn on a number of other philosophers, literary theorists and literary critics in producing a synthesis that I hope does justice to what I value and enjoy in the works I read and re-read.

PART I

CHAPTER 1

The Singularity of Literature

A CROSS-EXAMINATION

What is 'literature'?

Q *In 2004, you published a short book entitled* The Singularity of Literature *in which you advanced a number of interconnected ideas about the distinctiveness of the literary work as a cultural phenomenon in the Western tradition. Your account of literature emphasizes a number of special qualities which you claim literary works possess: for example, they expose the reader to otherness; they have the capacity to change the reader's ways of thinking and feeling; they stage the power of language as it operates in a number of different dimensions. In stressing these remarkable qualities, aren't you limiting the category of literature to a very small number of texts? Don't most works of literature provide their readers with pleasure of a more limited, but still valuable, kind? It could be argued that you've generalized from the experience a reader might have of* Les Liaisons Dangereuses *or* In Memoriam *or* Ulysses *to all literary works.*

A I accept that my use of the term 'literature' is narrower than some familiar uses, and it clearly has implications of value. Setting aside the employment of the word to mean 'all written texts' or 'all written texts on a particular topic', senses which are irrelevant for our purposes, it can be used more specifically to refer to all texts of a fictional nature, or all texts belonging to a recognizable literary genre, or all imaginative writing (though problems remain with the terms 'fiction', 'literary genre', and 'imaginative'). This is what has been called the *classificatory* sense of literature. But it's noticeable that dictionary definitions of 'literature' invariably include an evaluative element—just to pluck a few off the Internet: 'writings having excellence of form or expression and expressing ideas of permanent or universal interest'; 'imaginative or creative writing, especially of recognized artistic value'; 'written works, esp. those considered of superior or lasting artistic merit'.

Perhaps what we really need are two words, one for the broader category, without any implication of value, and the other for the narrower, evaluative category. One way of characterizing the difference might be to distinguish between the class of all works of literature and those we would want to call *works of art*—though I acknowledge that this still leaves all the problems of definition in place. (I shy away from using lower and upper case to mark the difference: to write about Literature would perpetuate exactly the kind of privileging I want to avoid.) What is distinctive about the texts that constitute the body of literature in the first, general sense, I would argue, is that these texts can be experienced as *events* in addition to being interpreted as sets of meanings, and that this experience involves a particular kind of pleasure for the reader. (I should note here that when I use the term 'reader' I'm in fact referring to all the ways in which literary works are received, including reading on the page, reading aloud, reciting from memory, listening to someone else read or recite, or watching a play or film.) Literature *as art* involves a particular kind of experience that, although taking a host of different forms, can be characterized summarily as an opening to otherness. One test that serves to differentiate between the two categories is *re-reading*: works that operate as literary works of art tend to gain richness and power with re-reading, while those that are literature only in the broad, classificatory sense tend to gain nothing, and perhaps to lose something; whatever they have to offer the reader is complete when the initial reading is over. This is not to imply that the literariness of the text—and from now on I will use 'literature' and its cognates to refer to the narrower category—is something fixed in advance of its being read; until an attempt is made to read it *as* literature (I'll come back to what this means) it isn't possible to say whether or not it belongs to this class.

Nor is literature by any means a permanently constituted body with clear boundaries: which texts turn out to have literary qualities varies from period to period, from cultural group to cultural group, perhaps even from individual to individual and, for the individual, from reading to reading. And in any period, there will be texts that are not conventionally labelled 'literature' that nevertheless lend themselves to a literary reading. I should add that to experience a text as a literary event doesn't preclude interpreting it in other ways at the same time: I can read Plato's *Ion* as a work of literature while simultaneously learning from it about the institution of the Ancient Greek rhapsode and following the stages of a philosophical argument about poetry and knowledge. I also need to stress that the division between what I'm calling literary works of art and other literary works is not a division between 'high' and 'popular' literature; a widely read crime novel may well be, for most readers at least, inventive (and if it stands the test of time, like the works of G. K. Chesterton, Dashiell Hammett, or Raymond Chandler, it probably is). Nor, of course, are the uses to which literature has been put immutable; there have been immense shifts in the social function of the works we now categorize in this way. This shouldn't prevent us from accepting that in the present cultural context they operate as art, whatever their original function; in discussing how literary practice takes place today we aren't engaged in an exclusively archaeological exercise.

Literature as art does more than provide pleasure, then: these are works that open the reader to new horizons, or, following Levinas, bring the 'other' into the reader's habitual frameworks of consciousness and affective life, and effect some degree of change in the reader. (The term often used in analytic aesthetics to refer to the response called forth by the artwork, 'appreciation', seems to me too limited, implying only that the respondent finds the work to be of value, but says nothing about the kind of value, or the kind of pleasure, at stake.) This may make it sound as if I'm limiting the category of literature to a few masterpieces, but this is not the case. I'm distinguishing between a reading experience that affords pleasure through the confirmation of existing attitudes and habitual values—the enjoyment of familiarity, as when a novel follows a formulaic plot with stock characters—and one that affords pleasure by revealing unexpected possibilities of thought and feeling (including new formal possibilities for the genre in question). A poem may use a metaphor that fuses two concepts hitherto kept separate in my mind; a novel may explore, through the depiction of a character, a quality of emotion I have not encountered before; a play may reveal the comic potential of a domestic situation in a way that is new to me.

To provide textual testimony, let me compare two novels I happened to read in sequence recently; both are indisputably literature in the classificatory sense, but I experienced their literary qualities as works of art very differently. The first was William Boyd's *Any Human Heart* (published in 2002) and the second Kate Grenville's *Sarah Thornhill* (published in 2011). Both are lengthy novels tracing the history of an individual in that individual's own voice, and thereby engaging with the wider history of a society during the period spanned by their lives. *Any Human Heart* is written in the form of a series of journals, stitched together by an anonymous narrator, reflecting the experiences of one Logan Mountstuart from his early twentieth-century childhood in Montevideo, Uruguay, to his death in France in 1991, aged 85. During his long life he meets, and in some cases becomes friendly with, many of the famous figures of his time, including Pablo Picasso, Ernest Hemingway, Virginia Woolf, Evelyn Waugh, the Duke and Duchess of Windsor, Frank O'Hara, and Ian Fleming, and witnesses at first-hand several of the century's most momentous events, including the General Strike, the Spanish Civil War, and the Nigerian Civil War. *Sarah Thornhill*, Grenville's continuation of the saga of the Thornhill family which began in *The Secret River* with the transportation to Sydney of William Thornhill, traces in a first-person retrospect the life of William's youngest child Sarah as she matures from headstrong adolescent to troubled adult with a growing sense of being the beneficiary of a historic wrong, and finally has to face and live with the knowledge of her father's vicious treatment of an aboriginal community. In discussing these novels, I am, of course, reporting my own response, though in doing so I am, as is always the case when one does this, reflecting the norms and expectations of a particular cultural formation. That many other readers with somewhat similar backgrounds would disagree with some or many of the points I'm making is an indication of the complex and contradictory currents that operate in the constitution of that formation.

My enjoyment of Boyd's novel as it unfolds stems largely from curiosity about the various worlds with which he engages—such as the world of the English public school and the Oxford college of the 1920s, Republican Spain during the Civil War, the Bahamas under the Governorship of the Duke of Windsor during the Second World War, the New York art world of the 1950s, and 1970s London and the Continent during the era of left-wing terrorism. Though the major characters are fictional, a large number of the walk-on parts are not, and the context in which they live their lives is equally a representation of historical reality. I have to trust that Boyd has done his research (the novel has footnotes and an index that help to bolster my confidence), and that I'm learning authentic facts about the way specific individuals talked, dressed, and went about their business. In other words, my pleasure is similar to that which I obtain from a well-written historical account—though that pleasure is somewhat reduced in the case of the novel because of the always-present possibility that a given detail is fictional.

Are there any aspects of my engagement with the novel that one could call specifically literary? The experience of the literary work, I've argued, always involves a sense of the language's power—to arouse, to dismay, to endear, to celebrate, to terrify, to console—and style is therefore central to the distinctiveness of literature. We enjoy a successful metaphor because it creates a new connection within our conceptual universe, but also because it shows off how language can be creative—and also how a skilled author can achieve such creativity in language. (The question of metaphor is the subject of chapter 6 of this book.) *Any Human Heart* seldom generates this sense: although

Mountstuart is supposed to be a successful novelist his journals are written in dull prose, having recourse to cliché in the occasional descriptive passages (her lips were a livid gash in her face, wraiths of steam rose from the manhole vents, the lake was a sheet of burnished silver). When, in old age, the journal becomes overtly 'poetic' in its descriptions of landscapes and sunsets, it never surprises the reader with a fresh simile or unexpected adjective.

There is also very little sense in the novel of the onward propulsion that characterizes many literary works: the establishment of a degree of tension that draws the reader on in the hope of resolution, what Roland Barthes termed the 'hermeneutic code'. The opening of any autobiographical text will invite some anticipation: how is this life, begun thus, going to turn out? But Boyd makes very little of this potential for the arousal of expectations: one episode simply follows another in a life that could take any direction at any time. While the journal form creates a certain immediacy (though it remains an implausible device, like the letters of an eighteenth-century epistolary novel), the lack of any authorial hindsight (apart from a few rather clumsy interventions by an older hand) removes one possible source of dramatic irony. Occasional enigmas arise—who owns the Miró paintings that provide financial stability for Mountstuart later in life? who is responsible for Mountstuart's incarceration during the Second World War?—but these tend to fizzle out without resolution. Late in the novel, the secret of the repeated defacement of a plaque commemorating the apparent Resistance hero in the village of Sainte-Sabine does create short-term tension, though the explanation is given woodenly in a 'memorandum'. By and large, the language is unexceptional and the ingredients of the life-story familiar, and there is a certain kind of pleasure to be found in this familiarity.

I'm not suggesting that content is relevant to the literary experience only in so far as it is put into play as enigma or plot-momentum; the opening up of previously unknown or unacknowledged territory is one way in which literary works—novels in particular—may change the reader's conceptual world. (Think of the impact of Chinua

Achebe's *Things Fall Apart* on its European readers.) One dimension of *Any Human Heart* that works in this way (for me, at least) is its portrayal of male sexuality; for instance, after thousands of novels in which the universal phenomenon of masturbation is silently passed over, it features as a normal part of Mountstuart's life. In this respect, the novel, by virtue of its content, is inventive as literature—not that one learns anything, but that a portion of human existence is given literary expression and thus one's sense of the operation and limits of literature is altered. The novel has been very popular, I would guess because it has much to offer the reader whose primary interest is in content, and particularly historical content. I must admit to being bored by it a great deal of the time.

Sarah Thornhill, by contrast, took hold of me at once. The distinctive and compelling voice that begins its own story conveys both a lack of formal education in its use of non-standard English and a creative capacity in the freshness of some of the language:

> The Hawkesbury was a lovely river, wide and calm, water dimply green, the cliffs golden in the sun, and white birds roosting in the trees like so much washing. It was a sweet thing of a still morning, the river-oaks whispering and the land standing upside down in the water.
>
> They called us the Colony of New South Wales. I never liked that. We wasn't new anything. We was ourselves.
>
> The Hawkesbury was where the ones come that was sent out. Soon's they got their freedom, this was where they headed. Fifty miles out of Sydney and not a magistrate or a police to be seen. (3)

Not only are we drawn to the speaker, we're given crucial information in an efficient but natural way; and our expectations of a narrative full of interest—we are to hear about a place of great beauty populated by ex-criminals—are aroused. (If we've read Grenville's earlier novel, *The Secret River*, this information is unnecessary, but the opening still works as a re-initiation into the magical and terrible world of the Hawkesbury.) We're kept involved by the inventiveness of style, the fascination of the subject-matter, and the tension in the unfolding narrative as young Sarah begins to understand the violent origins of her relatively comfortable circumstances (origins of which the reader may or may not be aware, resulting in two different reading experiences). The events of the novel have a larger significance, representing as they do the brutal treatment of the indigenous population of Australia by European settlers, a brutality which many readers will find wholly relevant to present conditions; but few readers will be ignorant of these facts before starting the novel. It works as literature not by imparting knowledge but by enabling the reader to feel, for a few hours (and then in memory), the intensity of a consciousness exposed to the particular passions, marvels and horrors of this time and place—and by generating pleasure in the author's handling of language. It's not possible for me to say how I was changed by my experience of Grenville's novel, but I'm certain that I was.

Literariness, I should add, is not a constant absence or presence in works like these. *Any Human Heart* comes to life as a literary work from time to time; *Sarah Thornhill* isn't artful uses of language all the way through. And different ways of reading will produce different works: reading for content and the enjoyment of the familiar will generate a different work from reading with an alertness to the new, to the inventiveness of language and genre, to the possibility of surprise. Once again, it's important to stress that these two modes of reading aren't incompatible: they can easily co-exist in a single encounter with a work, and in fact the first mode provides the necessary background to the second, since it's the expectation of continued familiarity that makes possible the experience of surprise. It's possible, of course, for a reader who has no desire on a particular occasion to do anything but read for the pleasure of the familiar to find moments of surprise merely irritating and a bar to full engagement with the work. My interest, though, is in the reader who is open to whatever challenges to the familiar the work has to offer. These need not be earth-shattering; works of literature can provide all sorts of minor pleasures of this kind, refreshing longstanding assumptions, casting old ideas in a new light, introducing unexpected formal variations.

Q *Isn't it the case, then, that in order to be realized as work of art the literary text has to be read by a special kind of reader, one who has been trained in a certain way and possesses certain skills of interpretation?*

A To be able to read in this way doesn't require a long apprenticeship; it's more a matter of attitude and willingness than expertise. Oscar Wilde names the 'temperament to which Art appeals' 'receptivity'; education, he says, is no guarantee of an ability to do justice to the work of art, since 'an educated person's ideas of Art are drawn naturally from what Art has been, whereas the new work of art is beautiful by being what Art has never been' (*The Soul of Man under Socialism*, xx). Dickens was a great innovator in the form of the novel, but most readers who enjoyed—and still enjoy—his innovations had and have no special training in the reading of fiction. Anyone can have the openness to new thoughts and feelings, the readiness to be surprised, the capacity for careful attention that literature demands. Having said this, there's no doubt that the more widely you read, the more fully you engage with your cultural surroundings, the more you gain a sense of earlier periods, the better reader you are likely to be. More texts will yield themselves as literary, and you will gain more pleasure, and be more affected by, the works you read.

Q *But are you arguing that we* should *use the term 'literature' in a normative way because it's more useful or clearer than current usage? Are you trying to impose a meaning on the term that it doesn't normally have?*

A Not at all: I'm trying to identify what is commonly meant by the term when it's used to name a positive experience, and a category of writing that elicits that experience. It's true that this usage can be vague, and doesn't always distinguish literary experience from other experiences—enjoyment of a good meal, say, or an attractive sunrise—but I'm trying to extract from the common way of speaking those features that distinguish literature as a distinctive cultural practice, a distinctive use of the language. 'I loved the way it introduced...'; 'There was such a vivid description of...'; 'I couldn't help laughing when...'; 'There was something creepy about...': these and a thousand other off-the-cuff comments are testimony to the experience of literature as a mental and emotional event that made a mark on the reader.

Q *But in* The Singularity of Literature *you claim that the term 'literature' isn't definable, because it challenges the very procedures of definition.*

A Yes, it's a claim I stand by, and I believe to do so is not out of line with the common understanding of the word. In an earlier book, *Peculiar Language,* I traced some of the attempts down the centuries to define literature (or 'poetry', as it was likely to be called in earlier periods), showing that a crucial element in the definition was always an indefinable remainder, a *je ne sais quoi,* and that in the end it was only this unspecifiable element that constituted the difference between the literary and the non-literary. This doesn't mean that the ways in which literature operates in our own culture are beyond description, but any attempt, including mine, to fix the centre and boundaries of the concept (which is not really a concept), and to predict its future, is subject to revision. 'Literature' doesn't name an object, but an experience that involves a particular type of engagement between a mind and a text; and it's a necessary feature of that experience that it challenges fixed boundaries and firm predictions.

The literary event

Q *A great deal of philosophical ink has been spilled, and a vast number of philosophical pixels activated, in pursuing the question of 'the ontological status of the work of art'. (Many of these are treated in Richard Shusterman's useful study,* The Object of Literary Criticism.*) You identify yourself with the tradition that sees the work as having its existence in the readings, or performances, given to it. As you know, this is one of many positions that have been adopted in these discussions, all of which have been contested by other philosophers and literary theorists. What is the basis of your claim?*

A My thinking has been animated for a long time by the question of literature's distinctiveness among linguistic practices: what is different about a novel or a poem in comparison with a letter, a factual article, an opinion piece, a sermon, a historical study, a scientific treatise, a philosophical argument, an after-dinner speech? Various attempts to distinguish literary texts from other kinds of text by means of the analysis of inherent features have failed; there is no way literature can be defined by its inherent properties, as I tried to show in *Peculiar Language*. Even if someone were to devise a computer program based on all existing works classified as either 'literary' or 'non-literary' and capable of making a sharp distinction between the two categories, the next significant literary work could defy its predictions and render the program worthless. Nor is it possible to determine what is literary by reference to the author's intentions; there are countless examples of texts written without the intention to produce anything like literature in its modern sense or that of any of its predecessors ('belles lettres', 'poetry', 'poesie') that we now happily read as literature, and many works intended as literary that we read as documents of another sort. And it's clear that we can't identify the work with any particular embodiment in a physical object: there would then be as many *Dunciads* as there are material copies. The literary work comes into being only in the event of reading.

Q *Wouldn't an alternative approach to the question be to understand the distinctiveness of the work of literature as a matter of* potential: *a work is literary if, when read in the appropriate manner, it provides the experience you are talking of? The work would then inhere neither in material instantiations nor in readings, but as a type, an ideal form, possessing certain properties.*

A This characterization runs into trouble when you take account of the fact that the body of potential literary works would have to include all texts that could have been read or at some point in the future could potentially be read as literature, even if this has never happened and will never happen. And it's hard to imagine *any* text that could be definitively excluded on this basis, given the changeability and unpredictability of the boundaries of what can be treated as literature. (We're in Stanley Fish territory here: he argues in 'How to Recognize a Poem When You See One' that no inherent properties are required for a text to have the potential to be read as a poem). We have no way of knowing whether any given text may, at some point in the future, be readable as a literary work.

Of course, this is a theoretical, universalizing rather than a practical, real-world statement. If we limit ourselves to a particular cultural context (which could be interpreted narrowly or broadly) the idea of literary potential becomes more usable. A work of literature as constituted within a given cultural context, then, would be a linguistic text that, when read in the appropriate way, yields a literary experience. (What we currently think of as 'literary experience' is itself open to change, of course; I'm only talking about the present state of affairs). However, we would still have no way of knowing the status of any particular text until the test of actually reading it had been carried out. Moreover, cultural contexts are unstable and changing, so literary potential is not a permanent characteristic.

Q *But surely the common understanding of a 'literary work' is that it is a thing, not a happening?*

A It's true that if pressed on the question of the status of the 'work of literature' most people would probably speak in terms of an object rather than an event (without thinking through what kind of object this might be). However, when someone refers in conversation to a 'work of literature' the phrase often carries the implication—not necessarily conscious—of an *experience* of enjoyment, interpretation, perhaps puzzlement, an experience recalled or imagined or heard about. In these cases it's neither a reference to an ideal object—the type of which all texts are tokens—nor to a physical object—the particular book in which the text is lodged, but to an event. A 'work of philosophy' or a 'work of scientific writing' seldom has the same connotations—or if it does, it suggests the speaker has read the work in question in part as a literary work.

Q *By treating literary works as events, you foreground the temporality of the reading process. Don't you overlook the importance of the* spatial *dimension of some works? Most of our reading is done through the eyes, not the ears, after all.*

A Yes, of course, space plays a crucial role in a number of our literary experiences. Free verse, to name just one example, relies on the spatial arrangements on the page to signal that it is poetry, and to enable the exploitation of both the consolidating effect of the line and the fracturing effect of the line-break. But literature's spatial properties are all perceived and processed *in time*; even concrete poetry has to be taken in by the eyes and mind as a sequence. My argument isn't confined to the obviously temporal arts like literature, music and film; painting and sculpture have their being as art in the temporal event of being looked at (and perhaps touched).

Q *It's noticeable that in discussing literary practice you use both* text *and* work*; yet you don't seem to use them in the way enshrined so influentially by Roland Barthes in the essay 'From Work to Text'. Are you deliberately challenging Barthes's use of the terms? What is the difference between them in your thinking?*

A Barthes's essay was important to me many decades ago in highlighting the creative role of the reader and challenging critical approaches which sought to limit the meaning of a novel or a play to what can be ascertained about its production. But if I ask myself what happens when I read literature (or most non-literature, for that matter) I have to acknowledge that I'm conscious of the fact that these words have been selected and organized by an author.

I may not know who the author is, or have nothing more than a name to go on, but the words have the quality of what I've called *authoredness*. (Kant's notion of 'purposiveness without purpose' bears some relation to this idea, though Kant finds this quality in nature as well as—and more importantly than—in art.) And when it's literature that I'm reading, this dimension is particularly important, because my awareness is of the author's inventive activity. So in referring to literary uses of language I like the word *work*, with its implication that that creative labour is not something left behind but something sensed in the reading. The other important implication of the term *work* is, as I've said, that the work's existence—its ontological status, if you like—is not as an object but as an event; *work* can be a verb, after all. If I wanted to be pedantic, I would use *working* instead; and it might be helpful to hear this behind my use of the shorter word.

The term *text*, on the other hand, refers to all types of linguistic entity. We can include in the category of 'text' the literary exemplar conceived simply as a string of words, as they might be 'read' by a computer. If I read *Conrad*'s novella 'Typhoon' in search of information about seafaring practices at the end of the nineteenth century and for that reason alone, I'm reading it as a text—a series of signifiers whose conventionally endorsed meanings I'm familiar with. (To be more philosophically precise, the text of 'Typhoon' is a type of which I'm reading a token, say the version published in a particular collection of Conrad's stories; there are many such tokens, but only one type, which has no material existence apart from its tokens. When I refer to the text of 'Typhoon', then, I'm referring to the type.) It's true that the marks on the page or sounds in the air are only language for someone who possesses the requisite knowledge that renders them legible as letters or phonemes, and words and sentences constructed out of these; nevertheless, it's possible to say that the text has a meaning independent of any reading—even if humanity were to be wiped out, a computer could still interpret stretches of signifiers as linguistic utterances.

If I read 'Typhoon' as literature, on the other hand, enjoying it as an event rather than trying to extract any information from it, I'm still reading the text, but I'm now experiencing it as a *work*. The 'workness' of the text, in other words, lies in the effects it produces in a reader—and this is something a computer could not be programmed to encompass. Strictly speaking, I don't read a work, I only read a text; but in reading it in a certain way (assuming it's the appropriate kind of text) it comes into being as a work. Large numbers of readers have read the text in this way, and each time this has happened the text has been realized as a work; but the work 'Typhoon' has no existence outside these readings (which include, of course, Conrad's own readings and re-readings as he wrote the text). It has, however, acquired a degree of stable identity as a work thanks to the process of repeated interpretations and correction of others' interpretations—what Stefan Collini has called 'cultural Darwinism' (*Interpretation and Overinterpretation*, 16). The literary text is one which is potentially a work for any reader who has the necessary skill. (As we've noticed, however, the test of literary potential is usable only within determined cultural limits.) I will admit that I sometimes use, as shorthand, formulations that fail to keep the work–text distinction clear: it's easier to say 'I read a work' than 'I read a text as a work'—but the former should always be taken to mean the latter.

Several versions of this distinction have been proposed by theorists of aesthetics. For instance, Mikel Dufrenne begins his magisterial *Phenomenology of Aesthetic Experience* by distinguishing between the 'work of art' and the 'aesthetic object' (where the word 'work' is on the side of what I'm calling 'text'). Genette comes closer to the terminology I'm using, as the following comment suggests: 'To identify a text... is one thing, to identify the work that immanates in it is quite another, for the work is the way the text *operates*' (*The Work of Art*, 245). (For Genette, 'immanence' names the object in which the work of art consists, in contrast to 'transcendence', which refers to the ways in which it may function beyond the presence of that object.)

Literary works may in time lose their literariness, and become merely texts that reinforce what is acceptable and familiar. Blanchot describes this process as follows: a work may become 'graspable' in time, and when this happens,

> it expresses or it refutes what is generally said; it consoles, it entertains, it bores.... At this juncture what is read is surely no longer the work; rather, these are the thoughts of everyone rethought, our common habits

> rendered more habitual still, everyday routines continuing to weave the fabric of our days. And this movement is in itself very important, one which it is not fitting to discredit. But neither the work of art nor its reading is present here. (*The Space of Literature*, 206)

Q *Where exactly is the work to be located, then? Is it a psychological event in the mind of the reader?*

A Not quite: the work is a realization of the text *as it is experienced in my reading* (that 'as' meaning both 'when' and 'in the manner in which'). If I'm attempting to write a critical study, the work I'm referring to is likely to be the product of several readings. In a statement like '*Moby-Dick* was published in the middle of the nineteenth century' it's to the text, that is, the type of which all material manifestations are tokens, that I'm referring; whereas the statements '*Moby-Dick* changed my sense of the natural world' or '*Moby-Dick* plays an important role in America's self-understanding' probably refer to the literary work—in the first case, to my experience of the text as a work of literature, in the second to a conception of the work as realized in its readings that has acquired broad agreement.

Q *What do you mean by the word 'experience'? It sounds like a rather vague term from traditional humanistic criticism, suggestive of individual psychology. How far would you agree with Adorno, who objects that without historical awareness, artistic experience 'degenerates into empathetic appreciation'? Adorno makes a strong pitch against the idea of the immediate experience of art—'Many artworks of the past, and among them the most renowned, are no longer to be experienced in any immediate fashion and are failed by the fiction of such immediacy'—and his recommendation is that a 'stubborn semblance of spontaneous accessibility . . . be destroyed to permit their comprehension'* (Aesthetic Theory, *348–9).*

A I realize I use the word 'experience' a great deal, and I need to clarify that I'm not employing it to refer to an empirical psychological event nor to a model of literary reading which privileges immediacy over cultural and historical depth. French and German present different terminological difficulties. In French there is no corresponding verb to the noun *expérience* (which can also mean 'experiment'); the nearest term is *éprouver*, with its suggestion of testing. Levinas says that he prefers to use the noun *épreuve* rather than *expérience*, because the latter implies the mastery of the I ('Entretien', 108). Adorno, following Benjamin, usefully distinguishes between *Erlebnis*, or an immediate experience in the present, and *Erfahrung*, or cumulative experience—the latter being appropriate to an understanding of the artwork. These terms are usefully discussed in Barbara Cassin's remarkable *Dictionary of Untranslatables.*

Adorno's complaint about the idea of immediacy is of a piece with his view that 'aesthetic experience first of all places the observer at a distance from the object' (*Aesthetic Theory*, 346). This argument worries me: to thus dismiss the reader's impression of an intimate connection with a powerful work of literature, the feeling that it speaks to one with transformative directness, sometimes to one's innermost being, is to elevate the academic's way of responding over that of the untrained reader. When Adorno says that it's essential to an experience of a Beethoven symphony that one hear in it the echo of the French Revolution (349), he is privileging a small minority of listeners—and, for that matter, offering a classroom cliché that is as likely to diminish as enhance a full engagement with the work. (I discuss this question of historical context more fully in chapter 5 of this book.)

In spite of what I've just said, I'm sympathetic to Adorno's contention that 'not experience alone but only thought that is fully saturated with experience is equal to the phenomenon [of the artwork]' (349)—though one might also advocate experience fully saturated with thought. I'm not arguing for total immediacy: what is distinctive about responses to artworks, in contrast to experiences of the world outside art, is an awareness of the medium—in literature, the creativity with which the language, the forms, the generic expectations, have been handled. (Chapter 9 deals with this question in relation to the affect generated by literary works.) The experience of a literary work is of a staging of reality, of emotions, of language's capacities.

The experience of immediacy that I value and that Adorno is so distrustful of *is* an illusion, brought about by a coincidence between two sets of norms that might be historically very distant, and to engage with the work fully is not to strip oneself of all one's inherited knowledge and predispositions ('prejudices', Gadamer would call them) but to bring them to bear on what one is reading, always ready to have them altered or challenged. A useful approach is that of Krzysztof Ziarek, who argues in *The Historicity of Experience* in favour of a notion of experience he calls 'poietic' (as opposed to psychological or empirical), stressing its capacity to transform the everyday.

An alternative would be to talk of the 'encounter' with the work, which has the advantage of lacking those psychological connotations you mention, but to me this word suggests a rather limited relation, in terms both of its intimacy and its duration. I sometimes find myself speaking of 'living through' a work of literature, a phrase that conveys a stronger sense of the closeness and fullness of the relation; but 'experience' remains the most convenient term, for all its problems.

Q *So the work of literature is a completely subjective event? One of your reviewers, Timothy Clark, commented that your critical practice 'can drift towards becoming a kind of particularized reader-response' and that 'something rather too close to subjectivism seems to threaten' (397). Is your position that of Pater, who famously wrote in the Preface to* The Renaissance, *in a rebuttal of Matthew Arnold:*

> 'To see the object as in itself it really is,' has been justly said to be the aim of all true criticism whatever; and in aesthetic criticism the first step towards seeing one's object as it really is, is to know one's own impression as it really is, to discriminate it, to realise it distinctly. The objects with which aesthetic criticism deals—music, poetry, artistic and accomplished forms of human life—are indeed receptacles of so many powers or forces: they possess, like the products of nature, so many virtues or qualities. What is this song or picture, this engaging personality presented in life or in a book, to ME? What effect does it really produce on me? Does it give me pleasure? and if so, what sort or degree of pleasure? How is my nature modified by its presence, and under its influence? (xxix)

A I like Pater's emphases on the importance of honesty to the critic's own response to the artwork, on the role of pleasure, and on the changes the work brings about; and I approve of his insistence that the work can't be considered 'in itself' separately from an individual engagement. (His approach to art is premised on the centrality of beauty, which—for reasons we will need to come back to—is not something I would agree with.) When I try to do justice to the power and value of a literary work in a commentary, of course, I have no option but to base my discussion on my own experience of it, though I hope to be able to enter into conversation with others in my community in order to sharpen and deepen that experience.

To call the experience 'subjective' is misleading, however, since this term implies random variation among readers, whereas any individual's reading of a work is determined by a personal cultural and ideological history, and a resultant set of techniques, preferences, habits and expectations, that overlap considerably with those of others in his 'interpretive community', to use Stanley Fish's phrase. That is to say, I belong to a group whose members share a great many of my own mental and emotional habits and norms—or, to be more exact, I belong to a series of groups that operate in concentric circles, each one sharing less with me than the one inside it—and my reading practices are in part determined by those habits and norms. Instead of the term *subject* I've used the term *idioculture* (derived from the notion of *idiolect* as the unique version of the language system employed by a single individual) in order to signal the cultural constitution of any reader.

It's also important to acknowledge, though, the individual reader's capacity for creativity, which would not be possible if reading was completely determined by past and present cultural norms and proclivities. Creativity is possible because an idioculture is a singular nexus of such materials, one in which contradictions and tensions keep open the chance of the emergence of the new, and thus of a challenge to the wider culture. We will have to come back to the notion of singularity, which is operative in the writing process as well, but I will postpone a full discussion to chapter 3.

Q *While we're on the subject of the literary work as event, it will be appropriate to quote part of the philosopher Peter Lamarque's response to a piece you contributed to the colloquium on his book* The Philosophy of Literature *published in the* British Journal of Aesthetics *in 2010:*

> To *identify* a work with each token reading... seems unmotivated and counterintuitive. It implies that to read a work is to read a reading; that a work only exists as long as a particular person takes to read it (after which it ceases to exist); that no two people ever read the same work; that authors do not create works, only readers do...; that there is no one work *Pride and Prejudice,* but as many works as there are readers of the text; that there is no difference between evaluating a work and evaluating a reading of a work; and as each work is identical to a reading, then no reading can be deemed inadequate or limited in relation to a work. (101)

That seems pretty devastating as a critique...

A I'm grateful to Peter Lamarque—with many of whose views on the nature and function of literature I am in sympathy—for pushing hard on this point, and making me articulate my position more clearly. Let me pick up Lamarque's list of objections, which he formulates as what he takes to be the transparently ridiculous implications of my argument.

'*To read a work is to read a reading.*' I'll be coming back on more than one occasion to the paradox involved in the reading of the literary work, whereby the work one reads only comes into being in one's reading. But to clarify my argument, let me reiterate the distinction between text and work: the object, or, more accurately, the set of verbal signs embodied in a particular object, that pre-exists my reading is the *text*. When I read this text with the openness and attentiveness demanded by literature, I experience it as a *work*. The statement 'I read a work' is shorthand for this process.

There's a different sense in which one reads a reading, however: to read a text as a work implies a certain awareness of what one is doing as one reads. Simply to consume a novel for its content, with no enjoyment of its form, no sense of an author, no pleasure in the handling of language, is to read it as a text; to read a work is to enjoy the experience of language's power to move, to inform, to dispute, to dismay, and so on.

'*A work only exists as long as a particular person takes to read it.*' For this to make sense in the terms I've been sketching, we need to revise 'it' to 'the text', or better 'the text as a work'. With this amendment the statement is almost true: the primary existence of 'Typhoon' as a work is in the readings given to the text. I say the statement in this revised form is 'almost' true because the memory of the works we've read also plays a part in our literary experience. If I can call to mind not just the content but the language of parts of 'Typhoon', and continue to enjoy it in this way (that is to say, as a temporal unfolding), it has an enduring life for me as a work.

'*No two people ever read the same work.*' I see no problem in this assertion, though for Lamarque it appears to be patently absurd. A clearer way of putting it would be that no two people ever realize the text as a literary work in exactly the same way (and the same is true of the same person reading the text twice). This principle of the infinite changeability of the literary work is an instance of what Derrida calls 'iterability', that is, the openness of the sign to new contexts that allows it to preserve its identity. If a work remained frozen in the contours of sense and feeling that it produced when first created, it would have no continuing life at all. Of course it *would* be absurd to say 'no two people ever read the same text'.

'*Authors do not create works, only readers do.*' While it is true to say that there is a sense in which readers may be said to create works—I've discussed 'creative reading' as the kind of reading that literature calls for—it's not true that literary authors just write texts which readers then make into works. The process of literary composition, as I've tried to show, parallels in many respects the process of literary reading; and to write inventively—which involves constant reading and re-reading—is to experience one's own emerging text as possessing literary qualities, as engaging with and making available the hitherto unthinkable and unimaginable. Authors, then, can be said to write *works*. Of course, the writer has to hope that his own sense of the 'workly' potential of his text is confirmed by his readers. The continuities and ruptures in cultural history, and the interactions constantly taking place among different cultures, mean that texts are subject to a variety of arbitrary forces making them available in one time and place as literary works and unavailable at other times and places.

'There is no one work "Pride and Prejudice", but as many works as there are readers of the text.' This statement constitutes no problem for me, if we change 'readers' to 'readings' and add, at the end, 'as a work of literature'. Again, the logic of iterability is what is operating here: *Pride and Prejudice* is only able to survive as a work because it is different each time it is read. There is only one *text*, of course, leaving aside the different versions an editor might uncover, which is the type of which all texts are tokens; but the work *Pride and Prejudice* is remade each time it is read. (Whether *Pride and Prejudice and Vampires* is an iteration of the work *Pride and Prejudice* can only be determined by the experiences of readers and the ensuing cultural discussion—if there is one.)

'As each work is identical to a reading, then no reading can be deemed inadequate or limited in relation to a work.' This is true, but tautological, which is of course Lamarque's point: no work can be inadequate in relation to itself. But the non-tautological version, 'No reading can be deemed inadequate . . . to a *text*', is clearly not true: many readings of *Pride and Prejudice* are inadequate and can be shown to be so through the invocation of appropriate generic, historical and linguistic norms. That there is no single adequate reading is, I think, uncontentious; this is due to the fact that every reading deploys a different set of strategies and criteria, emerges from a different cultural background, and distributes attention to different aspects of the text differently. Arguments about better and worse readings are often about which of

these is most appropriate, and although consensus may well emerge at a particular time or among a particular group, it's unlikely to be permanent.

Q *Is there such a thing as a 'correct' interpretation of a literary work, then?*

A If 'correct' means 'fixed for all time', then there isn't, for the obvious reason that the meaning of a work changes as the context within which it is read changes (while, thanks to the logic of iterability, remaining the same work). But if 'correct' means 'appropriate to the time and place in which the reading takes place', then the term has some purchase. At least it makes sense to have a discussion about the correctness of this or that reading of a text; there may be no final resolution, but we know the kinds of evidence that would be considered valid at the time of the discussion, and disagreements, if not abolished, can be refined. The dispute may turn out to be about the kind of correctness being sought—correctness for what purpose or in what arena. The once-famous debates between the New Critics or Scrutineers and the Old Historicists were debates about what an interpretation is and the relevance of historical and biographical evidence to it. (Two celebrated disputes erupted over Andrew Marvell's poetry: between Cleanth Brooks and Douglas Bush over the 'Horatian Ode' and between F. R. Leavis and F. W. Bateson over 'A Dialogue between the Soul and Body'.) Behind the debates about particular poems lay a much wider disagreement about the proper form of the study and teaching of literature. But may the readings not sit side by side as representing different kinds of correctness?—one a description of how a contemporary reader with some literary sophistication and a little general knowledge can enjoy and be affected by the poem in question, the other an attempt at a scholarly reconstruction of how the poem might have been read in its time. The interesting further point is that the former type of reader, studying an example of the latter response, might well find the poem has changed as a result of the historical information provided—a change which is not a matter of applying a new framework to the poem, but of actually *finding* it different, thanks to the newly acquired knowledge.

Literary invention

Q *You argue not just that what you call the 'act–event' of invention succeeds in introducing into the familiar landscape of a culture a way of thinking, seeing, feeling, or handling language that is new to that culture, but that its exclusion from the culture up to that point is more than a matter of chance. The culture, you claim, is sustained by its exclusions, and the artist finds a way of accessing a part of this excluded realm, through the inventive handling of the given materials of the art-form. Why do you think it's necessary to take this further step: isn't it enough to say that the writer brings into the culture something it has never before acknowledged, for whatever reason?*

A This may be the most challengeable part of my argument, and to some degree it's an empirical matter that has to be tested against literary history.

The theoretical argument goes as follows. Take a culture at a given moment in time (this, of course, is a simplification: there's no such thing as 'a culture', only cultural constellations, large and small, constantly changing; but the simplification will help us get to the heart of the issue): it's made up of the sedimentations of its particular history, manifested in the practices, dispositions, norms, limits, emotional tendencies and mental contents that characterize its members and sustain it as a viable, if fragile, whole. This is the context within which the artist works. The realm of ideas, feelings, technical possibilities and formal arrangements that the culture does not acknowledge is infinite, and most of the original works that artists or would-be artists create—works that differ, that is, from anything that has been created before within that culture, and hence draw on that infinite realm—have very little impact; they simply add something different to what exists. What the writer—the 'serious' writer, if you like—is striving for is an original creation that will effect a change in the culture, through the changes it brings about in its readers, and through the new possibilities it introduces for future works. This is what I've called *invention*, which names both the process and the artefact. (Sometimes the process is not conscious, as in the case of works whose literariness emerges only for a later generation.) I've distinguished between invention, which, although it's usually achieved by an individual, is something that happens to a culture, since it has never come into being before and opens up new possibilities for other artists, and *creation*, which is something that has never happened to the particular individual before—though it may have occurred to many other individuals. In 'What is Creativity?', Margaret Boden has termed these 'historical creativity' and 'psychological creativity'.

Such an invention can only come into being if the cultural norms are challenged by the new thing introduced, which means that in some way its relation to the culture is not neutral, but in tension, even antagonistic. I've stressed that the concept of otherness is necessarily relational, a point that not all users of the term acknowledge; to be other is to be other *to* an existing state or entity or subject. So the otherness which tests the culture, which demands a change in the culture in order for it to be apprehended, must be an otherness which the culture excludes, not one which just happens not to have been acknowledged. And for a culture to exclude a possibility, and to have to change if that possibility is to be admitted, implies that it has depended on that exclusion in order to sustain its existence.

Since this excluded realm is, by definition, out of reach to anyone constituted by the culture that has excluded it—that is, to any idioculture formed within the broader cultural context—the task of the writer is to exploit symptoms of the exclusions in order to make a space for otherness to enter. These symptoms are to be found in the inconsistencies, strains, fractures, and stoppings short that mark any culture at a given moment. Many features of the culture no longer possess the force and value they once did; they have become routinized, overused, exhausted. A somewhat similar argument in the realm of science that has become very familiar is Thomas Kuhn's theory of paradigms, whereby a governing set of assumptions about the world throws up an increasing number of anomalies until a breakthrough results in the establishment of a new, hitherto inconceivable, paradigm. The writer cannot know in advance what that otherness will look like: hence the repeated descriptions by artists of the created work as coming from somewhere else, appearing of its own accord, and hence, too, the frequent accounts of artists who doggedly pursue a hunch or uncertain glimmering of something to be achieved without any concern for the size of the potential audience or material reward. Let me quote just one of potentially thousands of comments; this is Zoë Wicomb:

> Not even for myself do I write: an impossibility, since in confronting the blank page there seems to be no pre-existing self. (The self I know would rather slouch in a hammock, sipping something or other.) Rather, eerily, in that process of forging a narrative, of discovering what I am writing, a strange self seems to wonder at the text that is painstakingly being formed. ('The Challenge is to Capture Marginal Stories').

In the Introduction, I quoted a fictional example from Coetzee's *Disgrace*.

Theoretical discussions of the coming into existence of the 'new' don't always acknowledge the testimony of creative artists (or, for that matter, scientists, mathematicians, philosophers, engineers and many others); Michael North, for example, has written an entire book with the title *Novelty* that makes no reference to such testimony or to the extensive discussion in continental philosophy of the 'other' and the 'event' (as an unpredictable occurrence—the arrival of otherness—that brings about a change). The logical problem North identifies in any concept of the 'new'—nothing can be new in itself, since newness names a relation with a previously existing state of affairs—disappears when we recognize that the grasping of otherness by means of an invention is an event (and, from the point of view of the creator, an experience). I tend to avoid words like 'new' and 'novelty' because, as North stresses, what is regarded as new is often a repetition of something old; 'invention', with its previous meaning of 'finding' and its links with words like 'advent' and 'event'—from the Latin *venire*, 'to come'—is truer to the phenomenon I'm describing. (Readers of Derrida will recognize my indebtedness to his essay 'Psyche'.)

I must stress that otherness, and hence cultural (and idiocultural) change can be of many kinds. One obvious area is ideology: the writer challenges reigning assumptions that arise from domination by a particular class by introducing perspectives that those assumptions exclude. But other possibilities lie in the texture of human relations, in the emotions that are allowable on particular occasions, in ideas about the physical or psychic world, in the formal arrangements of literary art. The exclusion I've referred to shouldn't be taken as necessarily something to be judged unfavourably; the example of ideology is somewhat exceptional in this regard, as most exclusions are not the product of a particular system of power.

The closest argument to mine that I've encountered is Wolfgang Iser's in *The Act of Reading*, building on Roman Ingarden's work. Iser's contention is that 'all thought systems are bound to exclude certain possibilities, thus automatically giving rise to deficiencies, and it is to these deficiencies that literature applies itself' (73). The reader, then, 'can reconstruct whatever was concealed or ignored by the philosophy or ideology of the day, precisely because these neutralized or negated aspects of reality form the focal point of the literary work' (73). By contrast, 'didactic literature', he notes, 'will generally take over intact the thought system already familiar to its readers' (83). Iser gives, as one example, the manner in which *Tristram Shandy* recodes Lockean philosophy, finding a solution to the weakness of Locke's associationist premises in human sociability. Iser's argument, however, leaves no space for other kinds of recodingr; for example, inventive writers usually produce formal and generic innovations as well as exploring new types of content or new modes of thought.

The model proposed by Bourdieu for what he calls 'great *symbolic revolutions*'—the specific example he discusses is Baudelaire—is also close to mine, although I would extend the model to all inventive artistic achievements. Such authors, he argues, all 'find themselves placed before a space of already made possibles, which, for them and them alone, designates in advance a *possible to be made*'. He continues:

> This impossible possible, both rejected and called for by the space which defines it, but as a void, a lack, is what they then strive to bring into existence, against and despite all the resistances which the emergence of this structurally excluded possible induces in the structure which excludes it and in the comfortably installed occupants of all the positions constitutive of that structure. (*Pascalian Meditations*, 92)

An example will, I hope, make this structural event clearer. Let's consider a young poet at the Inns of the Court in 1590s London by the name of John Donne. We know very little about the actual circumstances of Donne's composition of satires, elegies and love lyrics in this period, but we know that he circulated them to close friends but was opposed to wide circulation and even more to publication. Let's suppose the year is 1595 and young John is trying his hand at a love poem. We can imagine him reading Spenser's sonnet sequence, *Amoretti*, published in that year, and thinking, 'These are well-turned poems, but there must be a way of using the language to create something with more fire in it.' He would probably have got hold of a copy of the rather poor edition of Sidney's *Astrophel and Stella* published by Thomas Newman in 1591, and been somewhat more impressed by Sidney's ironic take on the Petrarchan tradition of passionate address to an idealized and resisting beloved than by Spenser's Neoplatonic encomia. We're told Donne was a great theatre-goer, and perhaps among the plays he had seen in the first half of the 1590s were some of Shakespeare's early works, which could have included the very different representations of sexual relationships in *The Taming of the Shrew*, *Love's Labour's Lost*, and *Romeo and Juliet*. He might well have wondered; Why can't the short poem achieve that degree of liveliness, that verbal manifestation of intense passion?. He had many opportunities to discuss poetry with other writers undertaking legal studies at the Inns of Court at this time, including John Marston, Joseph Hall, John Davies, and Edward Guilpin, and no doubt shared with them an admiration of the Latin verse of Juvenal, Martial, Catullus, and Ovid. Here a different question arose for him: how can the English language be made to achieve the vividness and directness of these poets—Juvenal's cutting satires, Martial's concentrated epigrams, and the erotic love poetry of Catullus and, above all, Ovid?

So Donne attempts a Petrarchan sonnet addressing a mistress. Too formal, too starchy, too rigid. Why not let the lines fall into different lengths, thus varying the iambic pentameter with shorter segments? And what about a rhyme scheme that doesn't follow an existing pattern, but will keep the reader on her toes? Why not vary the old ti-tum-ti-tum occasionally, as if the feelings being expressed are so strong they can't be restrained by regular metrical alternation? As he writes and rewrites, he finds his love-poem becoming a little drama, occurring in an identifiable scene that the reader is invited to imagine, rather than an unsituated, extratemporal declaration of feelings. What might powerful sexual attraction lead the lover to think or say—for instance, when the light of the morning sun penetrates the curtains after a night of delightful sex? Donne would have been aware of one precursor: the thirteenth poem of the first book of Ovid's *Amores* has the poet begging the dawn not to hurry, allowing that farmers should be called to the field, oxen to the yoke, plaintiffs to the law-courts, but not that he should be divided from the girl lying so sweetly at his side. But Ovid took nearly fifty lines to spell out this prayer; it would be more potent if something similar were done more economically (and sophisticated readers would enjoy the challenge to the classical precursor). Shakespeare had revitalized the old aubade tradition in depicting Romeo and Juliet's parting at daybreak, but that was in a play...

And from somewhere—inspired by the Muse, Donne might have said—the right words, in the right rhythm, capturing the right tone of voice, emerge:

> Busy old fool, unruly Sun,
> Why dost thou thus,
> Through windows, and through curtains, call on us?

Although Donne could not have written this opening without a mind furnished with lines and themes from his reading of the Latin love poets, Renaissance Italian and Spanish verse, and the writing of his English contemporaries and forebears (including Marlowe's translation of Ovid's *Amores*), it brings something new into English culture. Neither Spenser nor Sidney could have written it—not because they lacked the skill to do so, but because it was, to them, an unthinkable manner of writing, a manner that was not included among the possible options open to them. The courtly qualities that poetry embodied for them, in their different ways, would have been threatened by the unashamed individualism of this speaking voice, the forthright unbridledness of this outburst, the drama and immediacy of this evocation of sexual desire, the knowing absurdity of the conceit, the gaiety of the implicit laughter behind the preposterous dressing-down inflicted on the sun. The versification alone threatens the newly established decorum of English accentual-syllabic metre: a four-beat line with initial inversion allowing strong stresses at beginning and end is followed by a surprising two-beat line. (Such is the expressive dynamism of the voice that we scarcely notice the subtle play of sound, especially the repeated [ʌ] sound in *un-*, *Sun*, *dost*, *thus* (for the Elizabethan reader, *dost* probably doesn't belong here, but *Busy* does) and the rhyme of *fool* and *-rul-*. And any lingering sense of the old hierarchy of the gods and planets is brushed away with nonchalant ease.

The remainder of the poem, which we know as 'The Sun Rising', fully lives up to this opening: the tone remains vividly captured as the speaker turns from chiding the sun to welcoming it, on an equally implausible pretext; the sense of an outrage performed on all the courtly conventions of decorous speech and behaviour continues; and the rhythm tests the limits of metrical normality. The rhyme scheme turns out after all to imitate, distantly, the last ten lines of a Petrarchan sonnet (*a b b a c d c d e e*). Here is the first stanza in full:

Busy old fool, unruly Sun,
Why dost thou thus,
Through windows and through curtains call on us?
Must to thy motions lovers' seasons run?
Saucy pedantic wretch, go chide
Late schoolboys and sour 'prentices,
Go tell court huntsmen that the King will ride,
Call country ants to harvest offices;
Love, all alike, no season knows, nor clime,
Nor hours, days, months, which are the rags of time.

The second and third stanzas follow closely the metre and rhyme-scheme of the first: in this respect, Donne is quite conventional.

Q *Yet Donne didn't publish his poems—does this affect your argument about the inventive writer introducing into the English language and the English literary tradition new possibilities for other writers?*

A It's true that because of Donne's antipathy to publication or even wide circulation, very few writers were made aware of those opportunities at first (and others, like Ben Jonson, chose not to capitalize on them). During the seventeenth century, however, we can see very clearly how Donne's poetic breakthrough became an enabling resource for poets, especially after the first, posthumous, publication of his poems in 1633 and the second edition (in which, for the first time, the lyric poems were gathered together and given the title *Songs and Sonets*) in 1635. Many of the Caroline court poets, including Carew, Lovelace, and Suckling, show the influence of Donne's discoveries, as does the work of Katherine Philips. The writer who most fully absorbs Donne's innovations and uses them as a springboard for his own inventiveness is Marvell. But literary history doesn't follow a simple trajectory, and Donne's outspoken eroticism, outrageous conceits, and free rhythms were soon meeting with disapproval; as the century progressed, Denham and Waller helped to set a new tone in poetry, and Dryden cemented it. (There were eight editions of Donne's poetry within the century after his death, and then none for nearly a century and a half.)

Although Donne's reputation started to recover in the nineteenth century—Browning's dramatic monologues are hardly imaginable without the earlier poet's example—it wasn't until the early twentieth century that the possibilities inherent in his innovative intervention in the English poetic tradition once more became available to poets.

Q *While it's possible to see Donne as inventively changing the landscape for future poets, the example of his love poetry being a rather obvious one, it's not very easy to see every work of literature as having a comparable importance. Aren't you exaggerating the significance of inventiveness, in your sense?*

A I agree that Donne is an obvious example, but I wanted to show the operation of cultural invention at its clearest. But I do believe that every work that contains at least a spark of inventiveness is making a potential change in the cultural environment—I say potential because of course everything depends on the reception of the work, as we see vividly in Donne's case. Take the poetry of Sir John Suckling, for example, one of those minor Caroline court poets I mentioned. Here's a poem that bears the unmistakable stamp of Donne's love poetry:

Out upon it, I have lov'd
Three whole days together;
And am like to love three more,
If it prove fair weather.

Time shall moult away his wings,
Ere he shall discover
In the whole wide world again
Such a constant lover.

But the spite on't is, no praise
Is due at all to me;
Love with me had made no stays,
Had it any been but she.

Had it any been but she,
And that very face,
There had been at least ere this
A dozen dozen in her place.

Suckling makes no major intervention in the poetic tradition established by Donne, and yet this poem is not quite like anything Donne wrote; it's a singular invention that alters in a tiny way the available resources of English poetry. Part of the poem's originality is metrical: it uses the familiar four-beat rhythm that is the staple of the poem-as-song, but in a version that heightens the rhythmic swing by varying the disposition of stressed and unstressed syllables—the form sometimes known as dolnik. (Any attempt to analyse the metre in terms of classical feet would suggest a complex form involving trochees with missing syllables and sudden switches from trochaic to iambic meter, whereas part of the charm of the poem is the very simple, straightforward rhythm.) This in itself is far from original, but what is original is the way Suckling takes advantage of the 'virtual' beats that play a role in much four-beat verse. The first two stanzas follow the pattern of the ballad stanza and the common hymn measure so often used in song forms: four beats, three beats, four beats, three beats, but with a fourth 'silent' beat felt by the reader rounding out the second and final lines. (A basic musical setting would include a measure or half-measure of accompaniment here.) The last line of the third stanza is one where we expect three beats, and it can be made to fulfil this expectation without difficulty by letting the first stress fall, as it would in speech, on 'any'. This, of course, is where the poem surprises us by turning from a sardonic attack on the nature of love—three whole days is to be counted a triumph of constancy!—to an encomium on the beloved. Then comes the poem's most inventive moment: if we had been tempted to laugh away the apparent shift of tone, the line is repeated as the opening of the final stanza, a repetition that immediately creates a feeling of greater seriousness, as the speaker dwells on this idea; and the seriousness is heightened by the metrical demand that this be read as a *four*-beat line, inviting a stress on the first syllable. Suckling has one more surprise up his sleeve: the last line should have three beats, and so we would expect 'A dozen in her place'—so the extra dozen (numerically an extra 132) also produces a line that, although still metrically acceptable as it fills out the full length of the line, is itself excessive. Although this line marks a return to the panache of the carefree womanizer, it remains a compliment to the one woman. These are very small matters (we might also mention the striking visualization of Time moulting its wings), and similarly small discoveries and adjustments can be found in thousands upon thousands of poems, novels, short stories, and plays; this multiplicity of invention is what makes for the richness of the cultural sphere.

Does it make any sense to say that Suckling, in exploiting the resources of common measure to create a complexity of tone in a way that no-one had hitherto done, was introducing into poetic practice a possibility upon whose exclusion existing practice had depended? It would be a rather overdramatic way of putting it, perhaps, but if his poem is characterized by inventiveness, something like this must be correct. To unpack this complicated question further, it's necessary to introduce the distinction between originality and invention that I drew in *The Singularity of Literature*. Whether Suckling's poem was original or not is an empirical, historical question: it would require extensive research to establish whether any other English poet had accomplished exactly this combination of metrical and tonal expressiveness, and whether other poets had taken advantage of what he achieved in their own work. On the other hand, whether we can say now that the poem is inventive, in the sense in which I'm using the term, depends on the experience of reading it today: a work is only inventive for a reader, since inventiveness is only experienced in the act–event of reading. (The kind of thorough investigative analysis advocated—and undertaken—by Bourdieu into the conditions under which artistic breakthroughs occur deals only with originality, not with inventiveness.) Though I haven't done sufficient research to decide on the degree of originality represented by Suckling's poem, I do find it inventive. It produces a little charge of surprise each time I read it: in its use of sexual rakishness as a means to make an amorous compliment it ventures into an affective space I've encountered nowhere else and in its handling of poetic techniques to achieve this complex unfolding it possesses genuine singularity. This is what entitles me to say that, for me, it is a work of literature. If I were to discover that what seems fresh in Suckling's poem was actually derived entirely from another poet's work—in other words that it had no originality—I would probably find my sense of its inventiveness fading, though it's hard to imagine it disappearing. (If the poem was a word-for-word copy, I would simply transfer my admiration to the earlier poet; the *poem* would retain its inventiveness.)

The puzzle as to how in the early twenty-first century I can find poems written in the sixteenth and seventeenth century inventive, carrying me into new territories of thinking and feeling, showing off the power of the language and poetic technique in a fresh light, remains one of the most difficult phenomena in literary practice to explain, and we shall have to return to it.

Q *Your account of literary invention is largely based on theoretical deduction. Is there any concrete evidence for it?*

A Above all, I would appeal to the evidence of literary history: the activities of writers since the classical period, and the reports that have come down to us of readers' experiences. To trace artistic, including literary, history in the West is to follow a narrative of constant invention as each artist builds on and departs from previous art to offer a new apprehension of inner and outer worlds, and to find fresh ways of utilizing the materials of a particular medium to surprise and please the recipient. Chaucer adapted the Italian *endecasillabo* to create a medium for English verse, the iambic pentameter, that allowed him to capture subtleties of tone and humour hitherto unavailable to English poets; Sidney fine-tuned English prose to embody courtly virtues in the *Arcadia*; Shakespeare exploited the material potential of the new theatres in a way that appealed to the masses; and so on down to the current crop of writers each attempting to create a work that will strike readers as possessing distinctiveness, opening new horizons, and providing the pleasure that comes from inventiveness.

In assessing the history of readers' responses, however, one has to be careful. Many, if not most, written responses to literary works are responses to something other than their literary qualities and functions. These are far from unimportant—as I've stressed, literature has proved to be an invaluable mine of historical and biographical information, a comfort in times of distress, a rallying cry in times of revolution, a guide to living and loving, a masterclass in linguistic usage, and many other types of useful resource. But from time to time in literary history a response has been noted that, unlike all these, is peculiar to literature. Sidney's *Apology* explicitly pits poetry against philosophy and history to their discredit; and although his argument is directed toward the moral effectiveness of literature, his description of the peculiar power of poetry leaves one in no doubt of the specifically literary quality of the response he's describing. For instance, in contrast to the philosopher, the poet 'yieldeth to the powers of the mind an image of that whereof the philosopher bestoweth but a wordish description, which doth neither strike, pierce, nor possess the sight of the soul, so much as that other doth'. If we move to a later period, we find Coleridge's notebooks filled with vivid evocations of literary responses. For Shelley, in the *Defence of Poetry*, 'Poetry is a sword of lightning, ever unsheathed, which consumes the scabbard that would contain it.' Emerson's view was that 'It is the essence of poetry to spring, like the rainbow daughter of Wonder, from the invisible, to abolish the past, and refuse all history' ('Shakspeare; or, the Poet'). Emily Dickinson's comment is also well-known: 'If I read a book and it makes my whole body so cold no fire can warm me I know that is poetry. If I feel physically as if the top of my head were taken off, I know that is poetry' (Johnson and Ward, *Letters of Emily Dickinson*, L342a). In his 1933 Leslie Stephen Lecture, *The Name and Nature of Poetry*, A. E. Housman penned a famous statement that emphasizes the bodily response to poetry, and also nicely reminds us that poetry exists in the memory as well as on the page and in the ear: 'Experience has taught me, when I am shaving of a morning, to keep watch over my thoughts, because, if a line of poetry strays into my memory, my skin bristles so that the razor ceases to act' (47).

Q *We need to pick up the tricky question of the apparent transcendence of history involved in your notion of invention. What is the relation between a writer's inventive bringing into the world of a work of literature at a specific moment in history and the reader's experience of that work as inventive fifty, a hundred, a thousand years later?*

A This is indeed a tricky question, and not one that has been much addressed in literary theory, although it seems to me central to what is distinctive about literature. As Rita Felski has noted, 'We cannot close our eyes to the historicity of artworks, and yet we sorely need alternatives to seeing them as transcendentally timeless on the one hand, and imprisoned in their moment of origin on the other' ('"Context Stinks"', 575).

There is plenty of evidence for the experience of inventiveness as something happening in the present even while the reader is well aware that the work dates from the past. We can return to Donne for some examples of readers' testimonies. In *The Singularity of Literature* I quoted F. R. Leavis's account in *Revaluation* of his reading of an anthology of seventeenth-century poetry: reaching Donne's poems after ninety pages of work by other poets of the time, he says that 'we cease reading as students, or as connoisseurs of anthology pieces, and read on as we read the living' (18). For a more recent witness we can turn to Achsah Guibbory, the editor of the *Cambridge Companion to John Donne*, who opens an essay on Donne's erotic poetry with this: 'Even after four centuries, Donne's love poetry strikes us as fresh and immediate, with its urgent rhythms, its irregular, frequent stresses communicating the sense that passion cannot be contained within regular iambic feet' (133). One could multiply these examples from a number of academic and non-academic sources.

Leavis doesn't hesitate to identify the inventiveness he experiences in the poems as he reads them with the inventiveness felt by Donne's early readers: 'The extraordinary force of originality that made Donne so potent an influence in the seventeenth century makes him now at once for us, without his being the less felt as of his period, contemporary' (*Revaluation*, 18). And Leavis is surely not alone in making this claim: few readers who sense that the words of 'The Sun Rising' open up a fresh perspective on sensual love would hesitate to say that it's Donne's inventiveness that they are experiencing, rather than something the words are achieving by themselves, irrespective of Donne's creative efforts. (This is an aspect of authoredness, to use my coinage again; it's also perhaps reflected in our habitual use of the present tense in describing what happens in a literary work.) But is this simply an illusion created by the intensity of the feeling; are we really just experiencing the work's originality in relation to our own past reading and our own habits and expectations?

In attempting to answer this question, we must first return to the distinction between the scholar's sense of a work's *originality* and the experience of *inventiveness* described by Leavis (who distinguishes it from the scholar's way of reading). If I've read a great deal of sixteenth-century poetry, I will appreciate Donne's originality more fully than someone with only a limited acquaintance. That historical knowledge may well enter into my reading of the poem and may enhance my enjoyment—or diminish it, if it seems that Donne was less original than I had at first assumed. The experience of the poem's inventiveness, however, its introduction of something unanticipated in the reading process, doesn't depend on historical knowledge, although historical knowledge may feed into it. What it feels like is a transcendence or short-circuiting of history, a leaping over the centuries to share the adventure of creation with the writer. And, yes, on occasions it could well be an illusion: although there may be some historical evidence to confirm that what feels like inventiveness now corresponds to what was actually inventive then, such evidence can never be conclusive. My sense that I'm reliving the exhilaration of the original invention may indeed be only a reflection of the work's relation to my own culture, a purely contingent phenomenon, a happy coincidence.

However, there are reasons to believe that, at least in the case of works that can be said to emanate from a culture historically linked to my own, there is usually more than coincidence at work. When I read a novel and enjoy its forays into what feels like new territory, I experience a transformation in my own idioculture, which is, as I've said, a complex of attitudes, aptitudes, habits of thought and feeling, and pieces of knowledge, formed as the impress of the broader culture around me in a constellation that includes traces of my past cultural experiences. If I've absorbed a rich array of cultural materials and my culture has a historical connection with that of the work I'm reading, it's at least possible that the inventiveness I engage with is related to that of the writer. Although the feelings, discourses, and behaviours that constituted the experience of 'being in love' in the late sixteenth century were hugely different from their equivalents today, there nevertheless remains, when all the differences have been taken into account, a common residue that enables readers today to share something of the situations and emotions of individuals in loving relationships several hundred years ago.

While, as I've suggested, there can be no single 'best' reading of a work of literature—given the dependence of all readings on the situatedness of the reader—the better readings are usually those made by readers immersed in their own culture and informed, to some degree at least, about the culture in which the original work was written. At the same time, it's possible for the cultural context of the reader, crystallized in a singular idioculture, to create obstacles to good readings. Many commentators in the eighteenth and nineteenth century responded strongly but negatively to Donne's inventiveness. It was perhaps Dryden who established this commonplace, with his judgement in the Dedication to 'Eleanora' that Donne was 'the greatest Wit, though not the best Poet of our Nation' (*Poems 1685–1692*, 233). Hyppolite Taine can serve to furnish a fairly extreme version of a common Victorian view: 'Twenty times while reading him we rub our brow and ask with astonishment, how a man could so have tormented and contorted himself, strained his style, refined on his refinement, hit upon such absurd comparisons?' (*History of English Literature*, 204). Clearly, such readers were not participating in the excitement of Donne's own inventive explorations of the powers of English verse; they were simply registering the difference between his poetry and that of his forebears (and most of his successors until their own time). The otherness apprehended by Donne remained other to them because the poetic culture of their own period required that such ways of writing, thinking, and feeling be excluded in order for them to pursue their own composing and reading.

It could be said that the culture of Renaissance England—or, rather, those aspects relevant to the composition and reception of Donne's love poetry—were too different from those of the eighteenth and nineteenth centuries to allow the kind of transhistorical experience of inventiveness that later generations were able to enjoy. The situation is not essentially different when we're dealing with writing in different cultures arising in different parts of the world. If I read one of Rumi's love poems translated from Farsi, the chances are that any inventive encounter with alterity I experience has little do with the original impulse of creation—assuming I'm not expert in Persian literature and culture. This is not a reason for ignoring poetry from other cultures; it's an argument for trying to absorb some of their elements. And if I do find myself moved by a Rumi poem because it happens to chime with certain aspects of love poetry in my own culture, there's nothing illegitimate or reprehensible about the pleasure I feel—though it's not likely to be particularly deep or complex. This is an issue I explore in chapter 6 of this book.

Terminological questions

Q *You've identified three features of the act–event that constitutes the literary work of art, both in its coming into being and in its being received: otherness, inventiveness, and singularity. To clarify your argument, could you say more about these terms and how they are related to one another? Why do you need three terms?*

A We could think of these as three dimensions of the experience of literariness, in creation and reception. I'll say a little about each (which will involve gathering up some of my earlier comments); but it's important to remember that they are really different aspects of a single experience.

Otherness, or alterity, is a dimension of the literary experience that manifests itself as surprise or unfamiliarity, whether massive or minimal. Otherness, in the sense in which I'm using the term, is not just anything (idea, entity, person, culture) hitherto unencountered; it's that which is *unencounterable,* given the present state of the encountering mind or culture, what Levinas calls the 'same'. (As I've remarked, otherness is always relative to a state of things, in a certain time and place.) It is unencounterable because the modes of encounter made possible by the state of things (a state which could be described in both social and psychological terms, in the way that Saussure describes the system of language) do not allow for it. Otherness is not just out there, unapprehended because no-one has thought of apprehending it, or because it bears no relation whatever to existing forms of knowledge, but because to apprehend it would threaten the status quo.

It might be tempting to say that the other is not just 'other to' or 'other than' the same, but that it is 'the other of' the same, in that is related to the same by this necessary exclusion; this, however, would make the relation of other to same much too cosy and predictable, as though we could simply *derive* the other from the same. But we cannot, because the occlusion of otherness is itself occluded. This is why the artist works in the dark, by trial and error, waiting for signs of otherness to emerge, and pursuing these when they do—which has to be achieved by means of a readjustment of existing horizons and habits. And the literary reader, too, starts in a state of uncertainty, alert to what may arrive to challenge frameworks of expectation and allow otherness to be acknowledged. If the reader is different after having read a work, I believe, this is because of the otherness it has introduced him or her to; but again I need to stress that the change I'm talking about can range from a revaluation of the entire moral basis of one's life to a new appreciation of the power of the couplet.

Inventiveness names the production of or encounter with the work as an invention, a word which encapsulates both the act of making the work and the result of that making. To experience inventiveness as a reader thus involves an engagement with the maker as well as the made; it's therefore related to authoredness. I'm trying here to do justice to an important aspect of what it feels like to read a work of literature, one that I outlined earlier in discussing the question of historical transcendence: we're aware that the words we're reading bear the impress of a creative act—even a found poem has been transformed from its original condition by a creative process—and we take pleasure in reliving that act (or rather act–event). Not literally, of course, unless we've been studying the genetic history of the work; but imaginatively. As the words enter our consciousness it's as if we're sharing in their discovery by the artist. Furthermore, to think of the work as an invention is to emphasize its relation to the culture within which it was created: the writer who succeeds in writing inventively has absorbed her culture's norms, varieties of knowledge, store of earlier productions, predispositions and habits, as well as the available techniques and methods of the literary field—what Henry Staten calls *techne*—and used them to go beyond what has previously been thought and felt. As readers, we deploy a similar array of resources and find ourselves, if the work is indeed inventive, taken to somewhere new.

Singularity is also something we experience in any encounter that can be called literary: the work comes across as different from any other work we know, even though its materials—the various components of the techne that the artist deployed in creating it—may be familiar. Singularity is not opposed to generality or universality (as Hegel's 'particularity' is); it's a configuration of general properties that creates, for the reader, a unique experience. So the singular work does not have a bounded and unchanging identity; on the contrary, it's open to change and reinterpretation. The identity of any sign depends on its being interpretable in different contexts; were it not so, languages couldn't function, as it would be necessary to reconstitute the original context in order to understand an utterance. (This is the logic of iterability.) As Jonathan Culler puts it, 'The singularity of the work is what enables it to be repeated over and over in events that are never exactly the same' ('Derrida and the Singularity of Literature', 871). The singularity of the literary work goes beyond that which enables the sign to function, however, as it involves a cluster of signifying elements with complex relations to one another that are the product of an author's inventiveness, and have the power of introducing otherness as part of a reader's experience. Blanchot captures something of my sense of singularity in his characteristic style: 'The book which has its origin in art has no guarantee in the world, and when it's read, it has never been read before. It does not come into its presence as a work except in the space opened by this unique reading, each time the first and each time the only' (*The Space of Literature*, 194). I take up the question of singularity more fully in chapter 3.

To return to the point I began with: although these words name three different aspects of the literariness of the literary work, they aren't separable; they are, if you like, three different ways of looking at the same thing. If you try to imagine a work that is singular without being inventive or reaching out to otherness, you end up imagining only a work that is different from other works, with nothing in that difference that calls forth the response we think of as literary. (I called this 'uniqueness' in *The Singularity of Literature*, to distinguish it from singularity.) A work that is inventive is necessarily one that introduces otherness and is singular; a work that brings the other into the field of the same is necessarily singular and inventive in its handling of the available materials.

One more point needs to be made: although I've presented them as nouns, what we're really talking about are verbs, aspects of the event of literature. Otherness occurs in the apprehending of new thoughts and feelings; invention is the process that produces the work of art and the tracing of that process in a reading; singularity is the crystallizing of a work's special identity. In engaging fully with a literary work as literature one is experiencing all three of these as they operate together and reinforce each other in a single complex movement.

Q *What is the particular attraction for you of the term* performance? *What do you mean by saying that the reader—even the silent reader—*performs *the work of literature? And how does this relate to your argument that as readers we enjoy the revelation of the power of language?*

A Aspects of this question come up in my discussions of metaphor, knowing, and affect in chapters 6, 7, and 8, respectively, since all these features of literary practice involve performance. I find the theatrical metaphor useful, because I believe the event of the literary work puts on stage, as it were, the emotions, the mental and physical events, the apprehendings of the external world, it depicts. Unlike, for example, the historian describing as plainly as possible the mental state of a politician making a crucial decision, the novelist 'stages' the individual's mental processes, allowing the reader to bring these to life as events—while always remaining aware that they are being staged, and that it's not a matter of gaining direct access to mental worlds. We might compare the pleasure taken (by many viewers though certainly not all) in the utterances and actions of individuals being filmed in a reality TV show with the pleasure taken in the utterances and actions of fictional characters being acted in a good television drama. Our awareness in the BBC adaptation of *Parade's End* that it is Benedict Cumberbatch uttering words written by Tom Stoppard (who derived them from Ford Madox Ford) doesn't diminish our intellectual and emotional involvement in the character of Christopher Tietjens; in fact, our involvement is enriched by that awareness, and by our pleasure in the skill evident in the language, acting, *mise-en-scène*, and so on. (This awareness is related to what Roman Jakobson, putting it in terms of perception, famously called the 'set for the message'.) We are conscious—perhaps only barely conscious at times—of a significant distance between what we're watching (or in the case of a literary work, reading) and the world outside art, but it's a distance that multiplies the sources and types of our enjoyment.

At the same time, this enjoyment of what is achieved with language in a work of literature is also an enjoyment of what is revealed about the power of language, and of the literary forms into which it can be moulded. Blanchot stresses that this is true of all the arts: the work 'is what makes its nature and its matter visible or present, it is the glorification of its reality: verbal rhythm in the poem, sound in music, light become colour in painting, space become stone in the house.... The work makes what disappears in the object appear. The statue glorifies the marble' (*The Space of Literature*, 123). The literary work glorifies the language, we might add.

Q *Why do you feel it necessary to bring the rather awkward compound 'act-event' into the discussion?*

A There's a mountain of testimony from writers and other artists that in the process of creation the work seems to take over from them, have a life of its own, determine its own direction. The idea of 'inspiration' is, of course, one way in which this experience is captured, though there have been many other attempts to describe it. (Timothy Clark's excellent study *The Theory of Inspiration* gives a full account of its history since the Romantic period.) Just to take one example, J. M. Coetzee cites Gabriel Garcia Marquez in *Diary of a Bad Year*: 'I don't see [inspiration] as a state of grace nor as a breath from heaven, but as the moment when, by tenacity and control, you are at one with your theme.... You spur the theme on and the theme spurs you on too' (192). In discussing invention earlier, I quoted Zoë Wicomb's description of this strange process. We can either ignore this large accumulation of testimony, as many theorists of literature have done, or we can try to understand it.

When we read a work of literature, it too takes over, directs our thoughts and feelings, captures us, as if it had its own agency. Yet in both cases it's obvious that this event that befalls the writer or the reader is the result of willed acts (except perhaps in the very rare case of a line or a melody coming from nowhere into a writer or composer's head—and even then, it actually comes from a rich complex of absorbed knowledge, and has to be laboured on to become a work of art). The reader responds passively to the active work, but the work becomes active only because of the reader's activity—'tenacity and control' in Marquez's phrase. The two dimensions aren't separable: hence the compound 'act–event'. Blanchot, again, has his version of this impossible chronology: the call of the work, he says, 'only reaches the reader's ear because he answers it' (*The Space of Literature*, 196). John Dewey understood the dual character of response, and recognized that it isn't confined to art: conscious experience, he says, is a 'perceived relation between doing and undergoing' (*Art as Experience*, 46). He contrasts perception, as involving 'a series of responsive acts', with recognition, which is purely passive (52). And again, 'Perception is an act of the going out of energy in order to receive' (53). And in his discussion of rhythm he states: 'Esthetic rhythm is a matter of perception and therefore includes whatever is contributed by the self in the active process of perceiving' (163).

There is no simple chronology here; as Derrida demonstrates in his discussion of the 'yes' (see, for example, 'Ulysses Gramophone'), to affirm the work is also to bring it into being so that it may be affirmed. This is the paradox I addressed in responding to Lamarque's criticism earlier.

Q *Why do you feel you have to introduce the term 'idioculture' into critical discourse? What's wrong with the term 'subject', or, if you want to signal that you're not interested in the subject as a psychological entity but in its constitution by cultural conventions, 'subject position'?*

A I do indeed want to make it clear that I'm not dealing with the whole person but with the individual consciousness (and unconscious) as a nexus within culture; at the same time I want to emphasize that this constituted entity is immensely rich: it's the deposit within an individual of a multiple, compound, internally inconsistent, constantly-changing complex of cultural discourses and practices. 'Subject position' suggests an empty marker, a certain perspective on the world, and 'identity' implies a fixed, coherent unity; whereas 'idioculture' indicates a unique (indeed, singular) cluster of attributes, preferences, habits, and knowledges, not all in harmony with one another, and subject to continual evolution. The notion of idioculture shares with Heidegger's *Dasein* a resistance to conventional notions of individual, person, subject and so on, but resists in turn the generalizing implications of *Dasein*. My idioculture is not, of course, entirely accessible to me—many of its elements remain unconscious—but to the extent that it is conscious it includes processes of self-interpretation (processes that are themselves mediated by cultural norms, of course).

The model is the idiolect spoken by an individual (in contrast to the dialect spoken by a speech community); it is unique to that individual, and reflects her exposure to and participation in one or more linguistic worlds. My own idiolect is a manifestation of my upbringing in South Africa in an English-speaking family among isiZulu speakers, my twenty years in southern England, my five years in Scotland, my ten years in the United States, and my sixteen years in northern England. Think of Henry Higgins in Shaw's *Pygmalion* identifying the streets in which individuals were born and raised from their speech—though even he would probably have failed to detect all the layers in my accent. My idioculture is similarly layered and complex, as is everybody's. Most histories of literature, and of culture more broadly, focus on general trends and material conditions rather than on the individual idiocultures of writers and readers which they constitute; literary biographies, however, often attempt to describe the singular mental and emotional worlds of their subjects at different stages of their lives.

When a reader engages with a literary work, his idioculture provides the resources—linguistic and cultural knowledge, generic expectations, technical know-how, and so on—that make a literary response possible; likewise, the work is a product of the writer's idioculture. It's like two wedges kissing at their sharpest points: behind the touching of tips that takes place in the reading process lies, on each side, an enormous body of cultural materials. So when I say that a writer exploits the fractures and tensions in the culture of her time, what I really mean is that those fractures and tensions are embodied in her idioculture, and it's there that they present themselves and are manipulated in the act–event of invention. Hence the necessity for the writer to be thoroughly conversant with her cultural context, if she is to make an inventive intervention within it. Donne could not have achieved the impact he had on seventeenth-century culture had he not been attuned to the minutiae of poetic techne, to his culture's symbolizations of erotic experience, to the surrounding discourses of religion, courtship, politics, and a great deal more.

Pierre Bourdieu's term 'habitus' might seem to be an alternative to 'idioculture': it refers to the 'systems of dispositions' (*Rules of Art*, 214) or 'matrix of preferences' (363) that are 'the product of the incorporation of structures of the social world—and, in particular, its immanent tendencies and its temporal rhythms' (328–9). But to refer to the individual's habitus is to emphasize what unites him or her to a group with shared predispositions, whereas to refer to an idioculture is to give equal weight to the singularity of the individual's constitution by cultural norms. 'Idioculture' is also intended to encompass a broader range of conscious and unconscious mental, emotional, and bodily contents, habits and expectations than 'habitus', which, in Bourdieu's usage at least, is limited to dispositions to behave in a certain manner. (It is 'always oriented towards practical functions', as he notes in *The Logic of Practice*, 52.)

Media, periods, and genres

Q *You appear to move between literature as a specific art-form and art understood more generally. What is the real focus of your interest?*

A I would have to say that my real subject is the work of art in a wide sense. I would like to think that my arguments pertain as much to music and the visual arts as to literature, though of course some things would have to be re-articulated, especially in discussing responses to the visual arts, where the question of temporality presents itself in a different way. And instead of the use of 'reader' it would be necessary to use clumsy formulations like 'reader, viewer, or listener' or unsatisfactory alternatives like 'consumer' or 'receiver'. I apologize for the way I swing from 'literature' to 'art' in this discussion; most of the time the terms are interchangeable. The specificity of literature only becomes significant when the particular properties of a language-based art are at stake.

Let me sketch how one might extrapolate from my arguments about literature to other art-forms. (I say more about the visual arts in chapter 8.) It's much clearer that musical works, as with theatrical performances, film, and recited poetry, and many forms of avant-garde art, have their being as events. A musical score is the equivalent of what I've been calling a text that may be realized as a work by a reader: it's an inert body of symbols until it's performed by someone with the appropriate skills. Music, like literature, uses the resources of a particular artistic tradition to arouse and fulfil or defeat expectations for those who are familiar with that tradition, to deploy concord or discord as part of a continuous argument, to use the power of rhythm to involve the listener in an experience of onward motion of various kinds, and so on. And music can be listened to as a pleasant diversion (most music is received in this way), or it can be listened to as art—assuming the musical piece in question will respond to such listening—just as a text with the right properties may be read as a work of literature. Listened to in this way, with that mixture of active engagement and passive reception that characterizes all artistic act-events, music (if we exclude the further complication of the setting of words) introduces into the listener's acoustic and affective worlds—worlds which are closely linked to one another—intimations of dimensions of sound and feeling not fully part of the familiar pattern of hearing and feeling. As a result, the listener is changed, perhaps only in the degree of receptivity to certain chord progressions, perhaps in a deep emotional way.

Static works—painting, photography, sculpture, architecture (when it can be considered an art)—clearly don't have the same relation to temporality, and it's less easy to see that as works of art they have their existence in the events of viewers' experience of them. (Nelson Goodman, in *Languages of Art*, 113, calls these 'autographic' works, and defines them as works in which there is a significant difference between an original and a forgery, as opposed to 'allographic' works, which can be reproduced ad infinitum.) A sculpture seems so much a thing in its own right, not needing a viewer to be realized as what it is. But like a text, a sculpture is a material form that can be 'read' mechanically or creatively. If I simply register its shape, colour and texture, or, if it's a representational sculpture, the entity it represents, I'm doing no more than a sophisticated camera attached to a computer might do. But if I walk round it, move towards and away from it, let my eyes wander around its surfaces, watch the changing relationships among its planes, allow its mimetic properties to resonate with my own knowledge of the world, register its singularity and inventiveness, and open myself to its otherness, I'm experiencing the object in a different way: it's coming to life as a work of art in the event of my looking at it.

There is a tradition of contrasting poetry and the visual arts, the most famous articulation of which is perhaps Joshua Reynolds's statement (in which he gives a description of the former that captures nicely something I've tried to argue):

> Poetry operates by raising our curiosity, engaging the mind by degrees to take an interest in the event, keeping the event suspended, and surprising at last with an unexpected catastrophe.
>
> The Painter's art is more confined, and has nothing that corresponds with, or perhaps is equivalent to, this power and advantage of leading the mind on, till attention is totally engaged. What is done by Painting, must be done at one blow; curiosity has received at once all the satisfaction it can ever have. (*Discourses on Art*, 145–6)

The immediate blow of a painting that strikes the viewer instantaneously has no parallel in literary responses, of course, other than in a very limited way in some kinds of concrete poetry; but, *pace* Reynolds, this itself is an experience in time, and is usually only the beginning of a longer event of looking and feeling.

Of course, as with literature, works in other media can become so familiar that they no longer effect any alteration in their audiences—though it's usually the case, with great works at any rate, that a fresh context can always revive a work's transformative power. It's important to remember, too, that the way surprise works in art is not quite the same as it does outside art: I can be surprised by the rhythmically dislocated final chord of the Sibelius Fifth Symphony even though I've heard the piece twenty times and know exactly when it's coming. (It would be more accurate, however, to say that I register, or perhaps even perform, the surprisingness of the chord.) Works of music, then, if they operate as art, possess the three qualities I associate with literariness: singularity (the melodies, rhythms, and sound textures of Strauss's 'Beautiful Blue Danube' constitute a wholly distinctive deployment of the musical techne Strauss had available to him), inventiveness (whether in a minor degree, as in a folk song given unexpected rhythmic freedom by Leadbelly, or a major degree, as in the fresh possibilities opened up by Elvis Presley in his packaging of African American rhythm and blues for a mass audience), and otherness, in providing the reader with that sense of new vistas of sound and feeling. Visual works, likewise, may, in their singularity and inventiveness, introduce the viewer to fresh perceptual and affective worlds.

Q *Your account sounds more convincing for modernism than earlier periods and movements. Aren't you seeing the history of literature through modernist—and perhaps postmodernist—spectacles? There may also be some affinities with Romantic conceptions of literature, but surely we need a different set of tools to appreciate literature before that? Indeed, the very concept of literature as we now use it doesn't go much further back than the Romantic period.*

A It's an inescapable fact that we respond to literary works of the past from the perspective of present understandings of literature. The work's openness to change is a part of my argument that I've already stressed, and what keeps works written before the emergence of the modern concept of 'literature' alive is precisely their capacity to be read as literary. This doesn't mean we read Chaucer as if he were David Foster Wallace; part of our current understanding is our grasp of the intellectual and artistic contexts of works of art of the past (though of course this will vary greatly from person to person, cultural group to cultural group), and the works themselves signal their belonging to a culture different from our own. But my emphasis on singularity, inventiveness and otherness doesn't, I would argue, privilege modernist and postmodern works. As I've suggested, the history of Western art, in all its forms, discloses a long series of inventive interventions in cultural practice, a striving to produce singular works that exploit technical innovations in order to bring into being new ways of seeing the world and new aspects of the world to see. The discourse surrounding art may sometimes appear to have other values—such as the imitation of the classics, or the work of art as familiar companion—but the practice of artists and the occasional comments of readers, viewers, and listeners suggest that this discourse is largely self-directed and self-sustaining.

I am, it's true, privileging a term that has a certain history, and there is perhaps an anachronism involved in projecting it further back than the nineteenth century. Jacques Rancière, for instance, has argued strongly for the emergence of the 'aesthetic regime' at the end of the eighteenth century; and Derrida locates the beginning of 'literature' in the same period. But there are two justifications for this projection. One is that I'm considering literary practices today, and in this light there isn't a radical difference between the way we read Edmund Spenser and Aphra Behn and the way we read John Keats and John Masefield. The other is that although the word 'literature' wasn't used in this way in earlier periods—the nearest term in earlier centuries of English literature would be 'poetry'—the characteristics I've sketched remain valid: Christopher Marlowe's innovations in theatrical language and spectacle bespeak an inventive impulse not very different from Henrik Ibsen's or Edward Bond's.

Q *Your emphasis on linguistic innovation seems to imply that poetry is more 'literary' than the novel or drama, especially the realist novel or play. Isn't yours an approach that privileges certain forms over others?*

A I hope not. Linguistic innovation is only one of many ways in which a work of literature can be inventive. When you're dealing with poetry, you're likely to demonstrate inventiveness by means of short examples, but this is far from the only possibility. Balzac's novels may not explore new uses of language, but they achieve an unprecedented richness of detail in their representations of Parisian life; Brecht's 'alienation effect' involves a number of theatrical devices unthinkable in the traditional theatre before him. Poetry, I surmise, has a different relation to temporality from other literary modes; while all works take place as events in the reading, poetry is a genre in which the experience of the unfolding of language *in real time* is an important aspect, just as musical works rely on real temporal relations. A. C. Bradley saw this over a century ago: 'An actual poem is the succession of experiences—sounds, images, thoughts, emotions—through which we pass when we are reading as poetically as we can' ('Poetry for Poetry's Sake', 4). This means poetry has a distinctive repertoire of potential sites of inventiveness—but so do the other genres. One unavoidable limitation of this book is that I've had to ignore most of the differences among them in attempting to say something meaningful about the category of literature in general.

Q *Most of your examples concentrate on literary works read on the page; can you say more about drama, especially as it's experienced in the theatre (and perhaps film as well)? Your model of the reader who performs the text and thus brings it into being as a work of literature seems closer to the activities of the director and the actors than the audience member watching a play or a film.*

A It's true that the argument gets quite complicated here, partly because so many creative individuals are involved in the production of a play or a film. What exactly is authoredness in these cases? I think we still sense in most examples of theatrical events and movies a single meaning-making purpose, even though this may be a complete illusion, since the work we enjoy may be the result of a number of creative endeavours, perhaps not working coherently together at all. Clearly, there are productions that deliberately shatter this sense of a single purpose, but they use our expectation of authoredness as a resource to create effects of surprise. And after the experience, we have no difficulty in separating out our judgement of the work of the writer, the actors, the designer, the director and so on, though we usually have no way of knowing exactly what creative insight went into what feature of the performance—how did the director influence the actors, was the lighting designer consulted in blocking the scenes, who chose the music?

The other complication is that the text—if there is one—is already interpreted before the viewer receives it, and the viewer's response is an interpretation of an interpretation, the performance of a performance. Moreover, the temporality of the work is given, rather than created in the process of reading. (Of course, these complications are equally true of an audience listening to a poem being read aloud.) However, to respond to such works as art means to take an active part rather than simply becoming a passive recipient. We have no difficulty in interpreting—and evaluating—interpretations, and our sense of the passing of time is affected by the quality of our own engagement. This active engagement is a kind of performance of what we are witnessing, just as our active listening to a musical piece is a kind of performance of the performance we are hearing.

Q *And what about recent (and not-so-recent) challenges to traditional genres—site-specific performances or installations, theatrical events that involve the 'audience' as performers, aleatory events, and so on? Aren't you focusing exclusively on the conventional division of genres and art-forms?*

A I would argue that my approach is better suited to such challenges than most alternative approaches. One way of inventively opening an artwork—and art-work as practice—to otherness is by contesting conventional genre boundaries. These would include the boundary between art and non-art, a boundary which has increasingly come under pressure. In order to understand why such works are effective one needs to understand what the difference between the events of art and non-art consists in. In such works, the experience I see as characteristic of the reception of art may or may not be overwritten—or overridden—by other kinds of experience; in, for instance, works that problematize the distinction between artistic invention and documentary reportage, such as 'verbatim theatre' of the kind the Tricycle Theatre in London has become known for, the audience response is simultaneously to the arts of the writer, director and actors and to the factual representation of words originally spoken by real individuals. And an audience member who is invited to participate in a performance may experience various pleasures that are not those of a response to an artwork—pleasures that can actually interfere with the latter type of response.

Q *A number of critics have recently argued that the lyric has come to dominate our conception of poetry, and that we need to attend to the history of poetic forms in all their variety in order to counter this tendency and give proper weight to other forms. Doesn't your approach to some degree buy into this 'lyricization' of poetry?*

A Not at all: lyric is only one of a number of poetic forms in which the qualities I'm highlighting can be found. I would be happy if the term could be confined to short poems with song-like qualities, such as the Suckling poem I quoted earlier, but that's a battle that can't be won: effectively, the term has come to refer to just about any short poem, especially one that takes the form of a personal meditation or response. It's to be regretted that the other genres are to some degree eclipsed by the lyric at present, and it's worth celebrating the best epigrams, satires, novels in verse and other non-lyric forms. They are all singular achievements, using form to pleasurably open up new terrain for the attentive reader.

Q *You've focused on individual works of literature; but how does the singularity of an author's entire oeuvre fit into your argument?*

A As I see it, singularity operates over several domains at once, ranging from an individual metaphor to an entire life's output or the collected work of a group of writers who share artistic techniques and ideals. A reader familiar with the output of a particular writer may enjoy the sense of recognition that accompanies the discovery of a new work, while at the same time deriving pleasure from whatever differentiates the work from others in the oeuvre. Coleridge's comment on Wordsworth's lines, 'that uncertain heaven received/Into the bosom of the steady lake', is well known: 'Had I met these lines running wild in the deserts of Arabia, I should have instantly screamed out "Wordsworth!"' (*Collected Letters* I, 452–3). Yet we can be sure that Coleridge's excitement included a sense that Wordsworth had at the same time achieved something new by means of this particular verbal sequence. If we know who has written a work we're reading, this knowledge necessarily plays a part in our interpretation and enjoyment of the work; and one way in which this happens is the creation of expectations based on our familiarity with that writer's oeuvre that are then satisfied or defeated. Thus the singularity of the writer's oeuvre enters into our reading—and something similar could be said of a school of writers, or the writing of a particular period or a particular place.

Otherness and ethics

Q *Can you say more about the process whereby the writer in composing and the reader in reading apprehends* otherness? *Isn't 'the other' inaccessible by definition?*

A This is a point Derrida worried away at in his first essay on Levinas, one of his earliest publications. If the other is absolutely other, I can have no access to it at all. But as I've stressed, the other must be other *to*; it already has a relation to me, although this is not a relation that can be easily spelled out. In order to acknowledge the other, I have to find a means to destabilize or deconstruct the set of norms and habits that give me the world—my idioculture, in short—in such a way that that the force of that which they exclude is felt. (This is where the tensions and fractures in the culture prove important). The way otherness is felt is not as the sudden apprehension of what was hitherto unknown and unknowable, but rather in the changes the familiar world has to undergo in order for the newcomer to be acknowledged. But of course, once it is acknowledged, it is no longer other; it has become part of what is known and felt—though there is no guarantee it will not become unfamiliar once more.

Of course encountering unfamiliar formal devices or content in a work of literature does not necessarily mean it is inventive or that its strangeness is produced by the introduction of the cultural other; the experience it provides may be one of bafflement or boredom. In some cases, re-reading might serve to overcome this blockage; in other cases the work will remain merely odd.

Q *But a common feature of positive responses to a literary work is a feeling of* recognition, *of a writer finding words for something one already knew or felt but hadn't acknowledged...*

A Yes, the experience of inventiveness, singularity and otherness in a work includes, alongside surprise, a sense of *rightness*, a sense that what has been revealed is valuable and appropriate, often a sense of the recognition of something that has been known while not known. (We recall Keats's 'It should strike the Reader as a wording of his own highest thoughts, and appear almost a Remembrance' [*Selected Letters*, 97]; and Barthes, in *The Preparation of the Novel*, discusses the response to the literary work he encapsulates in the phrase 'C'est ça!', 'That's it!'

[76–82].) This apparent paradox is explained by the relationship between the other that the work introduces and the existing culture into which it is brought. As I've said, it's not a matter of simple difference but of a possibility excluded by the culture, a possibility that, once acknowledged, enriches the culture by making good what has been absent. The sense of recognition or rightness, it seems to me, stems from this process.

Q *In* The Singularity of Literature *and in its companion study* J. M. Coetzee and the Ethics of Reading *you make the claim that the writing, reading, and criticism of literature has an ethical dimension. You also bring in the notion of the* responsibility *of the writer and reader. Don't these terms belong rather to the realm of interpersonal and inter-community relations than to writing and reading? Surely we can't judge a writer as unethical if he writes in conformity to existing norms rather than searching for cultural otherness, or the reader if she reads carelessly or distractedly?*

A What I've already said about the value of literature is one aspect of what I think of as the ethics of reading. A culture which gives literature and art an important place is a culture in which openness to otherness, to the possibility of change, is potentially an active presence. Of course, the arts can be subordinated to political aims or economic interests; literature can be reduced to the formulaic satisfaction of existing desires. But the possibility is always there: that artists will create works that refuse to be instrumentalized, that readers will read with a readiness to be surprised and changed.

The question of responsibility arises partly from the idea of authoredness: in responding to a work one is responding to the creative labour of the artist, even if one has no knowledge of that artist as a historical individual, so there is a human dimension to the apparently lifeless words on the page. Of course, one can always be mistaken: I might enjoy the sculpted form of a piece of timber that then turns out to be nothing but driftwood; at that moment, it ceases to be a work of art for me. To respond responsibly to a work, then, is, in the first place, to read attentively and, in the second place, to read with an openness to that which one has never encountered before. An attentive reading, deploying all the codes and conventions one regards as relevant to the work, is the necessary foundation for the second kind of reading, what might be called 'literary' or 'creative' reading. Rorty makes a similar distinction between what he calls 'methodical' and 'inspired' reading, the latter being the kind of reading that 'has made a difference to the critic's conception of who she is, what she is good for, what she wants to do with herself: an encounter which has rearranged her priorities and purposes' (Collini, ed., *Interpretation and Overinterpration*, 106). If one doesn't do these things, if one reads carelessly or with a closed mind, one is failing to do justice to the work (which is to say to the work's singularity, inventiveness, and otherness) and hence to the writer of the work. Roman Ingarden's distinction between 'non-aesthetic' and 'aesthetic' reading is related to this distinction, but the latter type of reading, by means of which the 'work' becomes a 'work of art', assumes as its goal the grasping of the object as a harmonious whole, which is not necessarily the aim or result of what I'm calling a creative reading.

Now, of course a lot of the time one does read hastily, one skims or jumps or reads with a particular purpose in mind. I'm not suggesting that this is ethically wrong; although the notion of 'doing justice to' the work implies an analogy with court cases, in which the judge has to assess a singular case in the light of general rules, there is fortunately no parallel between the work read quickly before lunch and Pope's wretches hung so that judges and jurymen may dine. No-one is likely to suffer from my action if I skip a few pages of *Clarissa*. Nevertheless, I believe one is behaving ethically if one takes the time to read someone else's writing with care and an open mind, just as the writer who responds to his environment with full attentiveness and an openness to the new possibilities it contains can be said to be working ethically. This is not an ethics of rules and norms—not, that is, a form of morality—but of singularities that exceed the possibility of legislating in advance. As Derrida argues in *The Gift of Death*, one's ethical obligations are infinite, but this doesn't mean there is no such thing as an ethical response. I take up this question in chapter 2.

The aesthetic tradition

Q *The arguments you are presenting constitute a direct intervention in the discourse about aesthetics and aesthetic value. Yet you avoid the word. Can you explain this avoidance more fully than you did in* The Singularity of Literature?

A My compunction here is perhaps excessive, but I do want to distinguish between the specificity of art as a cultural practice and the discourse around the beautiful or, going back to Alexander Baumgarten in the mid-eighteenth century, the sensuous. Kantian aesthetics is not the only game in town, but it looms extremely large in much work on the subject, and Kantian aesthetics is not a theory of art, though it has been extensively mined for theories of art. I would rather let aesthetics stand, as it did for Kant, as the domain in which judgments of beauty (or ugliness) are made, and look more closely at those aspects of the experience of artworks that are peculiar to art. If we identify aesthetics with art, we have no language to talk about all those other experiences of the beautiful (or the sublime or the moving or the harmonious) that form part of our lives.

Someone whose account of the aesthetic pays close attention to the distinction between natural beauty and art, is Genette:

> Whether an object attains the status of a work basically depends, then, on whether its receiver considers the possibility that an aesthetic intention is present within it. . . . Just as, *for me*, an object is an aesthetic object when I enter into a relation of an aesthetic type with it, so it is a work of art *for me* when, rightly or wrongly, I decide that this relation can be traced to an authorial intention. (*The Aesthetic Relation*, 139)

Genette rightly stresses that it is 'the *ascription* of an aesthetic intention to the object's producer' that determines whether it will be treated as a work of art, though I'm not convinced that the intention needs to be strictly aesthetic: we may take pleasure in the artful shaping of Freud's narrative in his *Gradiva* essay without assuming he had an aesthetic intention. The notion of 'authoredness' carries no such implication. (Genette appears to modify his position later in his study: 'Thus something that was perhaps not produced as a work of art, something that the "historian of cultures" can, invoking this doubt, legitimately refuse to call a work of art, can legitimately be received as such by the art-loving public and function as such in its eyes' [*The Aesthetic Relation*, 210].)

Q *Some of the central terms in traditional aesthetics are missing from your account, notably 'beauty'. Isn't the enjoyment of beauty an essential part of the experience of the literary work as literature?*

A The simple answer is that beauty is not specific to art, and what I'm interested in identifying is what is peculiar to the experience of the literary work. But there is more to say. Let us take some lines that I think most readers who enjoy poetry would call 'beautiful':

> Now came still Evening on, and Twilight grey
> Had in her sober livery all things clad;
> Silence accompanied, for beast and bird,
> They to their grassy couch, these to their nests
> Were slunk, all but the wakeful nightingale;
> She all night long her amorous descant sung;
> Silence was pleased: now glowed the firmament
> With living sapphires: Hesperus that led
> The starry host, rode brightest, till the moon
> Rising in clouded majesty, at length
> Apparent queen unveiled her peerless light,
> And o'er the dark her silver mantle threw.
>
> *Paradise Lost*, Book IV, 598–609

What makes it easy to call these lines of Milton beautiful? First of all, clearly, the content: the silence of twilight in a sylvan setting, the singing of the nightingale, the starry sky, the moon appearing resplendent out of the clouds: Milton has brought together a series of images guaranteed, then as now, to play harmonious chords on the reader's aesthetic sensibility. Then there's the masterful handling of the iambic pentameter: take, for example, the line openings, moving back and forth between regular iambics—'Now came...', 'Were slunk...', 'With living...', 'The starry...', 'Apparent...', 'And o'er...'—and inversions—'Had in...', 'Silence...' (twice), 'They to...', 'Rising...' There are the varied lengths of the clauses, sometimes ending at line end, sometimes running on to produce a kind of counterpoint against the formal division into lines. There are the sound-effects, such as the rhyme between 'Had' at line-opening (a word that surely invites a stress) and 'clad' at the end of the same line, or the echo of 'queen' and 'peerless' against a backdrop of varying vowel-sounds. There are the metaphors that intensify the visual beauty of the scene: twilight as a tailor or tirewoman who dresses the world in the same grey clothes she wears; the stars as jewels then as a multitude; the moon as a gorgeously dressed sovereign.

Now this sounds like standard literary appreciation, the sort of account one would approve of in a student's essay. And that is as it should be. The passage is indeed beautiful, one of the most beautiful in the language, and to respond to that beauty is part and parcel of literary sensitivity. My point is just that its beauty, understood as a static property, is not part of what makes it literature. A starry sky, a nightingale's song: these are beautiful in themselves, and don't need poetry to enhance them. We find beauty in many places outside art. Even a text that straightforwardly described such a scene, without any literary qualities to boast of, would be likely to arouse an awareness of beauty in the reader.

What is literary about Milton's lines is *the use to which beauty is put*, something that we're less accustomed to talking about. For a start, we need to place the passage in its context in the poem: we reach it after receiving a powerful image of the beauty of Paradise as seen by a furious Satan, and learning of the angelic concern as to the vulnerability of the human pair. Milton's creation of Paradisal beauty is there to impart a sense of what we, his readers, have lost, according to Judaic and Christian theology, through the advent of sin, but also to increase the narrative tension of his poem, since we know this is a threatened beauty, and one that will soon be put out of reach of the couple now enjoying it. The sense of transience is heightened by the temporal nature of the beauty described: the passage is built on a sequence of moments, from the 'Now' of evening's arrival to the 'now' of the stars' appearance to the 'at length' of the moon's glorious unveiling (with a proleptic announcement of the nightingale's night-long performance). The sequence of verbs emphasizes that all is in motion—'came . . . on', 'clad', 'accompanied', 'slunk', 'sung', 'glowed', 'led', 'rode', 'rising', 'unveiled', 'threw'. The images of light move from an even sober grey to the glowing of stars, then to the special brightness of the evening star, then to the clouded moon, and finally to the silver light of what can only be a full moon fully visible. The subtleties of rhythm and sound I mentioned earlier play their part in this moving beauty, working as a sequence, not as a fixed set of properties.

The metaphors, too, are not merely evocations of beauty; they also play their part in the literary experience of the lines. For one thing, Milton, as often in the poem, uses comparisons from the post-lapsarian world, hinting once more at the distance we've travelled since Edenic times. The grey of twilight is like clothing, something as yet unknown in Paradise; the nightingale's descant is taken from the terminology of sophisticated vocal counterpoint; sapphires glow not in the earth but only when they have been cut and polished by human hands; and the passage ends with clothing terminology once more—the 'unveiled' moon casts its 'mantle'—the gorgeous robe of a queen—over the dark. Hesperus, too, belongs to the post-lapsarian world of Ancient Greece.

The word 'accompanied' in the phrase 'Silence accompanied' is also probably a metaphor, since it's used intransitively, which suggests, especially in the context of a description of sound, musical accompaniment. The paradox, of course, is that this accompaniment—to the visual scene—is not sound but soundlessness, an appropriate aural match to the visual uniform grey. (A descant is also an addition to some other melodic sequence, though here presumably silence is the ground to which it's added.) Another variety of metaphor, personification, runs through the passage, inviting further activity on the part of the engaged reader: the characters in this little drama are Evening, Twilight, Silence, the stars, and the moon; we also learn that the nightingale is female and in love, and that the sapphires that represent the stars are living. Perhaps the most risky of the personifications is that of silence: in addition to the already strange notion of silence as an accompaniment we are asked to make sense of the statement 'Silence was pleased'. Although I've modernized spelling and punctuation in this extract, I've kept Milton's original punctuation; a modernizer might be expected to insert a full stop after this phrase to link it more clearly to what has gone before, as it seems best understood as a response to the nightingale's singing. Even with this simplification, though, it tests the attentive reader: is it that the song and the silence produce a kind of perfect harmony, such that the listener can only imagine the receiving silence itself to be experiencing pleasure? No matter how many times we read the passage, the phrase will never fall neatly into a meaning we could paraphrase. John Wilson, writing as Christopher North in *Blackwood's Magazine*, articulates, somewhat awkwardly, the phrase's challenge to the intellect: 'There is here both a production and a variation of thought, beyond or after, or from what is given, proper to the understanding' ('Noctes Ambrosianae', 692). Wilson is correct, I believe, in arguing that this challenge produces a 'new different feeling', though the difference, as he indicates, is 'hard to define'.

There is more to say about these lines, but I hope this is enough to suggest that its power as literature doesn't lie in anything we might call its beauty as such, but in its mobilization of our attitudes towards and feelings about beauty, and of our awareness of the language and images whereby beauty is traditionally conveyed, so that we're taken up into the inventiveness of Milton's writing, and enjoy the evocative power of the language he has created—and, indeed, our experience of the power of which language is shown to be capable.

Q *Discussions of the aesthetic properties of works of art, including literary works, also usually stress the importance of unity, coherence, and balance. Doesn't your account suffer from the lack of any such requirement?*

A This question is closely related to the previous one, and my answer will be similar too. The concept of beauty includes some notion of unity and wholeness, and it's a quality we value in many places outside art: the perfect balance of features in a beautiful face, the ordered arrangement of natural elements in a beautiful landscape, and the like. It's not, therefore, a distinctive property of the literary work. But, as is the case with the more general idea of beauty, this is not to say that unity or coherence is unimportant in literature: it's a powerful resource available to the writer. This is because of its function as an expectation: to read a text as a work of literature is to anticipate that its parts cohere, that its opening and closing moments function to announce and to clinch the work, that the puzzles it presents will be solved and the loose ends tied up. While the expectation that a work will possess beauty perhaps varies from age to age, the expectation that it will be unified seems to be one of the most enduring of literary, and artistic, characteristics—however much it is challenged by actual works of art.

The writer may satisfy this expectation in the most obvious way, in which case unity plays only a minor part in the literary character of the work, providing some onward momentum and final release of tension. But the writer may satisfy the expectation for unity in an unobvious way, or only partially, or not at all. The conclusions of Dickens's novels, for instance, usually provide the reader with a sense of narrative strands being tied neatly together, more or less convincingly, but the literary pleasure this gives is not one of wholeness and unity but of a kind of retrospective meaning-making as the elements of the plot that had remained unresolved now find their resolution.

(On re-reading, of course, there is the added pleasure of knowing these resolutions in advance, and seeing through, as it were, the narrative mystifications.) Joyce's *Ulysses*, by contrast, leads the reader through hundreds of pages to what, by the norms of narrative structure, ought to be the culminating union of Stephen Dedalus and Leopold Bloom, fatherless son and sonless father, but turns out instead to be a parting of the ways. Here the thwarted expectations signal that we're in a different novelistic universe from most of Joyce's forebears.

Plot conclusions that round off the narrative in an obvious way can offer less in the way of literary pleasure than those that don't: it's quite possible to find the ending of the Lerner and Loewe musical *My Fair Lady*, in which Eliza Doolittle returns, humbly, to Henry Higgins, less satisfying than the ending of George Bernard Shaw's *Pygmalion*, in which her rejection of him is, it would appear, permanent. The expectation of closure in a conventional love story—that after negotiating obstacles the lovers will be united at the end—conflicts with the expectations aroused by moral demands—in this instance, that selfishness and misogyny will not be rewarded by a woman's devotion; in Shaw's play the second of these wins out, in Lerner's book for the musical the first does, to the disappointment of many in the audience.

We may turn to a short poem to examine how these issues play out over a small compass. Here's a well-known poem by Wordsworth that unquestionably possesses a roundedness and sense of completion:

A slumber did my spirit seal;
    I had no human fears:
She seemed a thing that could not feel
    The touch of earthly years.

No motion has she now, no force;
    She neither hears nor sees;
Rolled round in earth's diurnal course,
    With rocks, and stones, and trees.

It's possible that a reader will take pleasure in the wholeness and unity of this poem: there is the familiar ballad stanza or common measure with its alternation of four-beat and three-beat lines and an underlying dipodic meter that makes of the whole eight-line unit a single sixteen-beat ensemble with a satisfying feeling of completion on the last line; the balance between the content of the two stanzas, the unthinking and unjustified assumption of immortality during life complemented by the awareness of a different kind of permanence after death; the closural force of the regular iambic feet of the last line; the organizing power of the masculine *abab* rhymes. If this were to be a reader's response, it would be indistinguishable from the satisfaction taken in a smoothly rounded pebble or a perfect rose. But to read the lines as a poem is to experience an event, in which closure is something that *happens*; it's to be aware that this sense of roundedness, this rhythmic wholeness, is the product of a writer's inventiveness, evoking in a few words the movement from happy illusion to an acceptance of reality, the finality of which is both a kind of acquiescence in the inevitable and the registration of a terrible loss. It's not a matter of coherence but of the experience of cohering.

Coherence or cohering is, of course, a crucial factor in any interpretation: hermeneutic activity is necessarily based on the assumption that where there are alternative ways of understanding a word or phrase or sentence, the ones that fit best with the verbal context are to be preferred. This produces the familiar hermeneutic circle: we build up an interpretation by moving from the meanings of smaller items to the meanings of larger wholes, and these overarching meanings then enable us to refine and delimit our initial hypotheses about the finer details. The cluster of possible meanings suggested by the apparently mechanical terms 'motion' and 'force' in Wordsworth's poem, for instance, are retrospectively distilled to a more intense set when we reach the last two lines: we realize that they refer to the possession of life itself, although, against the literal sense of the lines, they also foreshadow the global movement of the earth which is now the only motion and force the dead woman has.

I might also mention the assumption of linearity here: that we read a work of literature from start to finish, and that each stage leads on to the next. Again, it's an expectation that the writer is able to use as a literary resource; in 'A slumber did my spirit seal' the linearity that leads from the first to the second stanza enables us to jump the gap between them, the gap in which the most significant event of the poem occurs. As we've just seen, the ending of the poem encourages a non-linear reinterpretation of an earlier line (though in re-reading, of course, we're already equipped to read that line).

Philosophical aesthetics, as the study of beauty in art and nature, relies heavily on notions of unity and coherence. For instance, when Ingarden, whose view of literary experience has some affinities with mine, turns from discussing literary works in the broadest sense, irrespective of evaluation, to the literary work as art, he speaks of 'the polyphonic harmony of its aesthetic value qualities' (*Literary Work of Art*, 369). He thus retains the sense of the work's sequentiality but stresses the beauty of relationships rather than the exploitation of the reader's expectations.

Q *Another term that doesn't feature in your argument is 'truth'. Do you have a use for it?*

A Clearly, there's considerably rhetorical efficacy in claiming that one's work, or the work of a writer one admires, tells the truth; and it may sound like an admission of literature's weakness to say that it doesn't do so. Once again, I must emphasize that I'm isolating only those aspects of the text that justify our calling it 'literary'; works of literature often do, of course, valuably convey truths about the world. As literature, though, they engage not with truth itself but with its modes of existence or non-existence—or its coming into, or fading out of, existence. A great many novels deal with the uncovering of truth, from crime fiction to such explorations of memory and veracity as Ford Madox Ford's *The Good Soldier* or Graham Swift's *Waterland*.

In saying this, I'm departing from the Adornian tradition of aesthetic theory, in which the idea of a work's 'truth-content' is central. However, Adorno's much-debated notion of truth-content is far from simple; it includes, for instance, a recognition of the importance of the artwork's incomprehensibility, which is not unrelated to what I'm calling 'otherness'. It's not the same as the work's meaning, themes, or content. And it doesn't refer to an unchanging, ahistorical truth but to a thoroughly historical form of truth, a paradox which lies at the heart of Adorno's thinking, and marks one of the great differences between his thinking and Heidegger's. (I don't find the latter's account of the work of art as the letting-happen of the advent of the truth particularly helpful, though Heidegger's readings are always worth attending to, however peculiar. Nor, for that matter, do I find anything useful in Badiou's idiosyncratic notion of truth.)

My own sense of the usefulness of a notion of truth also has a historical dimension. The otherness that I welcome in writing or reading a work of literature is, I've argued, not simply something outside of current conceptions but something *excluded* by current conceptions. To bring it into view is to act in the service of a kind of truth, a truth, we might say, hitherto universally unacknowledged. But the literary work doesn't present this 'truth' as an entity or statement to be contemplated; the reader experiences its coming into being as an event, perhaps as much by the slight realignment of existing patterns of thought as by the apprehension of something new.

Q *What then of that feeling we sometimes have in reading a literary work, expressed in the somewhat banal exclamation 'It's so true!'?*

A What this usually means is that the work carries conviction; that its handling of the available literary techniques is such that it achieves a particular vividness and forcefulness. (I've already touched on the sense of recognition that often accompanies a powerful reading experience.) If all it means is that its account of some reality corresponds with the reader's view of that reality, it's a reflection not on the literariness of the work but on its documentary usefulness or gratification. It's possible to read the poems of George Herbert or the later T. S. Eliot as a way of strengthening one's religious belief; but it's also possible to enjoy them as literary works without the question of the truth of Christianity becoming an issue. The narrower and more fixed one's sense of 'the truth' is, the less able one is to read certain literary works as literature. (I discuss the related idea that works of literature can possess knowledge in chapter 8.)

Q *One more term that gets short shrift in* The Singularity of Literature *is 'imagination'. Given its centrality to Romantic theories of art, and its frequent appearance in discussions of literary creation, doesn't it need to be part of your account?*

A I'm not as averse to the Romantic vocabulary of 'imagination', 'genius', etc. as many literary theorists have been over the past few decades, but these words need to be handled with care. One aspect of our enjoyment of literary works is our admiration for the inventive act that brought them into being, and words like these gesture towards this dimension of art. They arise out of an awareness that the act of invention is a mysterious one, involving as it does the apprehension of otherness; something which, though it's achieved through the deployment of existing resources and requires a deep knowledge of the cultural environment, involves a leap into the unknown. Similarly, a reading that does justice to a literary work is one that that draws on knowledge and understanding to make it possible for the unknown and the not understood to enter the world; the term 'imagination'—not just meaning the ability to create images—is one of the available names for this process.

Q *How important would you say the* feelings *experienced by the reader in engaging with the work of literature are?*

A Affective responses to literary works include many different elements, some of which are relevant to the literary work as literature, others that are not. As I suggested earlier, the enjoyment of beauty or wholeness is not a distinctively literary response; one could say the same of the pleasure one gains from acquiring new knowledge. Aristotle thought the pleasure of mimesis lay in the access to knowledge it provides, an idea in which there may be some truth, though it would apply to all forms of mimesis, including documentary accounts. Boredom with a work that seems to be going on for ever and pleasure when the end is in sight are also not relevant to my argument. I would argue, too, that the emotions aroused by fictional *characters*—hatred of villains, sympathy with victims, admiration of heroes—or depicted *events*—shock at a brutal murder, delight at an accepted marriage proposal, fear at the sound of footsteps in the night—are characteristic of much more than literary works: a strong historical account might well have similar effects on the reader. The feelings that form part of the peculiarly literary response are not direct responses to content, but are always mediated by *form*: they are coloured by the pleasure we take in the representation itself, in the language whereby the emotional response is invited. I may feel something like genuine hatred of Gilbert Osmond in *Portrait of a Lady*, but my literary response recognizes the fictionality of the character and admires James's skill in drawing him; it becomes, therefore, a kind of staged emotion, one that I don't fully subscribe to but acknowledge as appropriate. I discuss this question further in chapter 9, where I examine the arousal of a response of horror and dismay by a particular example.

Sources and parallels

Q *In* The Singularity of Literature, *you elaborated on your understanding of the nature and function of literature, and of art more generally, with only limited references to other theories and theorists. Can you say what the main sources of your arguments are?*

A Your question is closely related to the question I asked myself at the beginning of this process of exploration and theoretical formulation many years ago. From what mysterious zone do the words that I'm writing, and the ideas they express or make possible (since the ideas don't necessarily pre-exist the words), emerge? It's a question any writer, of literary as well as non-literary works, may ask—and in all likelihood, fail to answer. It's because of this unanswerable question that I felt it necessary to invoke the concept—though it's not really a concept—of the 'other'.

This is not an answer to the question, but the point I'm making is that there's no reason to assume that any author can give an accurate answer to it. In *The Singularity of Literature* I provided an appendix in which I tried to enumerate, with comments, all the authors and texts I was aware of having been important in developing the thinking spelled out in that book. The names that bore most weight there were Kant, Adorno, Derrida, Levinas, Blanchot, and J. M. Coetzee; but I added to that list many more writers and thinkers who played a part, and could have added more still. My continuing debt to Derrida and Levinas will be evident throughout this book, and it seems to me impossible to get to grips with the question of the literary without grappling with Kant's Third Critique. Adorno, important to me especially for *Aesthetic Theory*, also requires a good deal of grappling—which is usually rewarded, though I don't have Adorno's faith in the dialectic. It will be evident from my many quotations from Blanchot that I'm often taken by his specific formulations; however, I don't find his larger meditation on literature as *désoeuvrement*—'unworking' or 'worklessness'—helpful; my sense of the experience of literature is not rooted in negativity. Coetzee, in his interviews and non-fictional writings, presents one of the most compelling accounts of what it is to write literary works that I know.

The age-old discourse on the sublime, from Longinus to Burke and Kant and to much more recent discussions (one might include Lyotard on the 'presentation of the unpresentable'), is in the background, though I'm not concerned with a special variety of literary experience in the same way. The question of the distinctiveness of literature was a central focus of the Russian Formalists and the Prague Structuralists, and I absorbed their influence long ago, as well as that of the tradition of 1950s and 1960s stylistics addressing the same question. Since the publication of *The Singularity of Literature* I've read several others who have helped to confirm or sharpen my arguments. One theorist I failed to mention in that book, but whose admirably patient analyses of many dimensions of the literary has been a constant resource, is Gérard Genette. Many more names will come up in the course of this book.

It's also the case that my mode of argument has been more influenced by the analytic tradition than by the continental tradition: I seek to make each step follow logically and transparently from the previous one (a procedure very different from a writer like Deleuze or Badiou). I can't tell exactly how my reading, my attendance at lectures, my conversations, and my correspondence have operated together to produce the picture of literature that I now hold, though I'm extremely grateful to all those whose ideas have filtered into my thinking. (I've tried to say something, in a discussion with David Jonathan Bayot and Francisco Roman Guevara, about the intellectual paths that led to my current thinking in *Derek Attridge in Conversation*.)

Q *Many philosophers have made significant use of the term 'event', which is central to your arguments, but they have done so in very different ways. It would help clarify your position if you related your sense of the term's implications to these various uses of it.*

A The most important philosophers for my understanding of the event are Jean-François Lyotard and Jacques Derrida. The idea of the event was central to Lyotard's thought throughout his career, from his early 'libidinal' philosophy through his concern with postmodernism to the account of language games, phrasing and the *differend*. Geoffrey Bennington's admirable study of Lyotard's thought was aptly named *Writing the Event*. The significant properties of the event for Lyotard are its unpredictability and its unrepresentability—or, more accurately, the fact that it can be represented in various ways, all of which will fail to fully capture it. Any attempt at a universally valid representation of events will fail, not just logically but ethically, since justice for Lyotard inheres in multiplicity and singularity. Lyotard also put forward the idea that it's possible to 'act passively' as the best way to respond to events. My sense of the event of the literary work draws on all these features. Lyotard's later writing is indebted to Wittgenstein's concept of 'language games', and there is an affinity between the arguments I've put forward and Wittgenstein's explorations of the operation of language and the limits of universalizing philosophy.

Derrida's understanding of the event shares a great deal with Lyotard's, but introduces an important complication: the event is at one and the same time singular, unpredictable, unrepresentable *and* a repetition, an inscription in an existing code that is eminently repeatable and imitable. This is the paradoxical force of a number of Derrida's terms, such as *iterability, arche-writing,* and the *trace,* all of which seek to capture the inter-implication and inseparability of the new and the old, singularity and repetition, the spontaneous and the mechanical. I'll be returning to this paradox in later chapters, but the point I want to make now is that in talking of the literary work as an event, I have in mind both the singularity of the creative and receptive processes and their constitution by the systems and codes of the cultural context which enables them to occur even as they are challenged by those processes.

Other versions of the event in continental philosophy I've found less useful. Heidegger's *Ereignis* is often translated as 'event', but more accurately as 'event of appropriation' or 'enowning'; it is too embedded in Heideggerian thought to be itself appropriated in this discussion. The event is a key term in Gilles Deleuze's thinking, descending from Stoic philosophy and influenced by, among others, Leibniz and Whitehead; but Deleuze's concern with the relation between events and concepts, his notion of the 'pure event', and his postulation of a 'time of the event' which is different from historical time, bespeak a different kind of interest from that of Lyotard and Derrida, one that is avowedly metaphysical, albeit a metaphysics that is wary of anything like essence. Someone whose notion of the event is equally central to his thinking but is diametrically opposed to Deleuze's is Alain Badiou; in *Logics of Worlds* he boils the former's account down to four 'Deleuzian axioms of the event' and counters them with four axioms of his own, making precisely the reverse assertion in each case. But Badiou's version is no more helpful in discussing literary works than Deleuze's: it situates the event as an absolute break in politics, the arts, the sciences or love ('erotic liberation'), fidelity to which constitutes 'truth'. This grand proclamation of absolute verities offers little purchase on the experiences of readers as they find particular literary works moving and pleasing them. I've found in Foucault's work a more usable conception of the event, with its emphasis on discursive events and their role in the operations of power. Barthes's championing of *signifiance* over *significance* and *text* over *work* is a related endeavour to my mind, though I've already explained why I use the latter pair of terms differently. Some literary theorists have tried to employ Levinas's distinction between the *saying* and the *said* to argue for the non-conceptual, event-like nature of the artwork—something of a distortion of Levinas's thought, but useful in itself.

Among literary theorists, one whose position is close to mine and who is largely ignored in both analytic and continental traditions is Louise Rosenblatt, who was best known among teachers of English in schools and colleges across the United States. Rosenblatt, in works such as *The Reader, the Text, the Poem*, argues powerfully for what she calls 'transactional reading', emphasizing that what is important is what happens when we read a work of literature, not anything we might carry away from it. The meaning of a work lies in the reader's interaction with it, and each reader, with a unique set of beliefs and range of knowledge, produces a different work in the reading process. Although I discovered Rosenblatt's work late in my writing of *The Singularity of Literature*, it provided welcome support for my thinking.

Q *Could your theory of the literary work be described as a phenomenology of literature?*

A I recognize that the way I approach the question 'What is literature?' has much in common with the Husserlian tradition, in that I start from the individual's experience of the work but attempt to identify an underlying structural relationship rather than attending to the empirical facts of psychology. I am, in a sense, looking for the essence of the literary experience, keeping presuppositions about the nature of literature at arm's length and focusing on what is given; this is a paradigmatically phenomenological search. Also in tune with the fundamental insights of phenomenology is the treatment of works of literature as existing neither wholly objectively in the world nor wholly subjectively in the mind of the reader, but in the relation between them.

I've already mentioned Mikel Dufrenne's useful distinction between the work of art and the aesthetic object. Good phenomenologist that he is, he doesn't argue that the former is real while the latter is ideal: 'The work of art is outside consciousness, a thing among things, yet it exists only as referred to a consciousness' (lii). He explains that 'the work of art, as present in the world, may be grasped in a perception which neglects it aesthetic quality—as when I'm inattentive at the theatre—or which seeks to understand and justify it instead of experiencing it, as the critic may do' (lii). This distinction is useful in thinking about the difference between the text and the work, as I've outlined it: the text is not simply the material set of marks or sounds, but the verbal sequence as it is apprehended without the characteristic engagement that transforms it into a work of art—that is to say, without experiencing it as a singular transformative event revelatory of the powers of language. Dufrenne comes close to articulating the need to posit what I've called authoredness:

> The experiences of creator and spectator are not unconnected; for the artist becomes the spectator of his own work as he creates it, and

> the spectator associates himself with the artist, whose act he recognizes in the work. That is why, although limiting ourselves to the experience of the spectator, we shall all the same need to evoke the creator. *But the creator then in question is the one whom the work reveals, not the one who historically created the work.* (xlvi, my italics)

However, there is a major difference between a thoroughgoing phenomenological account of artistic experience and the argument I'm making. Dufrenne, who offers what is perhaps the most fully elaborated phenomenological account of the artwork, tells us that aesthetic perception

> must at once be distinguished from judgments, sometimes vociferously maintained, which express our special tastes, that is, affirm our preferences. The latter raise the vexing question of the relativity of the beautiful, for they make it appear that the aesthetic sensibility is limited, and at least partly determined by, the nature of the individual and his culture. These determinations bear primarily on our preferences, and our preferences are not constitutive of aesthetic experience but only add a personal note to it. (*The Phenomenology of Aesthetic Experience,* lxiii)

By contrast, my understanding of what is essential in responding to literary works assumes that my preconceptions, expectations, habits, stock of knowledge, and so on are what I respond *with,* and that what I have to account for are as much the differences among all readings of a text as what they share.

Another problem for a phenomenological account of the work of literature is that phenomenology treats *all* entities as coming into being in the relation between a subject and an object; literature is not something distinctive in this regard. The two theorists who have attempted to be more explicit about that distinctiveness are Ingarden and Iser, whom I've mentioned as offering accounts I've found helpful; their emphasis is on the essential incompleteness of the literary work. Ingarden's phenomenological description has some elements in common with mine, such as his rejection of both physicalism and psychologism, and at times his actual formulations come close to mine—for instance, his statement that 'the literary work of art constitutes an *aesthetic* object *only when it is expressed in a concretization'* (*The Literary Work of Art*, 372). Ingarden recognizes, too, that an individual's concretization of a work, influenced by a host of particular contingencies, demands creativity and will always be unique—though he privileges the single 'adequate' concretization that he believes is determined by the structure of the work, and sees, in a conventional manner, the establishment of a harmonious whole as a goal of literary writing and reading. Ingarden's main project, however, is to determine the mode of being of the literary work irrespective of its worth as a work of art, and thus he includes in his analysis all those more formulaic works I leave out of account.

Iser follows Ingarden in arguing that the work of literary art is produced in the reader's concretization of the text (and he uses 'text', as I do, for the words written by the author before they are read as literature), but goes a little further in allowing for the text's openness. He insists that the structures of the work are 'contained in the text' but 'they do not fulfill their function until they have affected the reader' (*The Act of Reading*, 21). Similarly, he asserts, 'relative indeterminacy of a text allows a spectrum of actualizations . . . [but] the mixture of determinacy and indeterminacy conditions the interaction between text and reader' (24). Although Iser is critical of Ingarden for allowing only a one-way relationship between text and reader (173), for arguing that the indeterminacies of the text demand, rather than stimulate, completions (177), and for failing to see that a work may be concretized in different, equally valid, ways (202), he himself constantly draws back from allowing any real creativity to the reader. Again, in trying to establish the mode of existence of the literary work, he is drawn both to the idea that it's an event—'the meaning of a literary text is not a definable entity but, if anything, a dynamic happening'—and an object, if a rather ghostly one: 'The work itself cannot be identical with the text or with the concretization, but must be virtual in character' (21). And Iser's 'implied reader' is, like the subject in phenomenology, 'a transcendental model which makes it possible for the structural effects of literary texts to be described' (38). He perhaps comes closest to my position in the final sentence of *The Act of Reading*: 'And if there is not *one* specific meaning of a literary text, this "apparent deficiency" is, in fact, the productive matrix which enables the text to be meaningful in a variety of different contexts' (231).

The other school of literary theory associated with phenomenology is the Geneva School, the most prominent member of which was Georges Poulet. Their focus on the act of identifying with the consciousness of the author has little in common with what I'm arguing. I'm more drawn to Hans-Georg Gadamer's revision of Husserlian premises: we interpret not in spite of but by means of our accumulated mental stores, imbibed from our cultural surroundings, from the horizon within which we read. This is not to say that we shouldn't try to become aware of the role of our prejudices in influencing what we make of a work; but we need to accept that most of what we bring to the act of interpretation is not conscious. I'm also sympathetic to Gadamer's appropriation of the hermeneutic tradition's idea that interpretation is endless.

Q *So yours is not a psychological account either?*

A I admit that I've found it difficult to delineate the distinction between the focus of my investigation and the somewhat different focus that would govern the work of a psychologist interested in the reading activity. Many of the terms I use, like *surprise, wonder, expectation, satisfaction,* and the term *experience* itself, refer to psychological events that could be studied by means of questionnaires or investigations of neurological activity, but what I'm attempting to isolate are the fundamental processes that underlie these subjective occurrences. I'm aware that I'm putting a great deal of weight on introspection, and it's possible that this limitation could be overcome by quantitative studies; but such studies still need careful interpretation if they are not to remain at the level of the contingent incidents that cluster around any reading activity.

Q *Perhaps your thinking owes as much to the pragmatic as to the phenomenological tradition?*

A I had read very little of Dewey's work when I was writing *The Singularity of Literature*, and now that I have greater familiarity with it, I realize that there is much in that book that has affinities with Deweyian pragmatism. Let me just give you a few quotations from *Art as Experience* (the very title of which resonates with my thinking) to illustrate some of the similarities. The first is from Dewey's opening paragraph: 'In common conception, the work of art is often identified with the building, book, painting, or statue in its existence apart from human experience. Since the actual work of art is what the product does with and in experience, the result is not favorable to understanding' (3). Dewey makes a distinction between intellectual and aesthetic experience that has some similarities with my formulations of the event-character of the literary work: in the former, he states, 'the conclusion has value on its own account. It can be extracted as a formula or as a "truth" . . . In the work of art there is no such single self-sufficient deposit. The end, the terminus, is significant not by itself but as the integration of the parts. It has no other existence' (55). And again: 'The value of experience is not only in the ideals it reveals, but in its power to disclose many ideals, a power more germinal and more significant than any revealed ideal, since it includes them in its stride, shatters, and remakes them' (322). Dewey also understands the need to distinguish literary reading from among the many other ways in which the literary text can be read: one of the two great fallacies of aesthetic judgement, he declares, is 'the confusion of categories': 'the historian, the physiologist, the biographer, the psychologist all have their own problems and their own leading conceptions that control the inquiries they undertake. Works of art provide them with relevant data in the pursuit of their special investigations' (317).

However, the main thrust of Dewey's argument (which is not concerned primarily with literature) is different from mine. His emphasis on experience derives from his desire to bring the practices of art as close as possible to other kinds of activity, and his notion of aesthetic experience, the exact nature of which is never fully spelled out, is predicated (like Ingarden's understanding of literary reading) on the achievement of unity and harmony. The formal characteristics of an aesthetic experience, says Dewey, are 'cumulation, tension, conservation, anticipation, and fulfillment' (145): this is a good summary of the processes at work in the onward drive of the literary work, but it's clear that for Dewey the achievement of the final term is crucial to what he means by 'aesthetic experience'.

Followers of Dewey have developing his thinking in a number of directions. Richard Rorty and Stanley Fish have, in their different ways, pursued the anti-foundationalist strand, and have valuably undermined an older faith in eternal aesthetic verities (some of which Dewey still clung on to). Perhaps the philosopher who has derived most from Dewey's work is Richard Shusterman, who has advanced a theory of pragmatist aesthetics with a strong emphasis on the continuity of aesthetic experience across traditional boundaries, including the boundary between mind and body. Most interesting for me is Shusterman's desire to draw from both the pragmatist and the continental philosophical traditions, and his critique of the fixation of analytic aesthetics on the art object. Thus he links Dewey's acknowledgement that 'the work's meaning and value can change with the changing realities and practices that condition our experience of it' to Adorno's remark that 'Works of art are not fixed once and for all, but . . . have a historical existence owing to their processual quality . . . [and] change in accord with the historically changing attitudes of people' (*Pragmatist Aesthetics*, 2nd edn., 26–7; citing Adorno, *Aesthetic Theory* [1984], 255–6). Shusterman defends Dewey's attachment to the idea of unity by suggesting that, for Dewey, it's never a final resting point, and in fact can be a spur to new activity. Nevertheless, in the light of poststructuralist thinking, he does attempt to do fuller justice to the fragmentary and unfinished than Dewey was able to do.

Politics and ideology

Q *One area in which you part company with a great deal of literary criticism over the past thirty or forty years is in your views of the social and political value of literature. You argue that although literary works can have powerful social and political effects, these don't arise from their operation as literature, but from non-literary ways of reading them. Can you clarify your claim?*

A Let's take one example that will throw some light on this question. It's widely accepted that Väinö Linna's Finnish trilogy *Under the North Star*, and in particular the second novel, *The Uprising*, published in 1960, had a profound effect on Finns' attitudes toward the civil war of 1918: it brought into the open what was in many respects still a taboo subject, and challenged the White-dominated accounts of the war by its full and convincing treatment of the Reds' experience. But did it do this as literature, or as historical documentation? There's no doubt that by presenting the historical material as a gripping novel, utilizing the resources of fiction such as suspense and characterization, Linna was able to reach an audience that a straightforward historical account would not have done, and readers were treated to a history lesson that gave them a new understanding of the war in a manner that afforded them real pleasure. But this is not quite the same as saying the work had an effect *as literature*; its literary value lies in the changes it brings about in its reader's grasp of the world, and these changes vary from reader to reader and are not predictable or controllable. The consequences of Linna's composition and publication of *The Uprising* are a matter of empirical fact and historical record; its importance as a book perhaps lies more in this history than anywhere else. But as literature its importance is not limited to a particular moment in Finnish history: it continues to be enjoyed as a literary work irrespective of the information it conveys.

The value of literature, then, can be approached in two ways. Certain literary works can be shown to have had specific effects on defined communities at particular moments in time, and the potential for new works (or rediscovered old works) having such an effect in future is a legitimate subject for discussion. Literary works, like many kinds of text, can be the bearers of wisdom. Equally, literary works can have regrettable effects, reinforcing racial stereotypes, for instance, or encouraging violence towards women, or distorting communities' histories. Because literature works in a manner that is particularly pleasurable and powerful, these effects, good or bad, can be very pronounced.

Alternatively, the literary domain can be seen as valuable for its cultivation of an openness to otherness, a willingness to change, an alertness to that which challenges preconceptions and fixed habits. Individual literary works—understood as having their existence in the events of reading they provide—can be discussed in both ways, for their tangible or potential effectiveness, and for their less tangible but no less significant capacity to open readers to new possibilities of experience. The event of the literary work of art, as I've suggested, leaves the reader changed (as opposed to the event of the work that is 'literary' only in the more general, classificatory sense, which leaves the reader just as she was). Iser sees this clearly: 'The completion of meaning gains its full significance when something *happens* to the reader' (*Act of Reading*, 158). He also acknowledges that 'the reader himself, in constituting meaning, is also constituted' (150).

I'm not, therefore, arguing for the traditional notion of the 'disinterestedness' of art; works of literature, I believe, are deeply engaged in bringing about change, first in individuals, then through them in society more broadly. But those changes can't be stipulated or predicted in advance; literature—as literature—is never in the service of a particular moral or political or religious program. Philodemus said it over two millennia ago: 'Poems, insofar as they are poems, do not provide benefit' (*On Rhetoric* 1,226, col. 21, 12–15).

Q *You appear to reject the study of literary works for the purpose of revealing their ideological biases—the hermeneutics of suspicion, symptomatic reading, the idea of 'reading against the grain,' in order to expose hidden prejudices and* *assumptions. These modes have been prominent in literary studies for two or three decades, and by not going along with them you appear to have been swimming against the current. Is this a fair assessment?*

A I need to stress yet again that what I'm trying to do is to isolate the operation—and the value—of literature (or art more generally) *as distinct from other cultural practices.* I'm not trying to give an account of everything that literature is or does; it may not even be a very important part of what literature does, at least at particular historical moments or in the case of particular texts. Literary works inevitably reflect the predispositions of their time, often in covert ways, and exposing these is an interesting and illuminating endeavour that has resulted in some outstanding works of literary analysis; but most other verbal and non-verbal artefacts are analysable in the same way. Rorty has invoked Kant's distinction between the *dignity* we accord people and the *value* (or price) we attach to things, suggesting that we treat literary works as 'honorary persons' (*Interpretation and Overinterpretation*, 106); and while I'm not quite proposing this strategy, it seems right that a full response to a work involves treating it not as a means to a predetermined end, which would be an instrumental approach, but as an end in itself. This is not to imply that works of literature are autonomous entities, any more than human beings are autonomous entities; texts are cultural products, as are readings, and both are interlaced with the circumambient culture at every point.

There is one strand of thinking about the relation of literature to ideology—it's associated particularly with the work of Pierre Macherey—that sees the specificity of the literary as lying in its simultaneous incorporation of and challenge to ideology. Readings on this basis are not suspicious of literary works, but rather applaud them for their subtle exposure of ideological operations (whatever the overt purpose of the author was). No doubt some works do achieve a complex relation of this kind to ideology, but this can't be held to be generally the case without a good deal of special pleading. (And it seems odd that the very same works that have achieved canonical status on the basis of their ideological conformism should *also* turn out to be exceptional for this opposed reason.) If works of literature are sites of resistance, they may or may not resist the dominant ideology, but, as Adorno saw (at least in his reading of modernist literature), they do resist a culture of instrumentalization.

As for the current against which I've been swimming, I've had the gratifying sensation that the stream has begun to flow more and more strongly in the same direction as me. For one thing, *The Singularity of Literature* received some warmly positive responses from fellow critics who had appeared committed to the symptomatic reading of literature. Then there is the movement known as 'the New Formalism' and, more recently, the flurry of attention to 'surface reading', about both of which I have some reservations, but which testify to a new willingness to develop other ways of reading literary works than historical or ideological analysis. Surface reading—at least as summarized in the Introduction by Stephen Best and Sharon Marcus to the 2009 special issue of *Representations* on 'The Way We Read Now'—can mean something close to what I think of as responsible reading as I've described it in chapter 2, but it can also embrace 'distant reading' or book history, which mark out a very different terrain. The assembled critics in the forum on the same topic put together by Lisa A. Freeman ('Why We Argue about the Way We Read') tend to reassert the value of suspicious reading, but make many gestures in the direction of its unsuspicious twin. Henry Staten and I, in our discussions of what is most essential to the reading and criticism of the poetry (published as *The Craft of Poetry*), struggled to find a satisfactory term for what we're advocating and attempting to practice: 'minimal reading', 'weak reading', and 'literal reading' were all possibilities. (We settled in the end for the first of these.) Heather Love, in 'Close but not Deep', prefers Erving Goffman's 'descriptive reading', though, following Bruno Latour, she also refers to her account of Morrison's *Beloved* as 'flat reading' (375). I rather like Sharon Marcus's term 'just reading', which she introduces in her book *Between Women* (75), not only for the senses she enumerates there but for its implication of doing justice to the work.

Q *Pierre Bourdieu begins the Preface to* The Rules of Art *with something of a rant against those who object that the sciences and social sciences lose sight of the 'singularity of experience' in their attempt to analyse literary practices (xv–xx). This appears to put your approach and Bourdieu's at opposite extremes. Is this the case?*

A I don't believe it is, at least not from my point of view. I've already noted some of the similarities between Bourdieu's account of the cultural and historical embeddedness of art and my own, and I've found Bourdieu's work extremely valuable in other ways as well. *Distinction* helped me articulate my overall project in my book *Peculiar Language* when I came across it in the final stage of writing. Perhaps I need to emphasize that my sense of the singularity of the work of literature (and of the author who wrote it and the reader engaging with it) is not of a replacement for the operation of social and historical determinants, but rather an attempt to grasp the remainder that is left when such explanations have been exhausted. Bourdieu in that Preface to *The Rules of Art* quotes approvingly a thought of Goethe's, which, he says, 'all natural scientists and social scientists could claim as their own': 'Our opinion is that it well becomes man to assume that there is something unknowable, but that he does not have to set any limit to his inquiry' (xvii). This seems right to me: scientific analysis should be taken as far as it will go, but there should also be a readiness to acknowledge that it can't explain everything. The power of literature may well lie primarily in what can't be scientifically explained.

The sociology of literature is an interesting and important field; it's just not what I do, nor do I feel it should be central to literary studies. It's a subfield of the sociology of culture, and is governed by scientific procedures; its aim is to achieve generalizations valid for large bodies of literature, not to do justice to the singularity of individual works or oeuvres. 'Distant reading', as practised by Franco Moretti and others, is one version of this sociological approach. It can be very revealing about the history of literary production and reception, and about patterns of literary activity today; it doesn't have much to tell us about why certain literary works repay re-reading, stay in the mind, or effect changes in their readers.

Q *The work of Jacques Rancière has been influential in recent years in reviving an interest in the relation between aesthetics and politics. Have you found it useful in developing your own views?*

A Rancière presents a strongly articulated account of the history of art, reaching, in the modern era (which he regards as starting with Vico), the 'aesthetic regime', whose capacity to re-orient political subjectivity stems from what he claims is the simultaneous assertion of the 'the absolute singularity of art' and the destruction of 'any pragmatic criterion for isolating this singularity'. Art is thus freed from any rule, and 'from any hierarchy of the arts, subject matter, and genres'. (I'm quoting from *The Politics of Aesthetics*, 23.) I'm not convinced by this historical narrative, as there's plenty of evidence of the continuing power of art's distinctiveness as a cultural practice, and its hierarchies and generic conventions, and so I find it hard to accept the claims based on this analysis. As I've said, literature can be highly effective in the realm of politics, and Rancière's account of art's capacity as a form of 'dissensus' to effect a 'redistribution of the sensible' is one of the ways in which this can happen; but such an outcome, like all literature's political effects, is not a function of its literariness.

However, when Rancière describes how 'political art' would function, it seems to me he does acknowledge what I've been insisting is the crucial dimension of the work of literature, or of art more generally:

> Suitable political art would ensure, at one and the same time, a double effect: the readability of a political signification and a sensible or perceptual shock caused, conversely, by the uncanny, by that which resists signification. In fact, this ideal effect is always the object of a negotiation between opposites, between the readability of the message that threatens to destroy the sensible form of art and the radical uncanniness that threatens to destroy all political meaning.
>
> (*Politics of Aesthetics*, 63)

Elsewhere, in attacking what he calls 'the aesthetics of the sublime', Rancière appears to give short shrift to what he here calls 'radical uncanniness' (see *Aesthetics and Its Discontents*, 20–2 and 88–105), arguing rather that art's political force stems from its simultaneous existence as art and as something other than art (36). I prefer the earlier version.

Q *You've contributed to postcolonial studies with books on South African literature, and you're on the editorial boards of leading postcolonial journals. How does the approach to literature you're expounding here square with this field, whose starting point is the history of political struggles and their aftermath?*

A I'd like to quote from the editorial of the first issue of one of those journals, the *Cambridge Journal of Postcolonial Literary Inquiry*, in which the editors put forward a view that is close to mine:

> In announcing our new journal venture . . . we gesture toward a mode of reading that stays with the text, lingers with it, and expresses a reluctance to depart from it . . . In other words, at the risk of echoing a well-known maverick philosopher, we *tarry* with the text. In bringing back the term *literary* to the idea of postcolonial inquiry, we signal the centrality of a paradigm of reading that we feel has been somewhat eclipsed in recent decades by the field's voracious extratextual and interdisciplinary perambulations.
> (Quayson, Ganguly and ten Kortenaar, 'Editorial: New Topographies', 5–6)

Postcolonial studies is a field which is made up of many disciplines, and literary studies is only one of those disciplines—perhaps occupying a larger space within the field than it should, as a result of the literary affiliations of many of its most influential practitioners. Within postcolonial *literary* studies, the kind of attention to the text promoted by the editors of the *Journal of Postcolonial Literary Inquiry* exists alongside more historical or sociological or explicitly political approaches, just as is the case in literary studies more broadly. My interest is in the contribution made by literary works to colonial and postcolonial struggles *as literary works*, which means first of all engaging with their singularity and inventiveness, and attempting to articulate the otherness they apprehend—which is often an otherness produced by the colonial situation.

Q *What would you say about literary works with objectionable content—say, Céline's* Voyage au Bout de la Nuit *or Sarah Gertrude Millin's* God's Step-Children; *do they work as literature to open readers to new experiences?*

A I would put the issue the other way round: if they do open readers to new experiences, they are—for those readers—literary works; if they simply confirm existing habits of mind and affective responses, they can't be called literary in the sense in which I'm using the term. I don't see literary works as any different from other kinds of text when it comes to content: if the represented scenes or individuals are repellent, we deal with them as we deal with repellent scenes in historical or journalistic accounts.

But this raises an important point that I've already brought up: openness to the other, though in itself a positive value, is no guarantee of a change for the good. The other you welcome might be destructive or dispiriting. Most readers new to the Marquis de Sade would be altered by the experience of reading *120 Days of Sodom,* but not necessarily for the better. As J. M. Coetzee's Elizabeth Costello argues in 'The Problem of Evil', there may be scenes of such dehumanized horror that it would be best for them not to be represented—which I take not as an endorsement of censorship but an ethical attitude which might lead to certain works not being recommended to acquaintances or children. The issue can be understood as one of *hospitality,* which I discuss in chapter 10: in principle there can be no limit on what can be said in a literary work; in practice, there are many safeguards in place against the potential harm certain texts might cause.

And to conclude...

Q *What are the critical consequences of your theory? Isn't it just a version of New Criticism or Practical Criticism? Aren't you just clinging to the version of literary criticism you learned as an undergraduate in the 1960s?*

A Clearly, one's early training has a deep effect on one; I can't pretend that all those hours I spent analysing poems and short pieces of prose haven't had their effect on me. The beneficial result has been a lasting admiration for critics and philosophers who write accurately and illuminatingly about texts (the names would range from Cleanth Brooks and Hugh Kenner to Jacques Derrida and Cora Diamond), and an interest in the mechanics of literary language. I get impatient with criticism that fails to take account of the singularity of the text and the reading experience; Moretti's 'distant reading' holds no attraction for me. I believe in the importance of teaching our students to respond accurately as well as imaginatively to literary works.

There are, however, some significant differences between the kind of close reading I would advocate and that championed by the New Critics and, rather differently, the Scrutiny school headed by Leavis. My emphasis on the literary work as an event gives rise to an understanding of literature's operation rather different from the 'well-wrought urn' of the New Critics, while my version of the ethics of reading shares nothing with Leavis's promotion of literature as the repository of the virtues of the English yeomanry. (I exaggerate, but readers of Leavis will know what I mean.) Both these schools (and before them Richards's 'practical criticism') operated on the assumption that they were advancing the 'correct' reading of the text under discussion; there was no sense that their responses were being made in a particular time and place by a singular individual shaped by a specific cultural history. My preference is for critical readings that are aware of the temporal determination of the work of literature, and attempt to take into account the situation of the critic by allowing for other readings from other positions.

I accept the argument, influentially made by W. K. Wimsatt and Monroe Beardsley, that the writer's intentions, as mental acts or dispositions prior to the work, or his later comments on his own work, can't override what the text itself offers when it is read—though I do believe we have to take into account the fact that such biographical details and authorial comments, once the reader is aware of them, can impact upon the understanding of the work, and no amount of theoretical argument will make any difference. This does not mean such readings are, *ipso facto,* better or worse than readings ignorant of biography and authorial comment. And in the concept of authoredness (which I believe is implicit even in the most staunchly anti-intentionalist account) I've already suggested a modification to orthodox New Criticism.

As for the role of historical context, another bugbear of both schools of close reading, it seems to me that it too, whether we like it or not, plays a part in interpretation and enjoyment. (I've discussed the whole question of context in an essay that forms chapter 5 of this book.) The old idea of the 'autonomy' of the work of art seems to me fundamentally wrong; the work exists in the closest of relations to the culture in which it is read, having come into being in the closest of relations to the culture in which it was produced—those cultures being reflected in the idiocultures of writer and reader.

Q *You've published several books on rhythm and metre. Is there a connection between your work on prosody and your thinking about broader theoretical issues?*

A It's hard for me to say exactly how this work has fed into my wider ruminations, but it undoubtedly has. My sense of the importance of bodily responses to rhythm—something ignored in the many accounts of metre which treat it as 'abstract'—has helped me to see the importance of the somatic dimension of literary response, both directly to sounds and rhythms and via verbal sense to content. My close analysis of the rhythmic and sonic patterns of many poems, as they interact with their semantic properties, has probably enhanced my sense of the singularity of the experience of a poem. And of course, there are endless examples of inventiveness in the prosodic domain.

Q *Since the publication of* Singularity *ten years ago, has your further reading influenced your thinking about literature as a cultural category and practice? Have you been persuaded to modify your views in any way?*

A As I've continued to read newly-published articles and books, and also caught up on some of the work I wasn't aware of before *Singularity*, I've sharpened rather than changed my thinking. I've tried to define more clearly my agreements with and differences from analytic aesthetics, as represented, for instance, in Lamarque's book *The Philosophy of Literature*. One venue was a section of *The British Journal of Aesthetics* devoted to this book and responses to it, including mine. (I discussed a part of this published conversation earlier in this exchange.) I've discovered the work of Richard Shusterman, mentioned earlier, which has many similarities with mine, such as an emphasis on experience, an acceptance of the multiplicity of interpretations, and an assertion of the constitutive unpredictability of future developments in art. Shusterman's concept of 'somaesthetics' chimes well with my wish to include bodily responses in my account of literary experience; but I am sceptical about his category of immediate, uninterpreted understanding of language. This may be an accurate description of what it feels like when understanding happens; but logically, it seems to me, there can be no pre-interpretative moment when language somehow conveys its meanings without reference to the code that makes it language. I have a similar objection to the theory that proposes an immediate, pre-semantic, affective response to words; my discussion of affect in chapter 9 elaborates on this objection. Of course, the sounds and rhythms of stretches of language, especially in poetry, can have an unmediated effect—an effect that is felt by anyone hearing the words, whether or not they know the language, and in fact probably more strongly by those who don't. But I would argue that this effect is tiny in comparison with the effect of the meanings that emerge for the speaker of the language as soon as the sounds (or letters on the page) are perceived as words.

A work that appeared in the same year as *The Singularity of Literature* and advances a theory that has much in common with mine is Krzysztof Ziarek's *The Force of Art*. Where I talk of the artwork's operation as, simultaneously, act and event, Ziarek uses Heidegger's terms *machen* and *lassen* to similar effect. He, like me, exploits the double meaning of 'work', stating, 'Revealed in its full complexity, the artwork is the reciprocal animation of the nominal and the verbal sense of "work", the event of the actualization of art's status as an object into the performance of its work' (9); and argues, as I do, that art 'escapes the logic of commodity, both its paradigm of exchange and its corollary tendency toward fetishization', making vital that we understand 'the way in which art calls this dominant practice into question and opens the possibility of a nonproductionist (in the widest possible sense) way of being' (15).

Q *To end with, can you say how your account of literature manifests itself in the classroom?*

A As a teacher, I do, of course, operate on a set of principles that I believe to be appropriate in the pedagogic context, and that I would wish to be observed more generally, but it's not a set of principles that I've deduced in some mechanical fashion from a prior understanding of my responsibility to and for the other. Were I to make an attempt to spell out these principles, they would sound all too familiar, since they were imbibed from the best of my own teachers, and stem from widely influential moral and pedagogic traditions. They involve, inevitably, constant compromises: there is never enough time or energy, and there are never enough material resources, for education to happen as one would want it to. When, however, it does happen, in a stronger sense than the imparting of knowledge and skills (not that this aspect of teaching should in any way be devalued), I believe it happens as an inventive act–event in which the student (and sometimes the teacher) is changed by an apprehension of otherness, of that which had been outside the realm of the known and felt. There can be no pedagogic method, no transferable skill, that can guarantee the occurrence of such events, so any programme of teacher training must, in addition to the important task of providing such methods and skills, encourage and leave a space for the encounter with otherness, the taking of risks, which will sometimes mean the bending of the institution's rules and procedures. Derrida says that when a decision that really is a decision (as opposed to a calculated action) occurs, it's not the subject who decides but the other, the other in (though it's hard to talk of inside and outside at this point) the subject. I would add that when teaching takes place that is more than the inculcation of knowledge and skills, or charismatic entertainment, it's the other who teaches—and the other who learns.

There can be no recipe or formula whereby the other can brought into the field of the apprehensible; this is just what we mean by calling it other. All the recipes and formulae which we possess are capable only of producing further versions of the same. But we might be able to increase the possibility of encountering the other, or of the other's encountering us, by the attentive reading of what is around us. That is to say, to become aware of patterns of silence, inconsistency, over-insistence, avoidance, repetition, exhaustion, and so on in a cultural, textual, philosophical, or psychological field (one's own 'character', for instance) might be to open oneself to excluded alterity. The classroom is one space in which this kind of reading (and writing) could be fostered.

PART II

CHAPTER 2

Justice

Doing justice

Can we do justice to literature? More specifically, can we do justice to literature *as literature* when the institutions within which we engage with it—as teachers, students, researchers, and critics—exert constant pressure on us to treat it instrumentally—to reduce it to a set of rules, or a source of information, or a deployment of skills? The first thing to say is that, of course, much, perhaps most, of what we write and what we teach as specialists in literature *is* a matter of rules, information, and skills: we have to imbibe and impart all those techniques of reading and analysis spelled out so carefully by school and college authorities; we have to absorb and convey large amounts of factual information; we have to endure and encourage a great deal of sheer hard work. And we're failing if we don't find and communicate real pleasure in undertaking this work, whether it be ascertaining a complex publication history, analyzing an intricate syntactical structure, or exploring a long-lost archive.

Nevertheless, it's also essential to acknowledge that literary works—like all works of art—operate in our culture in a way that is not, finally, reducible to these instrumental, objective techniques. Although in retrospect we may see artistic development as following a coherent, even logical path—which it's the task of the literary historian to trace—when an artwork that's genuinely new appears, and transforms the genre or genres from which it takes its bearings, it always, and necessarily, blasts apart the carefully orchestrated predictions of the cultural analyst. The same is true of the rediscovery and re-evaluation of artworks of the past: we can't predict which author or painter will surprise us in ten years' time with the apparent contemporaneity of her work. There seems to be something in the practice of art in western culture that exceeds all attempts to subsume it under positivist principles;[1] and my claim is that this excess is not just an empirical fact about the history of art but constitutive of art as art.

One common approach to the question of art's unpredictability and resistance to instrumental analysis is to understand all artistic practices, in both production and reception, in terms of the operation of ideology: any claim for a special status for art is regarded as a form of mystification, functioning to entrench a particular class-based power structure. The 'original' artist is understood only as the one who has most successfully assessed the cultural climate, in order to produce the appropriate frisson among the art-appreciating minority. (Some artists, it is argued, overdo their innovativeness, with the result that their achievement is appreciated only after their deaths; in which case their heirs are the lucky ones). The vast educational machine that we as English teachers and scholars are engaged in is seen as a state apparatus designed to inculcate this ideology and buttress the class system it underwrites.[2]

There's much in this description that I agree with: art clearly functions as cultural capital, and educational institutions clearly play a significant part in sustaining the class contours produced by the uneven distribution of that capital. But the power of the work of art in challenging norms and habits, in disrupting the field of the same by introducing the hitherto unthinkable other, in resisting the profit-and-loss calculations of the marketplace, includes the power to contest the totalizing reductiveness of an appeal to ideology as full and final explanation. If we spend our time as teachers showing how literature exemplifies and reinforces ideology we're not treating it as literature

[1] I examine some key moments of this history in *Peculiar Language*.

[2] See Pierre Bourdieu's work for an elaboration of this approach to literary culture, notably his path-breaking sociological study *Distinction*.

but simply as one among many types of discourse; if, instead, we direct our energies to examining the subtle ways in which it can be seen to undermine the ideology it apparently endorses, we're doing more justice to its ability to escape the determining impulses of its time—but we still risk reducing its field of operation to the restricted realm of existing ideological structures.

An alternative approach sometimes encountered in the critical arena is one that takes art's resistance to objective analysis as a sign of its essential ineffability, and deduces from this the pointlessness of all analytic endeavour. One version of this is appeal to the slogan 'we murder to dissect', another the claim that 'it's all subjective'; those of us who teach literature are familiar with these attitudes in the responses of some of our students. Though it's easy to dismiss such assertions as unsophisticated, I believe we ought to pay attention to the impulses that lie behind them, since they do articulate a part of the truth. The first slogan, borrowed from Wordsworth and redolent of Romanticism, is an exaggerated version of what I'm arguing—that objective analysis, though it can be an immensely valuable adjunct, cannot exhaust the literary work as literary work; the second one registers the open-endedness of literary interpretation and evaluation, a characteristic which also renders the literary work resistant to objective methodologies. What is needed is an account of literature and the literary that's cognizant of these limitations upon objectivity but doesn't slide into mysticism or wholesale subjectivism.

Let me return to my original question, which immediately leads to a second question: what would it *mean* to do justice to a literary work? We don't hesitate to say, such and such a review does justice to—or doesn't do justice to—the work on which it's commenting; but we seldom stop to enquire what this might imply. In thinking about this question I've found Derrida's writings on justice particularly helpful, most notably the essay 'Force of Law'. Here's Derrida's summary of the paradoxical nature of the just decision:

> If the act [by which justice is exercised] simply consists of applying a rule, of enacting a program or effecting a calculation, we might say that it is legal, that it conforms to law, and perhaps, by metaphor, that it is just, but we would be wrong to say that the decision was just. To be just, the decision of a judge, for example, must not only follow a rule of law or a general law but must also assume it, approve it, confirm its value, by a reinstituting act of interpretation, as if ultimately nothing previously existed of the law, as if the judge himself invented the law in every case.... It must conserve the law and also destroy it or suspend it enough to have to reinvent it in each case, rejustify it, at least reinvent it in the reaffirmation and the new and free confirmation of its principle. ('Force of Law', 23)

Derrida is not, of course, talking about literary criticism, but one doesn't have to look far in his writing on literary texts to find similar structural paradoxes, and similar imperatives for responsible judgement, being articulated. In two essays on works of literature, the idea of the law is directly interrogated: 'Before the Law', on Kafka's parable of the same name, and 'The Law of Genre', on Blanchot's fiction 'The Madness of the Day';[3] in each case, the problem of justice, and its relation to the law, is implicit both in the text being discussed and in Derrida's own approach to it. For the problem of justice, as Derrida insists, is the problem of the relation between the *absolutely singular* and the *wholly general*: a relation which is at once that of mutually defining opposition and necessary inter-implication. 'How are we to reconcile the act of justice,' he asks, 'that must always concern singularity, individuals, irreplaceable groups and lives, the other or myself *as* other, in a unique situation, with rule, norm, value or the imperative of justice which necessarily have a general form, even if this generality prescribes a singular application in each case?' ('Force of Law', 17). Hence the necessity to go beyond (while affirming) the law: 'Each case is other, each decision is different and requires an absolutely unique interpretation, which no existing, coded rule can or ought to guarantee absolutely' (23).

[3] See Derrida, *Acts of Literature*, 181–252 for these two essays.

The literary text I read is singular, yet that singularity is constituted and conveyed only by its participation in general laws: laws of genre, convention, language, discourse.[4] My response to that text is singular—at least it's my obligation as critic to strive for a singular appreciation of its singularity, since no other response will do its singularity justice—yet it's arrived at and articulated only by means of norms and conventions. The act of criticism, the decision or the judgement whereby the reader assents to the singularity of the text (and thereby produces it *in* its singularity), is an affirmation that doesn't simply *follow* rules but rather suspends and reinvents the rules by which the text is rendered readable. It passes, as Derrida says any decision must, through 'the ordeal of the undecidable' ('Force of Law', 24); if it did not, it would merely be the application of an algorithm; a calculable, programmable reaction.

It's impossible therefore, to do justice to a literary text; not because of the infinite richness of literary language or the sad limitations of readers, but because the act of critical judgement is an impossible, though always necessary, act. It's impossible because the text is other, and our reading of it can be said fully to do justice to it only to the extent that it's a response to that otherness (most readings, inevitably, are exercises in converting otherness to sameness); but there's no way we can represent that otherness, to ourselves or to anyone else, without contaminating it with, or rather without finding it *already* contaminated by, the same. Once again, it's necessary to emphasize that the otherness and singularity of the literary text is not an ineffable, inaccessible essence; indeed, it may well be in its very *readability* that a text manifests its otherness.

Implicit in what I'm saying is that the link between legal and literary studies is in large part an ethico-political one. It's not, however, a

[4] For a fuller account of singularity, see the following chapter. Rodolphe Gasché, discussing Derrida's essay 'Before the Law' in *Of Minimal Things*, gives an excellent account of the relation between the generality of the law and the singularity of the text (285–308, especially 296–8).

question of the moral power of great literature as traditionally taught in humanistic criticism, nor of the detection of morally and politically suspect ideological positions concealed in literary texts, but of the supremely difficult ethical act of responding to the singularity and otherness of the unique instance—whether person, act, or text—while bringing to bear on it, without merely *applying* them, all the general laws and norms which constitute both it and the judging discourse. This is not to decry critical analysis which operates by means of the application of rules; as I've been stressing, most of what we do as scholars and critics is just such an activity, and the skills involved in this activity form the foundation of all reading. But just as no *literary* text is ever entirely the programmable reaction to events or experiences, but reinvents the very rules which enable it to come into being in a way that surpasses the logic of computers or psychological and sociological rules, so no *critical* text that may be said to do justice to literature, and to the specific literary work it's answering to and affirming, can be solely a skilful application of existing rules. Its singularity affirms, and makes possible, the singularity of the other, of the work, but also necessarily betrays it, does violence to it (otherwise it could not be a singular, but merely an algorithmic reaction); and we touch here on the difficult, and essential, question of the violence at the heart of any ethical relation.

The judge in the law court appears to be passing judgement on an individual, but in fact is judging an *event*: the act which the defendant did (or did not) carry out. Doing justice to a literary work—and here I want to depart from the immensely powerful Kantian inheritance and from what we think of as the tradition of the aesthetic—is, in an even more essential way than in the law court, a matter of engaging with an event, not of assessing an object. The event of the work takes place, first as the event of its invention, then as the event of its reading; outside of its readings, it's nothing but a structure of inert signs.[5]

[5] See Part 1 for a discussion of this distinction, captured in the contrast between *text* and *work*.

(I would argue that this is true of all artworks, but it's perhaps clearest in literature, film, and music.) And it seems clear that the event of the literary work is a *formal* event, involving, among other things, or rather among other happenings, shifts in register, allusions to other discourses (literary and non-literary), the patterning of rhythms, the linking of rhymes, the ordering of sections, the movement of syntax, the echoing of sounds: all operating in a temporal medium to surprise, lull, intrigue, satisfy. I'd also include—and this might at first sight seem surprising—the *meanings* of words and sentences, for once we conceive of the work as an event, meaning becomes an occurrence, not a substance or an abstraction. Meanings unfold, intertwine, fade, echo, clash; we rely not only on our internal lexicon and familiarity with linguistic and literary conventions to handle the semantic dimension of literature, but on memory (both its powers and its limitations), predictive ability, and the capacity to orchestrate several levels of sense at once. What's traditionally called 'form' is one aspect of this moving complex, inseparable from what's traditionally called 'content'. This is not the familiar idea of form that matches content, sound that echoes sense; it's a question of a single indivisible process.[6] (Only if we read a text as a verbal text and not a work of literature, to return to the distinction I outlined in Part 1, can we separate form and content.) And because meaning—the occurrence of meaning, meaning as a verb—is so integral an element in the event of the literary work, its relation to the many contexts that determine it is also an integral element. A responsible reading of the words on the page, therefore, can't avoid attending to the strands that tie them to the world they arose from—nor, for that matter, the associations they evoke in the world of the reader.

[6] I mentioned in Part 1 A. C. Bradley's understanding of the 'actual poem' as the series of experiences passed through by the reader; he understands also the implications of this view for the relation of form and content (or 'substance'): 'They do not "agree", for they are not apart: they are one thing from different points of view, and in that sense identical' ('Poetry for Poetry's Sake', 15).

An example: Dickinson's 'As imperceptibly as Grief'

What does it mean to say that when we pick up a poem or a work of fiction and start reading we enter the realm of responsibility—which is to say, the realm of ethics, at least in some sense of that rather problematic word? I don't mean in terms of the characters in a novel or a play, who have their own ethical dilemmas and responsibilities to deal with, but in terms of the reader's own obligations towards the work. One perfectly reasonable answer would be that we clearly don't: we pick up a book freely and put it down again freely, and it's entirely up to us whether we read carefully or casually, from cover to cover or jumping about indiscriminately. No-one benefits (apart from ourselves) if we do the former; no-one is harmed if we do the latter. If we convert our reading into 'a reading', questions of ethics, at least of a minimal kind, clearly do arise: if we offer, orally or in writing, an interpretation of the work, we can do so responsibly or irresponsibly, thereby benefiting or harming the author (or the author's memory) and perhaps our own hearers or readers. The ethical stakes are usually not great, but they are real. However, for the moment, I want to concentrate on the act of reading itself—or what I've called the 'act–event' of reading, since it's a curious blend of doing something and having something done to one. Pierre Bourdieu calls this the 'active surrender to the singular necessity of the literary object', a phrase I like (*The Rules of Art*, xix).

Although the reasons for hesitating to invoke ethics in a discussion of reading are undeniably well-founded—there are so many domains in which ethical questions are more pressing and more far-reaching—much traditional literary criticism and teaching of literature implies that reading does have an ethical dimension. To advance a particular reading or to advocate a particular strategy of reading (and often these are done simultaneously, at least by implication) is to make a claim about its value: this reading or this type of reading does fullest justice to the specificity and the worth of the work or works being addressed.

Although 'responsibility' is not a word that all such readers would employ in justifying their choices, few would disagree that there is some sense in which a 'good' reading must be a 'responsible' reading. Anyone making a case for *irresponsible* reading—and as we shall see, there could be reasons for doing so—would be using the term in the knowledge that it contradicts norms of common sense.

But what does responsibility mean in this situation? Here's a well-known poem by Emily Dickinson:

As imperceptibly as Grief
The Summer lapsed away –
Too imperceptible at last
To seem like Perfidy –
A Quietness distilled
As Twilight long begun,
Or Nature spending with herself
Sequestered Afternoon –
The Dusk drew earlier in –
The Morning foreign shone –
A courteous, yet harrowing Grace,
As Guest, that would be gone –
And thus, without a Wing
Or service of a Keel
Our Summer made her light escape
Into the Beautiful –

(*Poems*, 399)

Am I under an obligation to read these lines in any particular way? Obviously not: I can glance at the words, I can read them inattentively, I can even read them backwards—and if I didn't understand English I couldn't read them at all and couldn't be blamed for this failure. What I wish to argue, though, is that to read these lines *as a work of literature* is to be put under an obligation of a kind, or, more accurately, to find oneself already under an obligation. And I believe the word 'responsibility' is a useful one to refer to that obligation, suggesting not so much a duty which binds the reader (like a moral code) but a certain attitude or disposition and a certain practice or mode of behaviour.

If we think of responsibility in the strict sense of answerability or accountability, we have to ask: before or to whom is the reader responsible? Who does the reader have to answer to for his reading? There's no judge or court before whom I will be held to account for dealing well or badly with a literary work. (Of course, a reading in the other sense may well be put before judges who will pronounce their verdicts on it—examiners, journal editors, the academic public—but I am, as I've said, concerned for the moment with the process of reading, not the spoken or written aftermath.) To call such a reading *responsible* must mean that it's one which the reader would be willing to be judged by, whether or not judging is ever likely to take place, and with the full awareness that one's later reading may displace the current experience. In a similar sense, a responsible driver is one who is prepared to be judged by the highest standards; a responsible builder is one who would be willing to have his work assessed according to the strictest codes.

We mustn't overlook the ethical dimension of our use of this term, however. Responsible driving is not the same as *skilful* driving, though it depends on being able to drive skilfully; the implicit judgement is not about speed or elegance at the wheel but about road safety. A sceptic will ask: Isn't good reading just like skilful driving, a matter not of ethics but of expertise? One way of approaching this question is by looking at the prepositions we might use. A crucial aspect of a driver's responsibility is not responsibility *to* but responsibility *for*: for passengers, for other road users and pedestrians, for the wider community. Their lives, or their well-being, are in the driver's hands, quite literally. A responsible car driver is therefore one who takes full account of the safety of others, with all that this entails: thorough training, physical alertness, skilful handling, conscientious attention, careful anticipation. The responsible builder takes into account those who will live in the house being built, as well as those who will look at it and those who will be affected by the choices of materials, site, and so on. The crucial issue here is the question of *others*, or in the language of philosophical ethics, *the other*.

So: what 'other' is the literary reader responsible for?

In the first place, the 'other' could be said to be the work itself. Here we touch on one defining attribute of the literary work—and the art work more generally—that I've discussed in *The Singularity of Literature* and elsewhere. Literature in the strictest sense, I've argued, is always characterized by a challenge to the habits and norms by which the reader relates to the world; it may be a minimal challenge, the highly familiar in slightly unfamiliar garb, or a frontal assault on our sensibilities or our linguistic expectations.

But how can the reader be held responsible for the otherness of the literary work? What is important to acknowledge, I believe, is that otherness is not an inherent and unchanging property of the work. Literary history is in part the history of the changing way in which works present their challenge, some becoming unreadable, others becoming so readable as to cease to operate as literature. The reason why this happens is that cultures and therefore readers alter, and otherness exists only as it's produced by a particular relation between a reader and a work. Otherness is always otherness *to;* it's not an intrinsic feature. A responsible reading, then, is one that recognizes, affirms, and sustains that otherness, in and for a particular time and place. A reading that glides over the work's challenges, or converts otherness to sameness by imposing a common meaning on an uncommon one, or that disregards the context within which the work is being read, is refusing to accept the responsibility being demanded.

Dickinson's poem is not hard to understand, yet it's full of strangeness. To do justice to the poem as we read is to *experience* that strangeness, which is not a matter of being bemused or amazed by its departure from what we expect, but of attempting to account for it. We register its otherness *in the effort we have to make* to adjust our own habits of thinking and feeling, and in the sense that despite all our efforts we have not reduced alterity to sameness. This is different from, say, encountering an unfamiliar word in a text, looking it up, and then finding that the sentence in question becomes perfectly comprehensible.

Let's take the first four lines. (I should stress that I'm not offering a 'reading' of the poem, just writing about what it might be like to read it.) The first surprise is that the opening simile equates 'the summer' with 'grief', an equation that seems an affront to our common understanding. The ground of their likeness is the manner in which they both 'lapse away' (itself an unusual phrase): they do it 'imperceptibly'. With a little thought, we can understand the logic: grief for a lost loved one does not disappear overnight, so that we can observe its passing—rather, it lessens so gradually that we're not aware of its going. A diminishment of grief would feel like a betrayal of the one we are mourning, and we are only spared that sense of betrayal by the imperceptibility of the process. In the case of the summer, however, the perfidy that we would otherwise feel is not our own but that of the season itself, making the simile a far from simple one. However fully we're able to explain the comparison, the contrast between the two words, and the distinct affective universe each conjures up, is not entirely banished, and when we come to read the poem again, it's likely to retain a trace of that power to disconcert.

I could go through the poem's surprises like this—the ambiguous grammar of 'distilled' and 'long begun', the striking idea of a distilled quietness, or of Nature as a solitary individual, or of the morning as an embarrassed guest—confident that most of them would be registered as surprises by other readers as well. Had Dickinson published the poem immediately after she had written it, it would have surprised readers of the time even more, and perhaps in different ways. One feature of the poem has probably always carried a charge of surprise: the final word. It seems to have either too much or too little meaning, a confident Platonism or a desperate nominalism. Is it an appeal to memory, to the aesthetic, to a principle of evanescence? A responsible reading keeps these all in play, acknowledging the resistance of such multiplicity of suggestion to the demands of logic and rationality.

Another aspect of a reading that does justice to a work's otherness is, as I've noted, that it treats the work not as an object but as an event. In the case of a poem, this means reading it aloud, or at least in real time in one's head. (Or, of course, hearing it read.) Only then can its deployment of rhythm, its patterning of sound, its linear progression of expectation and satisfaction, tension and release, be fully experienced. Crucial to the way the reader registers the poem—or the poem registers upon the reader—is its rhythmic movement. Responding to the movement of Dickinson's poem doesn't require any specialized knowledge of formal poetic structures. The English-speaking reader who has encountered nursery rhymes, popular songs, advertising jingles, ballads, and/or rap will slip immediately and unselfconsciously into the regular rhythm, what I've called elsewhere the 'four by four' metre, four groups of four beats, repeated in this case four times. It's a rhythmic form common in many other languages as well, especially in children's verse. The first two lines announce the unmistakeable rhythm of the hymn-book's 'common measure', which is also the basis of the familiar ballad metre: lines of four, three, four, and three beats; the fourth beat of the shorter lines being virtual rather than realized:

```
As imperceptibly as Grief
   B      B    B     B
The Summer lapsed away—
     B       B        B     [B]
```

The quatrains that follow vary this by moving into the 'short measure' form, in which the first line too has only three realized beats:

```
A Quietness distilled
   B   B     B     [B]
As Twilight long begun
     B     B      B   [B]7
```

[7] For a full discussion of four-beat metres, see Attridge, *The Rhythms of English Poetry*, 76–122.

That unexpected silence after three beats contributes to the quietness evoked by the line—but I want to stress that we don't have to be *aware* of the metrical structure in order for it to do its work. A responsible reading, then, gives itself over to this rhythm, which is a physical more than an intellectual process, not so as to override the delicate variations of each line, but to experience the poem as an event given momentum and rhythmic shape by its engagement with deeply-rooted habits of the body.

The event of the poem is also, of course, the unfolding of its meanings, of its argument, of its narrative, all carried by that rhythm. In the case of prose, the articulation of individual words and the onward drive of rhythm may be less important to the sense of the work as an event, but a responsible reading will be alert to narrative, character development, dialogue, the creation and resolution of enigmas and many other features that take place as the work unfolds in time. This is not to say that the *visual* dimension of literary works is irrelevant: looking is as much an event as listening, and reading something aloud on the page combines the two. Part of the event of Dickinson's poem is responding to the dashes, the upper case letters, and the lack of additional spaces between the quatrains, none of which would be evident if we merely heard it.

Treating a work as an event means finding in that event the value of the work, not in anything to be learned or deduced from it. Certainly, we can and often do learn from works of literature, but to that extent we're treating them as if they were something other than literature. Dickinson's poem, we might say, is about the experience of loss—specifically, the loss of the beauty of summer as the year turns to autumn, but perhaps by analogy other losses as well. 'About', however, is an inappropriate preposition: it suggests that the poem's purpose is to provide information. The event of the poem involves the reader in an experience that is somehow connected with the experience of loss, but it isn't actually that experience. We don't feel we are losing something as we read the poem. What happens can only be expressed metaphorically: the poem *stages* loss, and stages the emotions aroused by loss. It does this not by naming those emotions, but by a vivid representation of seasonal transition that appeals to our shared store of affective responses. When a literary work moves us to tears or to laughter, it's through the power of its stagings, not through the direct apprehension of reality. If we shed tears at Cordelia's death, they are very different from the tears we shed at the death of a friend, though their origins are not entirely foreign to one another.[8]

Two further characteristics of the literary work operate in conjunction with its otherness. In responding to Dickinson's poem we are registering not just its challenges to our familiar ways of thinking, but its *singularity*. It has an identity that marks it off from every other literary work, an identity that is not fixed (partly because what it's defined against changes constantly) but that nevertheless enables us to say this is the same poem that its first readers encountered. We also respond to the work's *inventiveness*. When Dickinson wrote 'As imperceptibly as Grief / The Summer lapsed away' she brought into being a complex of idea, image, and affect that introduced something hitherto unknown into the world; she produced a pair of lines that were not only unlike any others that had been written, but which expanded the reach of the English language itself. This quality of inventiveness, like the singularity and otherness of the lines, remains potent today, as if in reading the poem (and even in re-reading it several times) we were experiencing an echo of its original explosion onto the nineteenth century American scene. Familiar though it is, it has not been wholly accommodated within our habitual patterns of thought and feeling.

In speaking of Dickinson's act (or act–event)[9] of bringing the poem into being, I've introduced the issue of the *writer's* inventiveness, not just the poem's. And this adds a further dimension to the

[8] For further discussion of affective responses to literary works, see chapter 9.

[9] Bourdieu's comment on the 'active surrender' to the literary work I quoted earlier continues with the observation that the work itself 'more often than not, is itself the product of a similar submission' (*The Rules of Art*, xix).

responsibility of the reader. There is a sense in which our responsibility is demanded not just by the work but also by its author (even if we know nothing about that person, or persons). The inventiveness of 'As imperceptibly as Grief' is Emily Dickinson's; she achieved its singularity in engaging with what was other to her; in finding ourselves responsible for these qualities of the poem, we find we have a relation to its author as well. It's not a matter of responsibility to or for the historical individual, however; it's a responsibility for her singular inventiveness as registered in the poem.

'Responsibility for the other' is a phrase associated, above all, with the ethical philosophy of Emmanuel Levinas, and I've argued elsewhere that—although Levinas would not have accepted this extrapolation—some of the terms he provides are useful in thinking about our responsibility as readers of literary works. In particular, we can draw on Levinas's insistence that responsibility is not something we choose to take on, but something we find ourselves already seized by—in fact, we only come into existence as fully human subjects through that responsibility. Thus I would argue that we are *constituted* as literary readers by the responsibility for the work that imposes itself upon us. We can refuse that responsibility, read rapidly or rigidly or carelessly, but doing so will not erase it. It is Levinas too, who stresses that we are responsible *for* the other—ultimately, for the other's survival. And similarly, it is our readings that keep literary works alive. Our responsibility is to affirm what is singular, inventive and other in the work, experienced as an event, and thus conserve it and pass it on.

It may sound as if I'm advocating a reading of the literary work as nothing but 'words on the page', divorced from any cultural, social, or economic context. This is because I've been imagining a reader coming to the poem without any background knowledge. But a responsible reading of the words on the page can't avoid attending to the strands that tie them to the world they arose from—nor, for that matter, the associations they evoke in the world that surrounds, and informs, the reader. Readings improve as familiarity with the author grows: those upper-case letters don't seem quite so locally functional when you've read fifty of Dickinson's poems. A question arises at this point, however: is a truly responsible reading one that has exhausted all the possible avenues of research that could throw light on its meanings, its contexts, its origins, its allusions? Is anything that falls short of this ideal to be deemed failing in its responsibility?

Levinas helps us again here. For him, the demands made by responsibility for the other are infinite—but this does not excuse us from those demands. That first-time reading, without any background knowledge or familiarity with Dickinson's work, can be responsible if it's attentive and open to the event of the poem. Ignorance can produce bad readings, but if the reader is excusably ignorant about a particular point, this can't be termed irresponsibility. At the same time, if there is an opportunity for further exploration of the poem's content and context, a responsible reading is one that takes this further step. And, as Levinas insists, there is no determinate end to the possibilities that offer themselves.

Signature and counter-signature

What if we move from reading to writing, to a 'reading' of the poem for a student paper or a published article? The same responsibility applies; but there is now the added responsibility of creating a verbal work that does justice to the original. It can't simply repeat the original, but every word that is added to the work is necessarily a deviation from it. However, there are different kinds of unfaithfulness. The responsible reading finds a way of being unfaithful that nevertheless affirms the singularity of the work—hence it involves a risk, a plunge into the unknown. (Just as the original act of creation did.) There can be no recipe to fall back on, since to affirm singularity requires that one produce an answering singularity.

In approaching this paradoxical situation, Derrida uses the analogy of the signature and the counter-signature, an analogy that I find useful in thinking about one's responsibility for the event of the literary work. When I sign a document, I testify that I'm physically present, here and now, and that I approve what I've signed; and I promise to acknowledge that presence and that approval at any future date. However, my signature will only work as it's supposed to if it's at once *unique* and *recognizable*. To be unique is to be different each time; if on inspection a signature turns out to have been produced mechanically, it fails, since it no longer testifies to the presence of the signer. (By convention, a mechanical signature is accepted in certain contexts, on a banknote, for example, or an e-mail, even though it doesn't testify to the presence of the signer. What such examples disclose is that a signature can always be mechanically reproduced or forged—it wouldn't function as a signature if it could not.) But to be recognizable is to be repeatable: a signature that's too different from the same individual's other signatures will also fail. Hence the paradox of the signature: to function, it has to be both the same and different, on the one hand a unique testament to an unrepeatable here and now of an individual, and on the other a reproducible inscription participating in general codes and processes. 'Usually interpreted as one's very own mark,' writes Derrida elsewhere, '[the signature] is instead what I cannot incorporate, cannot make my own' ('I have a Taste for the Secret', 85). The signature of *Ulysses* is that which makes it unique among literary works, but is also constituted by those many features it shares with other works, by Joyce and by other authors. If it were wholly unique, it would be completely unreadable, as there would be no codes and conventions by which to read it. If it were wholly a repetition of other works, no-one would bother to read it. A successful reading of *Ulysses* is one that does justice to both these dimensions.

In using this analogy to throw light on the operation of literature I want to stress two features of the signature. First, it's very much a matter of *form*. Simply to write one's name is not to sign: content alone is insufficient. What makes the signature recognizable, and what makes it unique each time, is its form. Of course, what's being formed is the name, so there's a sense in which content, or reference, is implicated in the form. The second feature I want to stress is that the signature—as it functions in our transactions—is not so much an object as an event. We should be talking perhaps about 'signings' rather than signatures. The signature we see on the page is, it's true, a *record* of an event, but it's something more than that if it's attesting, validating, promising: it's in our reading of it *as* a signature (and not just a written name) that it does its work. In the event of our reading we activate its power to do more than refer to a named individual.

If the literary work is like a signature, what of the critic's response? Here Derrida introduces the notion of the *counter-signature*: a signature that affirms another signature, which would otherwise remain invalid, unwitnessed, a possible forgery. The counter-signature—possessing exactly the same paradoxical properties as the signature—constitutes the first signature as a signature, not just a written name. Which is to say that the event of counter-signing—think of witnessing someone's signature on a legal document—validates the event of signing. The critic who does justice to the literary work counter-signs its signature, writes a text that affirms the work's uniqueness and identity by its own uniqueness and identity. In fact, you might say that the work's uniqueness and identity don't exist as such until responded to by readers in this way. The implication, of course, is that all good readings are different, though all find ways of responding to the work's singularity.

A counter-signature can also be a commitment that involves trust and the taking of a certain risk, as when I sign in order to attest to my willingness to underwrite someone else's financial obligation. Like the signature, the counter-signature is both an affirmation and a promise: I affirm in the present, and I promise to stand by this affirmation in the future. It's an exercise of responsibility, and not just responsibility *to* but, as I've suggested, responsibility *for* the other. In affirming a literary work through my critical response to it, I'm helping to keep it alive for this and future generations.

It's not possible to offer any kind of blueprint or programme for the response to a literary work that can be said to do justice to it: this, I'm arguing, is because of what it *means* to 'do justice'—to respond inventively to invention, singularly to singularity, in a way that doesn't simply implement existing protocols or conventions. It follows that there can be no guarantee that anything I say or write will do justice to the work I'm commenting on; this can only be a judgement of other listeners or readers, who do or do not find that my response brings the original work to life in a new and valuable way. Nevertheless, I'll risk a few suggestions about literary criticism today, always remembering that there are no rules, and that the next literary study I read may contravene everything I say here and yet be remarkably successful in doing justice to its subject. I say 'literary criticism today' because the needs of the time change; we're not dealing in eternal verities, and though we may hope to be read by future generations we write as critics for the present (and the same is presumably true for artists). When I use the word 'criticism' here I'm including any verbal response that aims to do justice to what is of value and importance in a literary work, or group of works, or oeuvre. And in talking about criticism I'm also talking, *mutatis mutandis*, about teaching.

The best criticism, I would argue, is personal, written by a critic willing to acknowledge the particular, unique history that has formed him or her, and the specific situation from which he writes. Philosophers may write as if their words were impersonal expressions of truth, *sub specie aeternitatis*, but the critic doesn't need this illusion: we write as individuals, with individual combinations of knowledge, prejudice, skill, and sensitivity. In reading a commentary that retains the note of the personal we're able to appreciate the direct effect of the work discussed on another mind and body. This is not to fall into the 'everything is subjective' position I mentioned earlier: the subject who responds, like the subject who wrote the original work, is a singular nexus within a complex, shifting, cultural matrix—what I've called an *idioculture*, on the model of the idiolect each of us speaks, a unique version of the dialects around us.[10] The criticism I'm advocating is aware of these cultural determinations, and is also alert to the

[10] See *The Singularity of Literature*, 21–2 and *passim*, and part I of this book.

demands and needs of the particular time and place, of the conversation it's joining, of the values it's endorsing or challenging; and it has an important relation to the future, implying as it does a promise, a trust, perhaps even a risk. Because of its awareness of its cultural situatedness it's also aware of its provisionality: it's not claiming to reveal truths about the work that all previous, and less able, critics have failed to see, nor is it assuming its judgements will remain valid for all time.

The best criticism is alert to both the originality and the inventiveness of the work. By originality, I mean its newness in the context of its time, opening up new possibilities for literature, for the articulation of feeling and thought in language. (To respond to a work's originality, of course, implies a degree of historical knowledge, which, it's important to remember, is never complete and is always subject to revision.) By inventiveness I mean its capacity to convey *in the present* a sense of that opening up (whether or not this reproduces the inventiveness of its moment of production). Such criticism is, by the same token, alert to the work's strangeness, to the demands it makes upon the reader to expand her sympathies, imagination, intellectual reach, or emotional range.

The best criticism *affirms* the work it responds to—as I've suggested, it's through our responses that we keep artworks alive—but this doesn't mean it eschews negative judgements, though it does mean making an effort to appreciate the work on its own terms. If the critical response is an attempt at an honest reflection of the experience of reading, of performing, of living with and living through a literary work, it's likely to include moments of disappointment, of valleys as well as peaks. It's also likely to express doubts and uncertainties, a recognition that both one's understanding and one's ability to express what one perceives are being tested to the limit. And it affirms the work as an event, an event in which what are traditionally called 'form' and 'meaning' are inseparable. In doing so, it's informed by accurate knowledge of the materials of literature: the sounds and structures of language, the conventions of genre, the materials of history, the techniques available to the writer.[11]

Finally, the best criticism is rigorous in reflecting the critic's actual experience of the work and in resisting the ever-present temptation to exploit the powerful machinery of critical discourse to make ingenious points. This is a topic I will take up again in chapter 4; it's also at the heart of the book written in the form of a conversation with Henry Staten.[12] Let me end with a comment from Don Paterson that sums up what is to be avoided: 'My definition of overinterpretation is the avowal of the presence of effects which you neither felt nor intellectually registered in the process of your open and direct engagement with the poem—but instead discovered in your post-reading critical vivisection' ('The Domain of the Poem', 2010, 83).

[11] Andrew Miller's account of what he calls 'implicative criticism' has some affinities with the approach I'm advocating here. Implicative criticism, he states, 'is not justified by its conclusions, by any facts established, information conveyed, or judgments made; instead it is successful to the extent that it implicates, it enfolds its reader' ('Implicative Criticism', 347).

[12] Attridge and Staten, *The Craft of Poetry*.

CHAPTER 3

Singularity

Unpacking singularity

What exactly is *singularity*, in the sense in which I've been using the term? The word of course carries with it a considerable load of historical baggage, and in employing it a certain amount of unpacking is necessary. Looking back over earlier uses of the term 'singularity', we might place Spinoza at the origin of the term's philosophical pedigree, but his notion of 'singular things' (*res singulares*) doesn't have a great deal in common with more modern meanings. Kant's proposal that the faculty of intuition apprehends the singularity of things without the mediation of concepts, although hardly unproblematic, is closer to contemporary uses, introducing as it does the idea that singularities are sites of resistance to the universal; and his argument that judgements of *taste* are necessarily singular judgements, in which there is no possible appeal to a governing concept, runs along similar lines.[1] Hegel's term *Einzelnheit* is often translated as 'singularity', though it also appears in English versions as 'individuality'; and in distinguishing singularities from, on the one hand, universals and, on the other, particulars, as the three 'moments' of the 'concept', Hegel invites us to think through what it means for a singular entity to be made up of perceptible particulars and at the same time to partake of universality. We'll come back to these distinctions in due course.

[1] Analytic of the Beautiful, §8, in the *Critique of Judgment*. See also Plotnitsky, 'Thinking Singularity'.

More recently we find a number of philosophers employing the term. Gilles Deleuze makes use of it in a sense derived partly from Spinoza and Leibniz,[2] often in the plural. 'Singularities,' he states, 'are turning points and points of inflection; bottlenecks, knots, foyers, and centers; points of fusion, condensation, and boiling; points of tears and joy, sickness and health, hope and anxiety, "sensitive" points.... The singularity belongs to another dimension than that of denotation, manifestation, or signification. It is essentially pre-individual, non-personal, and a-conceptual' (*The Logic of Sense*, 52). The term is important for Alain Badiou as well—he goes so far as to say that 'the problem that defines contemporary thought' is 'what exactly is a universal singularity?' This statement comes after a disagreement with Deleuze, whom he charges with being able to think singularity only 'by classifying the different ways singularity is not ontologically singular' (*Theoretical Writings*, 82). Although he doesn't use 'singularity' consistently, Badiou's most important claim involving the term is that 'if it is true that every truth erupts as singular, its singularity is immediately universalizable. Universalizable singularity necessarily breaks with identitarian singularity' (*Saint Paul*, 11). Elsewhere, 'singularity' occurs along with 'normality' and 'excrescence' as one of the three ways in which a term can relate to a situation; a singularity belongs but anomalously so.[3] Giorgio Agamben's best-known use of 'singularity' is in the phrase 'whatever singularity' (*la singolaritá qualunque*) in *The Coming Community*, designating that which is itself without respect to any particular common property, and thus is neither particular nor universal. Rather startlingly, Agamben explains this notion of singularity by explaining that it is that to which love is directed (*The Coming Community*, 2).

Peter Hallward, in *Absolutely Postcolonial*, a book that is subtitled *Writing between the Singular and the Specific*, chooses to use 'singular' to

[2] 'Thus [Leibniz] cannot give himself a kind of universal mind. He has to remain fixed on the singularity, on the individual as such' ('On Leibniz').

[3] See Hallward, *Badiou*, 99–100.

refer to an entity that has no relations outside itself—the debt to Deleuze and Badiou, in spite of their differences, is evident here—and 'specific' to refer to an entity that is constituted by such relations. Thus, according to Hallward, the weakness of postcolonial theory, until his own 'specific' work, is that it is dominated by ideas of singularity; see *Absolutely Postcolonial*, 1–61. A literary theorist who developed a strong version of singularity, not unrelated to Hallward's, was Paul de Man, who, like Deleuze and Agamben, uses it in a sense opposed to Hegel's. As Rodolphe Gasché puts it, 'absolute singularity' in de Man's work implies 'the thinking of a singularity that has no relation to, and thus withstands the dialectic of universalization' (*The Wild Card of Reading*, 266).

In attempting to understand the operation of literary works, I haven't found any of these recent deployments of a notion of singularity particularly productive, although in their diversity they usefully demonstrate the difficulty of describing a type of entity that is not immediately recuperable in the universality of the concept. Nor has singularity as I'm using the word have much to do with *technological* singularity, the posited moment in the future when artificial intelligence advances beyond human intelligence (though this will certainly be a singular event if it ever happens); nor with *mathematical* singularity, a point at which a function takes an absolute value; nor with *cosmological* singularity, which is a region in space-time at which matter is infinitely dense.

The most fruitful uses of the term for my purposes involve the conceptualization of a singularity that can be encountered rather than one that is completely inaccessible to thought or feeling, that is not simply opposed to generality or universality, and that is as much an event as an object. Jean-Luc Nancy's version of singularity has more to offer than those I've mentioned, with its rejection of essence, its emphasis on singularity as the event of singularization, its differentiation of the singular from both the particular and the individual (a distinction developed from Hegel and shared by Agamben), and its insistence on existence as co-existence—thus using the term in the way Hallward uses 'specific'. Here's a typical comment:

> The concept of the singular implies its singularization and, therefore, its distinction from other singularities (which is different from any concept of the individual, since an immanent totality, without an other, would be a perfect individual, and is also different from any concept of the particular, since this assumes the togetherness of which the particular is a part, so that such a particular can only present its difference from other particulars as numerical difference). (*Being Singular Plural*, 32)[4]

However, it's Jacques Derrida's use of the term that I've found most valuable in discussions of the literary work. Derrida's understanding of singularity welds it to his notion of iterability: a date or a signature, for instance, is irreducibly singular—it's a one-time-and-one-place-only event—yet its singularity only has any purchase outside itself, and is only intelligible because it is repeatable (and in its repetitions, in new contexts, it's constantly a new singularity). Leonard Lawlor gives an economical account of iterability, which he sees—rightly, I believe—as a central concept (if one can call it a concept) in Derrida's thought:

> [Derrida's] basic argumentation always attempts to show that no one is able to separate irreplaceable singularity and machine-like repeatability (or 'iterability', as Derrida frequently says) into two substances that stand outside of one another; nor is anyone able to reduce one to the other so that we would have one pure substance (with attributes or modifications). Machine-like repeatability and irreplaceable singularity, for Derrida, are like two forces that attract one another across a limit that is indeterminate and divisible. ('Jacques Derrida')

[4] Nancy's Heideggerian interest in Being—the three words of his book's title work together in a variety of ways made possible by the lack of punctuation—is not something I share, and makes for a difference in our use of the concept of singularity. And I'm less convinced by Nancy's originary 'co-' than by Derrida's originary *différance*, trace-structure, arche-writing, etc. See also Nancy's discussion of singularity (differentiated from individuality) in relation to finitude and community in *The Inoperative Community*.

A similar logic applies to exemplarity: the literary work is absolutely singular yet it stands for a great deal beside itself (or, to be more precise, *because* it is singular rather than merely particular it is also exemplary). Singularity is indissolubly linked, too, to the event; it's not an immobile and permanent feature but something that *happens* (as Nancy also implies)—which is why singularization might be the more accurate term. In order to come about, however, it must partake of generality or universality: the signature must use the inscription codes of a particular language, the date must draw on a system of chronology, the literary work must engage with generic expectations, and so on. In the interview I conducted with Derrida in 1989, he gave a lucid account of this aspect of the singularity of the literary work. 'Attention to history, context, and genre is necessitated, and not contradicted, by this singularity, by the date and the signature of the work', he said, and 'absolute singularity is never given as a fact, an object or existing thing in itself'. He further explained:

> An absolute, absolutely pure singularity, if there were such a thing, would not even show up, or at least would not be available for reading. To become readable, it has to be *divided*, to *participate* and *belong*. Then it is divided and takes *its part* in the genre, the type, the context, meaning, the conceptual generality of meaning, etc. It loses itself to offer itself. Singularity is never one-off, never closed like a point or a fist. It is a mark, a mark that is differential, and different from itself; different *with itself*. Singularity differs from itself, it is deferred so as to be what it is and to be repeated in its very singularity.[5]

Nor is singularity only on the side of the writer and the text; the reading too—or at least one that can be said to do justice to the work—must be singular, and the same apparent paradox is evident here too: 'You have to give yourself over singularly to singularity, but singularity then does have to share itself out and so compromise itself' (69). The

[5] '"This Strange Institution Called Literature"', 67–8 (translation modified; see the original French text '"Cette étrange institution qu'on appelle la littérature"', 286).

same goes for all the other ways in which literary works live on; Derrida takes the example of *Romeo and Juliet*, the subject of one of his essays:

> *Romeo and Juliet* . . . takes place only once. This singularity is worked, in fact constituted, by the possibility of its own repetition (readings, indefinite number of productions, references, be they reproductive, citational, or transformative, to the work held to be original which, in its ideality, takes place just one single first and last time). Reading must *give itself up* to this uniqueness, take it on board, keep it in mind, *take account of it*. But for that . . . you have to sign in your turn, write something else which *responds or corresponds* in an equally singular, which is to say irreducible, irreplaceable, 'new' way. ('"This Strange Institution"', 69–70)

So singularity, or singularization, is something that happens over and over, each time differently, in the life of the literary work; the work, that is, comes into being only in the event of its being read, or performed, or witnessed, within particular historical contexts.[6] Nor does singularity imply a whole, unified work; it can be a feature of a phrase, a chapter, or even the output of an entire creative life.

The promulgation of this version of singularity has given rise in literary studies to what has been called a 'school of singularity'. Timothy Clark, who coined this term, has provided, in *The Poetics of Singularity*, a book-length account of what he regards as the four most important founders of this 'school', Heidegger, Gadamer, Blanchot and Derrida.[7] Clark's own interpretation of singularity—what he calls 'post-existentialist' singularity, referring, I think, to Heidegger's brand of existentialism—builds on this tradition but, I would argue, makes of it something closer to de Man's and Hallward's absolute

[6] For valuable accounts of Derrida's notion of singularity, see Gasché, *Inventions of Difference*, 13–16; Kronick, 'Between Act and Archive', 55–9, and Szafraniec, *Beckett, Derrida, and the Event of Literature*, chapter 2, 'A Singular Odyssey'.

[7] See also the chapter entitled 'The Event of Signature: A "Science" of the Singular?', in Clark's book *Derrida, Heidegger, Blanchot*. Clark is especially illuminating on Derrida's discussion of the signature in *Signéponge*. Derrida's treatment of the singularity of the poem is also given astute attention by Clark in his chapter 'Dictation by Heart: Derrida's "Che Cos'è la Poesia?" and Celan's Notion of the *Atemwende*', in *The Theory of Inspiration*.

singularity than to Derrida's sense of the necessary interplay of text and context. His description of the encounter with the literary work has much in common with the traditional notion of autonomy:

> To read a text solely as itself and on its own terms, in its singularity: no idea might seem simpler—not to make the text an example... but merely *to affirm it in itself and as it is.* The point is not to interpret the singularity of the text but to move towards a point, never finally attainable, at which the text is being understood only on its own singular terms. That is to say, the reading attains a space in which the text is felt to project itself so specifically that the terms of any mode of interpretation one might want to apply begin to be felt as inadequate. (9)

And again: 'To treat something as singular is to move towards the idea of seeing it as irreplaceable, sole witness of what it says, an example only of itself, and thus "free" in the sense of not being fully intelligible in the broadly deterministic categories of culturalism' (12). I find it difficult to conceptualize the work's capacity to impose its own terms upon the reader, irrespective of any cultural norms operative in its production or its reception. (I've already suggested that far from being only an example of itself, as Clark claims, the work is intelligible only if it is exemplary.) There are echoes in Clark's account of the criticism of F. R. Leavis[8] and American New Critics like Cleanth Brooks and W. K. Wimsatt, none of whom Clark mentions, and whose massive contribution to the development of a scrupulous literary criticism was limited by their unwillingness to take into account the operation of extrinsic forces upon their, and everyone's, literary interpretation.

While it's not difficult to sympathize with Clark's antagonism towards instrumentalist critical approaches that reduce the work of art to its historical or present-day social, cultural and economic determinations and effects, this is not to say that such contexts are

[8] See, for example, Leavis's objections to Marxist, sociological, and philosophical critical approaches in the chapters of *The Common Pursuit* entitled 'Literature and Society', 'Sociology and Literature', and 'Literary Criticism and Philosophy', and his debate with F. W. Bateson on the question of historical context reprinted in *A Selection from Scrutiny*.

irrelevant. Singularity as I understand it, and I'm taking my lead from Derrida here, is nothing but a particular constellation of cultural norms—a constellation made possible for both creator and reader by habits of interpreting, thinking, and feeling, inculcated in the course of an existence within a culture or cultures and crystallized at any given moment in what I've called an idioculture.[9] That it's a constellation which exceeds and challenges all existing configurations of cultural norms does not mean that it exists in some realm entirely outside culture, whatever or wherever that might be. As Rodolphe Gasché puts it: 'Paradoxically, even the most radical singularity must, in order for it to be recognized for what it is, have an addressable identity, guaranteed by a set of universal rules that, by the same token, inscribe its singularity within a communal history, tradition, and problematics' (*Inventions of Difference*, 2).

In his discussion of Flaubert, Pierre Bourdieu, though hostile to some versions of singularity, promulgates an understanding of it that is not far from Gasché's or mine. It's worth quoting Bourdieu at some length, as his comments demonstrate how an attachment to sociological explanation need not completely eliminate an appreciation of literary singularity:

> It will be up to the reader to judge if, as I believe (having experienced it myself), scientific analysis of the production and reception of a work of art, far from reducing it or destroying it, in fact intensifies the literary experience.... Such analysis seems to abolish the singularity of the 'creator' [a word Bourdieu dislikes because of its association with irrationalism] in favour of the relations which made the work intelligible, only better to rediscover it at the end of the task of reconstructing the space in which the author finds himself encompassed and included as a point. To

[9] See *The Singularity of Literature*, 20–1. The term *idioculture* is sometimes used in sociological studies to refer to the shared knowledge, habits and beliefs of a small, relatively homogeneous group (the example often cited is a sports team). I'm appropriating it for the constitution of a *single* subjectivity by such a set of knowledges, habits, and beliefs, though to the extent that the members of a small group possess a similar set, there can be no objection in using the term in this expanded way. See also my comments about this term in Part I.

> recognize this point in the literary space, which is also the point from which is formed a singular point of view *on* that space, is to be in a position to understand and to feel, by mental identification with a constructed position, the singularity of that position and of the person who occupies it, and the extraordinary effort which, at least in the particular case of Flaubert, was necessary to make it exist. (*The Rules of Art*, xix)

Bourdieu's belief that the great work of art is solely a matter of extraordinary effort flies in the face of most accounts of the creative process by artists themselves and betrays a touching faith in sociological explanation, but if we modify his account to allow for the irruption of the unforeseen as part of that process and give to the term 'singularity' the force that Derrida gives it, it's possible to assent to this description. So while I'm in agreement with Clark (and with Leavis and the New Critics) that '"Singularity" includes the provocation of what cannot be fully understood by being situated back into its historical context' (32), I am by no means convinced that 'the work itself' can, without contextual references, tell us what it is and how to read it. Michel Chaouli seems to me closer to the mark when he says, echoing Pater's rewriting of Arnold's dictum, 'What interests us is not the object "as in itself it really is", but the object as its force registers in a human being with his or her own history and style' ('Criticism and Style', 332)[10]

Clark devotes his first chapter to the question of *freedom*. What he opposes is the idea of freedom as autonomy, which he traces back to Kant and associates with liberal and capitalist notions of individualism.

[10] Chaouli uses the notion of 'singularity' in a manner that resonates with mine:

> I recognize that the artist has arranged words or images or sounds or just space in a way that could only have emerged from a singular imagination with its own history and affective charge, yet I also recognize that the very singularity of the arrangement somehow calls to me. It is not clear what I 'share' with the artwork or the artist, if I share anything at all. I do not find myself in an alliance of experience, the way I do when I am in solidarity with a cause. Perhaps I am driven to take note of the way my own singular experience—my style—opens to this other way of being singular. (340)

A notion of autonomy that presupposes a creator and a reader free from all constraints is clearly untenable, so to speak of the work's freedom is to speak of a freedom that goes no further than its ability to have effects that exceed explanation in terms of cultural determinism. I wouldn't link this to an argument about 'the work itself', however. If writer and reader have freedom, it's not owing to their total autonomy as individuals, but to their ability to deploy the cultural resources available to them in such a way as to allow otherness to enter the familiar sphere of thoughts and feelings—in other words, it's owing to their *inventiveness*. In the case of the writer, the result is an inventive work of literature; in the case of the reader, it's a modification of his habitual mental and emotional worlds. Clark acknowledges this:

> At issue in reading a literary text, however gently, is the force of a possible discontinuity, that the understanding achieved by the minute discipline of following its terms is not a kind of continuous progression of insight, but—somewhere—a jump. In other words, such 'understanding' (if that is still the best word) is not the modification or enhancement of an underlying consciousness or identity that would end the text as it began it, bar a little increase in its mental stores, but a becoming-other of that consciousness itself, whether minutely or significantly. (304)

I'm not sure that what happens is always a jump—I think the transformation can happen more stealthily than this—but I'm in agreement with the general point being made here.

In discussing a concept whose constitutive feature is its resistance to all conceptuality one runs the risk of falling into a kind of mystical materialism. To speak, for example, of 'the text itself' refusing all interpretative strategies may make it sound as if each literary work, or perhaps each literary work worthy of the name, possesses an unreachable, ineffable core that we can respond to but that we cannot analyse. It's important to remember Derrida's statement that singularity is 'never closed like a point or a fist'; he is punning here on the French homophone *point/poing*—a characteristic literary device which exemplifies, while it addresses, singularity. So it's precisely in its openness to alteration in new contexts that the work manifests its singularity. And its openness to the future stems from its having no unchanging core: it's constituted by the very norms and rules that it exceeds. Singularity is not universal or transcendent. In this lies its difference from particularity: a particular is the other face of a universal—this pen is particular, the concept 'pen' is universal, and what distinguishes this pen from other pens can also be specified as particulars (this is Nancy's 'numerical difference'). But the singularity of a novel—which is to say, its singularization in an attentive reading—although it's produced by various kinds of generality such as generic codes, habits of interpretation, and so on, can't be subsumed under a concept. This is only true of the novel *as literature*, however; as I've noted, there are many other legitimate ways of reading it which are not matters of singularity—for instance, as a linguistic text, as a historical record, as an autobiographical expression, as a moral treatise, as a philosophical argument.

Describing singularity, as I do, as the welcoming of alterity may also sound like an ascent (or descent) into the realm of the numinous. But the other is not some other-worldly, alien existence: it's that which is other *to* an existing way of thinking or configuration of knowledge or habitual emotional response, it's what those familiar modes of being exclude in order to be and remain what they are—and it's what the artist, often without being fully aware of how it is happening, is able to apprehend and articulate by reforming and revising the forces that are excluding it. Thus the truly inventive artist is someone who is unusually alert to the tensions and fractures in the *doxa*, and can exploit these to make the unthinkable thinkable, the unexperienceable experienceable. To read a poem and feel one is entering a new world of thought and feeling, to find oneself laughing at a surprising passage in a novel, to have one's breath taken away by a speech performed on stage—these are experiences of alterity, of the impossible suddenly made possible, of the mind and, sometimes, the body being changed by new configurations, new connections, new possibilities.

Singularity and ethics

Where are we to situate ethics in this account of singularity, inventiveness and otherness? In order to approach this issue, it's first of all important to distinguish between the ethico-political effectiveness of literary works *as literature* (in the sense I've been developing) and their effectiveness as other types of discourse. I've already made the point that literary works can function as historical documents, autobiographical investigations, psychological models, ethical treatises, theological arguments, stylistic exemplars, cultural explorations, political exhortations and many other things. It might seem that in these instances we're talking about texts rather than works, given the distinction I made between these in Part I; but in many cases at least it's as works that they are most effective. If readers find in *Brideshead Revisited* a compelling portrait of 1920s Oxford it's not because they are provided with a certain number of facts but because of the novel's power as a literary work: the acquisition of knowledge is a consequence of the experience of literariness (which is a matter of language, genre, and form). To learn moral lessons about judgement and deception from *Portrait of a Lady* is to treat the novel as something other than a literary work, but any such lessons will only offer themselves as effects of a literary reading. Wordsworth's *Prelude* provides a great deal of information about the poet's early development, but the fullest understanding of his years of poetic apprenticeship comes from a reading of the work as a poem and not as the rehearsal of a number of facts. Of course it's always possible to read a work as a text, to glean historical details from Sheridan's plays or to trace the arguments about history in *War and Peace*, and this is an entirely legitimate activity; but it's not a literary activity.[11]

[11] Genette makes a similar point with regard to art more generally:

> Our relation to works of art is often not aesthetic but, for example, scientific or scholarly (historical), as when we are trying to determine a work's author or date, or practical, as when a believer goes into Chartres cathedral simply to follow the mass, or when Duchamp or Goodman, deliberately ignoring the

What, then, is the ethico-political function of literary works, taking place in literary readings? As I've suggested, the event of a work takes place as an event in a culture, whether this is the event of creation or the event of a creative reading, that is to say, a reading open to the otherness offered by the work. Since, by definition, an event is unpredictable (though in retrospect it may be possible to trace the steps which made it inevitable, or at least which now make it seem inevitable) it cannot present moral truths or injunctions in the context of a fixed scheme of right and wrong. Nor can its effects be known in advance: they may be good or bad, when judged by existing moral or utilitarian norms. The ethical charge of the literary work arises from the fact that an event always involves a change; it's the introduction of alterity into the more or less smoothly working machine of the same. A literary experience, then, is the experience of a shift in mental and emotional ways of being in order to apprehend and incorporate otherness. Wolfgang Iser articulates a position close to mine when he writes in *The Act of Reading*:

> Reading has the same structure as experience, to the extent that our entanglement has the effect of pushing our various criteria of orientation back into the past, thus suspending their validity for the new present. This does not mean, however, that these criteria or our previous experiences disappear altogether. On the contrary, our past still remains our experience, but what happens now is that it begins to interact with the as yet unfamiliar presence of the text. This remains unfamiliar so long as our previous experiences are precisely as they had been before we began our reading. But in the course of the reading, these experiences will also change, for the acquisition of experience is not a matter of adding on—it is a restructuring of what we already possess. (132)

Putting this in simpler terms, to read a poem or a novel that merits the term 'literature' (which, it will have become clear, I'm using in an unashamedly evaluative way), or to watch a successful theatre piece,

artistic nature of the object, imagines using a painting by Rembrandt as an ironing board, blanket or shutter. (*The Aesthetic Relation*, 121–2) is to feel oneself taken into a new realm of thought and feeling, perhaps only fleetingly and temporarily, but occasionally with profound and long-lasting effects. A fresh metaphor will fuse together two domains of meaning and produce a tiny alteration in one's cognitive map; a powerfully drawn character will modify one's perception of other selves in the world; a finely articulated couplet will enhance one's sense of the expressive potential of the language.

These multiple possibilities of change, large and small, when multiplied across thousands or millions of readers, are what makes literature (and art more generally) an effective social agent, quite apart from its potency when treated as something other than literature in the ways I've described.[12] Because there can be no advance guarantee that the changes brought about by art will be beneficial, the channelling of these effects is conducted by other institutions; in a healthy society, good effects will be applauded and disseminated, bad effects limited.[13] There is another ethical dimension to literature understood as event and experience, already touched on in Part I: a culture in which literature, and art more generally, are actively engaged in is one in which a degree of openness to otherness is valued, and this can only be an ethical good.

I've given some attention to the term *responsibility* in the previous chapters, a term which I take, of course, from Levinas, and from Derrida's interpretation of Levinasian ethics; and I've stressed the importance of the phrase 'responsibility *for*'. As I've suggested, the preposition is significant, since we tend to think more readily of

[12] A study that puts the transformation of readers' cognition at the centre of its claims for literature's social effectiveness is Mack's *How Literature Changes the Way We Think*. Mack, however, understands this transformation solely in terms of the undermining of the fictions that 'keep us enthralled', so that we're offered a choice 'to either continue to live these fictions or to sever our subservience to them, thus changing our cognition and potentially our behaviour' (92–3)—a narrow and, to me, unconvincing account of the transformative power of literature.

[13] In chapter 10, I discuss the relationship between two forms of hospitality to the other, unconditional and conditional; reading, as unconditional openness to whatever may come, is regulated by the conditions imposed by the social and moral institutions within which it takes place.

responsibility *to*—to one's family, one's country, or whatever it might be that demands our loyalty. To be responsible *for*, say, one's family involves a stronger obligation: it's to take upon oneself the duty of protecting, safeguarding, keeping alive, acting in the best interests of. The writer who succeeds in creating an inventive work that welcomes the other—for instance, an author who writes a poem that enacts, for the first time, a particular affective-intellectual complex challenging the barbarism of war—writes out of a responsibility to that other but also, more importantly, *for* that other, in giving it verbal realization and in allowing it the chance to live across future generations. The reader who responds inventively to the poem, who finds her own singularity reshaped through the event of reading, is one who accepts a responsibility for the poem and for the complex of thought and feeling it embodies. Through repeated readings of this kind, the poem is kept alive in its singularity. The readings need not be sympathetic to what the poem does: a reader who is angered or upset by the poem, but whose response stems from an openness to the poem's effectivity, is still acting out of a responsibility to and for the work, and still helping it to survive. Laughter, too, is a responsible response when it's appropriate, when it signals an intimate involvement with the words, their movements and meanings, their feints and surprises.

Now, what kind of ethics is this? It's not difficult to see that the artist who is responsible for the marginalized or excluded possibilities of thought and feeling that characterize her time and place is acting ethically, even though this may take the form of a certain kind of passiveness, a willingness and an ability to perceive the pressure of alterity upon the habitual world and to allow the words to shape themselves accordingly. And we must remember that this passiveness is possible only as the outcome of a process of intense activity—the activity of becoming profoundly familiar with a language, a genre, a tradition, a culture, techniques of composition, procedures of reading, and so on). This responsibility to and for the otherness that arises from a culture's exclusions is also often a responsibility to and for individuals and groups—those who have been silenced, disempowered, deprived of social and individual goods. The ethical responsibilities engaged with by, say, Coetzee or Ishiguro or Walcott or Pinter are clear, and even writers less obviously fired by evident injustices are often exploring hidden areas of social existence or individual lives that form part of a pattern of exploitation, oppression, or exclusion.

However, it's not so easy to see where the act of *reading* a literary work abuts on the ethical. Responsibility for complexes of thought and feeling, responsibility for sets of words: this is not what we usually consider the domain of ethics. Do I have an *ethical* responsibility to read carefully, without skipping or letting my thoughts wander, to keep my mental and emotional receptors open to the advent of the other as I experience the words? Isn't this to empty the word 'ethics' of all its serious content in a world of injustice, oppression, misery, and inequality?

I accept that this is a danger, and I certainly don't want to say that reading quickly, or putting a book down after reading a few pages, are irresponsible acts, that such a reader is somehow ethically at fault. But I do want to argue that reading a work of literature (or listening to a symphony or taking in the details of a painting) with the kind of attention and commitment I've described has an ethical dimension. Like the writer who finds a way to be open to the otherness obscured by the society in which he works, so the reader who is able to respond to the alterity made available by the literary work—which is to say to its singularity and inventiveness—is acting ethically, both in relation to that alterity and to the writer who has introduced it. And in order to do this, the reader must bring to the work an alertness to his own socio-cultural environment, for though the work may be experienced as an address to the singular individual who is me, my singularity is the product of my own history in a particular temporal, geopolitical, social, and cultural space. The reader who is detached from the forms and circumstances around her, who attempts to read in a vacuum (an impossibility, of course), is unlikely to be able to do justice to a literary work that speaks to those forms and circumstances. The freedom of the reader—like that of the author—is a curious freedom, as it arises not from the actions of a sovereign, autonomous self but from a subject willing to be disarmed and, if necessary dismayed, by the intimations of an otherness excluded by its familiar world. It's close to what Heidegger called *Gelassenheit*, a will-less thinking, and to *hineni*, 'Here I am', the utterance of Biblical patriarchs in response to divine appearances adopted by Levinas as a statement of readiness to do whatever is demanded by the other.

I must stress once more, though, that I'm not talking about the ethical value of bringing new *knowledge* into the light: literary works may well do this, but in so doing they are not working as literature. I may learn a number of facts about Indian caste divisions from reading Vikram Seth's *A Suitable Boy*, but it's my living through the vivid representations of those divisions as they impact upon individuals, and the shifts, partly affective, partly intellectual, in my grasp of what happens in the world, that constitute the ethical experience.[14] (There is a great deal to be said about the astonishing fact that works written hundreds of years ago can still operate in this way; I broach this subject below in chapter 5.)

I need to repeat one further clarification: the ethics of openness to alterity does not imply that the outcome of this openness will, in every case, be good. This is not a utilitarian ethics. Otherness is otherness: there is no way of knowing in advance whether its advent will be beneficial or disastrous. The writer who brings into the world hitherto unavailable ways of thinking may be doing a disservice to humanity; the reader who undergoes a powerful experience of new possibilities may be led into terrible crimes. Fortunately, otherness can never enter as a pure force: as I stressed earlier, in order to be apprehended it has to become part of a system of norms and conventions, and these will usually be sufficient as a guardrail to counter malign effects.

[14] For a lucid account of the difference between the knowledge one might take away from a work of literature and the experience of knowing that constitutes the work as literature, see Hurley, 'How Philosophers Trivialize Art'. Hurley usefully refers to a number of philosophical discussions of the role of knowledge in art.

Openness to the other is a form of hospitality, and hospitality, as we shall see in chapter 10, though it's informed by an unconditional openness to whoever or whatever may come in through the door, is, in actuality, always conditioned by limitations and rules.

A singular invention: Donoghue's *Room*

Singularity, then, as I conceive it, names a feature of literary works that acknowledges both their specific mode of being—realized as an event of reading—and their close engagements with two contexts: that within which they were created and that in which they are read. The ethical importance of literature lies in this engagement, which I understand as the apprehension of otherness through an inventive event of writing and of reading—though this ethical importance is not to be understood as the conveying of moral maxims or the representation of moral truths; it's a matter of an experience that brings about an unpredictable alteration in individuals—and, perhaps, through individuals, the collectives they constitute.

As an example, I've chosen a recent work that is a singular, inventive intervention in the cultural discourses of our time, Emma Donoghue's 2010 novel *Room*. I want to use a passage from this novel to discuss the actual experience of engaging with a text that takes the reader in unexpected directions and thus could be said to invite an opening to otherness. As I've stressed, the other to which we are introduced in such a reading must be other *to*; it's not absolute in the sense of having no relations outside itself but it already has a relation to me, albeit a negative relation. In order to acknowledge this otherness, I have to find a means to destabilize or deconstruct the set of norms and habits that give me the world—my idioculture, in short—in such a way that that the force of that which they exclude is felt. Or, putting it differently, I have to allow the novel to destabilize those norms through its grasp on otherness. (This is where the tensions and fractures in the culture prove important.) The *way* it is felt is not as the sudden knowledge of what was hitherto unknown and unknowable, but rather in the changes the familiar world has to undergo in order for the newcomer to be acknowledged.

Room is told from the perspective of, and in the language of, a five-year old boy. One can cite many precursors who have emulated a child's way of speaking—in Irish writing alone, instances include James Joyce in *A Portrait of the Artist as a Young Man*, Roddy Doyle in *Paddy Clarke Ha Ha Ha*, Hugo Hamilton in *The Speckled People*, and Eimear McBride in *A Girl is a Half-formed Thing*—but Donoghue succeeds in doing something new, as she leads the reader slowly to a realization of the boy's unique circumstances and of the mother's ingenuity in providing him with as rich a life as possible under highly straitened circumstances.

The slight estrangement produced by the child's failure to observe the rules of style and grammar begins from the opening sentence, 'Today I'm five', a locution that captures the child's sense of magical transformation where the more normal, if less logical, 'Today I turn five' wouldn't. But the reader quickly realizes that the oddness of the language is due not only to the youth of the speaker: there are peculiar designations of objects with proper nouns, Wardrobe and Bed, and the further strangeness of a child going to sleep in the former and waking in the latter. These are, of course, enigmas that we expect to be solved as we read on, part of what Barthes called the hermeneutic code; but they are also inventive challenges to the norms of verbal reference and daily behaviour that introduce an otherness we don't yet know what to do with. For the moment, the puzzles only multiply: while we don't find anything remarkable about a mother's recourse to fantastic explanations of conception and birth in addressing a five-year-old, the particular fantasy is not one of the usual ones:

> 'Was I minus numbers?'
> 'Hmm?' Ma does a big stretch.
> 'Up in Heaven. Was I minus one, minus two, minus three–?'
> 'Nah, the numbers didn't start till you zoomed down.'
> 'Through Skylight.' (3)

We're being asked to imagine why a mother might need to invent this tale of conception, and we're taken even further out of the familiar territory of birth stories by the boy's extraordinary comment as he looks at the room's rug, 'There's the stain I spilled by mistake getting born.' Through the innocence of Jack's outlook on his life, repeating what he has been told in his own ungrammatical fashion, comes an intimation of something untoward, something not quite in the same key as the happy birthday chatter. The darkness shadowing the cheerful scene grows stronger when we encounter the first pronominal reference whose referent is unknown to us, and remains unknown because of the mother's reluctance to speak of it: 'I don't think he came last night after nine, the air's always different if he came. I don't ask because she doesn't like saying about him' (4).

There is not much darkness in the scene that follows, in which Ma allows Jack to unwrap his birthday present, which is a drawing of him she has made while he was sleeping—except, of course, that the exiguousness of the gift makes it clear that the woman has no access to any resources outside her own ingenuity and the most minimal of materials. Again, we find ourselves invited to participate in the imaging of a world that is not aligned with that of the book's likely readers. Jack then takes care of the picture:

> I pin Ma's surprise drawing on the very middle cork tile over Bed.
>
> She shakes her head. 'Not there'.
>
> She doesn't want Old Nick to see. 'Maybe in Wardrobe, on the back?' I ask.
>
> 'Good idea'.
>
> Wardrobe is wood, so I have to push the pin an extra lot. I shut her silly doors, they always squeak, even after we put corn oil on the hinges. I look through the slats but it's too dark. I open her a bit to peek, the secret drawing is white except the little lines of gray. Ma's blue dress is hanging over a bit of my sleeping eye, I mean the eye in the picture but the dress for real in Wardrobe.
>
> I can smell Ma beside me, I've got the best nose in the family.
>
> 'Oh, I forgetted to have some when I woke up.'
>
> 'That's OK. Maybe we could skip it once in a while, now you're five?'

> 'No way Jose.'
> So she lies down on the white of Duvet and me too and I have lots. (5–6)

We stay in the five-year-old's world of objects as characters with personalities—Wardrobe is 'silly' because 'she' squeaks—and allow our own adult horizons to shift accordingly, taking in the boy's struggles with grammar and logic—'my sleeping eye, I mean the eye in the picture but the dress for real'. And now the mysterious 'he' is named—at least that's likely to be our guess—as 'Old Nick', and the reader may experience a frisson at the devilish connotations of the name, combined with Ma's refusal to let this individual see the drawing of her son and the reference to the bed. It's only later that the true horror lying behind the boy's happy chatter and the mother's resourceful dealings with him becomes clear: that the woman was kidnapped as a teenager and has been imprisoned since then in a single locked room, that she is forced to have sex regularly with her kidnapper, and that Jack is the second of two children, the first of whom died at birth. The significance of Jack's puzzling statement about Wardrobe and Bed emerges when we learn that before Old Nick—Ma has no doubt chosen the name as one the boy will find unthreatening—enters the room to rape her, Ma has Jack lie down to sleep in the wardrobe. When he has gone she moves the sleeping boy into their bed, where he wakes up in the morning.

Now, the question is: what exactly happens as Donoghue's inventive and singular deployment of the English language and the available techniques of the novel introduce otherness into the reader's fiction-comprehending framework? Take the last few lines of this passage. It isn't the case that 'I have lots' is at first completely inaccessible and then, when realization dawns, wholly accessible; we understand it immediately as a reference to a child's consumption of food, but what kind of food it is remains unclear until we shift our frames of reference to accept the idea of a five-year old boy at his mother's breast as a normal part of his daily routine. We now understand that 'have some' and 'it' refer to breastfeeding, a topic that doesn't have to be named as it's so familiar to both of them. It's the mental shift, making possible the accommodation of the new idea, that is the literary experience. And what is of particular importance in understanding how literature works is that we can re-read the passage and still experience the shift. There's always the possibility in this kind of experience that what at first seems other eventually becomes wholly familiar; this can happen when an artistic invention gets repeatedly imitated, or when we find that what seemed strange in a work then appears in one's own environment often enough to become normal. But unless the image of the mother and boy trapped in the room—and all the linguistic details Donoghue employs to convey its singularity—become part of the reader's familiar world, the book is going to retain at least a good part of its otherness, to be experienced in the adjustments and recalibrations it demands each time we read it.

Of course encountering unfamiliar formal devices or content in a work of literature doesn't necessarily mean it is inventive or that its strangeness is produced by the introduction of the cultural other; the experience may be one of bafflement or boredom. In some cases, re-reading might serve to overcome this blockage; in other cases the work will remain merely odd. When a work introduces an unacknowledged way of thinking or feeling that fills a gap in cultural understanding, the experience is, as I've noted before, often one of rightness or truth—Barthes's 'That's it!' So in the case of *Room*, many readers are led to appreciate aspects of childhood and motherhood—both linguistic and psychological—that don't form part of the general perception of these states, but that ring true when fictionally made real. More specifically, although cases of kidnapping and incarceration receive wide media publicity, it's possible that there has been a failure to fully comprehend the nature of the experience—especially the experience of children born under such circumstances.

Room is, admittedly, the product of a writer's creative imagination, and thus lacks the authenticity of an autobiographical account; but, thanks to its literary technique, it possesses an immediacy and intensity that invite readers to employ their own imaginative powers in engaging with it. Singular but far from autonomous, it engages closely with the social realities of its—and our—time and with the discourses of childhood, parenting, education, crime, sex and more; and if its inventive embodying of otherness effects a change in the reader's mental and affective hold on the world it can be said to work ethically—perhaps only in a minimal way, but out of such small adjustments much larger transformations may grow. All over the world injustice is being done as a result of the fear and hate of 'the other', from the United States to China to France and South Africa. A feeling that certain groups are inassimilably other feeds conflict all over the globe—at the moment of writing, Sunni against Shia in the Middle East, Dinka against Nuer in South Sudan, Catholic against Protestant in Northern Ireland, Jew against Arab in Israel...the list could go on and on. I'm not proposing a direct link between the openness to alterity encouraged by literary works and the exercise of generosity towards other cultures and communities—for too long literary critics have made exaggerated claims about the political efficacy of their readings[15]—but I don't think we should assume that the two are entirely unconnected.

[15] Bourdieu puts the matter trenchantly: 'It is the typical illusion of the *lector*, who can regard an academic commentary as a political act or the critique of texts as a feat of resistance, and experience revolutions in the order of words as radical revolutions in the order of things' (*Pascalian Meditations*, 2).

CHAPTER 4

Criticism

The critical tools we have at our disposal today—enshrined in a thousand guides to reading and teaching literature, analyses of individual works and oeuvres, and decades of classroom practice—are extremely powerful. Thanks to the brilliant examples of Empson and Richards, Wimsatt and Brooks, Jakobson and Genette, and many others, we've inherited techniques of analysis that can be widely taught and put to use, even by those who are left unmoved and unchanged by the works they are analysing. So much that is written or spoken about literary works is governed by an external need—the need to complete a student essay, to give a class, to achieve publication—rather than by a demand made by the work upon a reader, and we freely detect alliteration or allegory, historical reference or cultural allusion, biographical revelation or ideological deformation, without pausing to ask if this is what the event of the work insists upon when we read it with full attention. I'm not suggesting that we abandon these techniques, just that we make sure they're used to clarify and explain the experience of the work's singularity, inventiveness and alterity in an alert and committed reading. It's all too easy to allow the effectiveness of the critical apparatus to determine what we say about a work. Michel Chaouli describes the situation well:

> One way of seeing our disciplines is as a measure of the lengths to which we go to keep at bay the force of artworks, the same artworks whose ability to snap us out of our torpor drew us to them in the first place. How curious it is that we dig wide moats—of history, ideology, formal analysis—and erect thick conceptual walls lest we be touched by what, in truth, lures us. ('Criticism and Style', 328)

One way of approaching the question of the dangers that lie in our extremely powerful critical tools is to ask what the relation is between powerful critical writing and the power of literature. Does the former increase (or, when hostile, diminish) the latter, or does it reveal the power that is already there? Can the criticism be too powerful for the poem? We may take as examples a powerful critic, Christopher Ricks, and a powerful poet, Paul Muldoon.

Critical power: the critic

Christopher Ricks is a critic in the tradition of Eliot, Richards, Empson, and the American New Critics, and, to a lesser extent, Leavis. This remains the dominant tradition in the close reading of poetry in the English-speaking world, its influence observable in reviews, in classrooms, in critical studies of poets, and in those moments when predominantly historical, theoretical, political, or sociological interpreters decide to take a close look at poetic examples. It's the tradition in which I received my own training, giving it a certain naturalness for me, and I derive immense enjoyment from a display by a master of the craft like Ricks. Setting aside my partiality as far as I can, however, I'd like to look more closely at what happens when Ricks gets to grips with the language of a poem, on the assumption that, since we're examining this type of criticism at its best, anything problematic that shows up will be an inherent weakness in the method.

Although not given to theoretical statements, Ricks begins one of his books by raising the question of the critic's relation to the artist. He rejects the suggestion that the former's power can be at the expense of the latter's by way of a story told by one of his critical predecessors about another one:

> As a student at Cambridge long ago (1928?), the young William Empson impressed his teacher, the not much older I. A. Richards, by his spirited dealings with a Shakespeare sonnet. 'Taking the sonnet as a conjurer takes his hat, he produced an endless swarm of rabbits from it and ended by

> "You could do that with any poetry, couldn't you?"' But only if the poetry truly teems, and only if the critic only *seems* to be a conjurer. (*Dylan's Visions of Sin*, 1)

'Only if the poetry truly teems': this is the Ricksian yardstick by which we are to judge the responsible critic, who is not up to any tricks and reveals no more than is actually there. Empson's sceptical suggestion in the anecdote—that what is revealed in bravura criticism is the skill of the critic, not the value of the poetry—is brushed aside. Ricks seems to suggest, perhaps inadvertently, that the critic *is* a master of illusion—the illusion that he's a conjurer dealing in illusions, when he's really a hard-headed discloser of realities. But his drift is clear: *pace* Empson, it's not just any work of literature that will yield fruit in the hands of the skilful critic. What then, we might ask, is the function of the rhetorical flourishes, the humorous patter, the graceful motions, characteristic of much of the criticism we enjoy, if not to bamboozle the audience into taking illusion for reality? Is it not the task of the critic, like the conjurer, to *persuade* us that the rabbits really were in the hat? Is there, perhaps, a danger that the critic will persuade *herself* that they were? I want to use a tiny specimen of Ricks's own criticism to pursue these questions.

The work I've just quoted from is Ricks's 500-page study of Bob Dylan's lyrics, first published in 2003 and probably his best-known book among the wider public. I don't believe it's representative of Ricks's criticism at its best; however, my point is not to pass judgement but to examine a technique, and this study is useful because it exposes Ricks's critical method with great clarity. We'll have to let a small example do duty for many lengthy discussions of Dylan's words. Here's Ricks's analysis of two lines from 'Lay, Lady Lay':

> I long to see you in the morning light
> I long to reach for you in the night
>
> —where there are not only the parallel syntax and the rhyme but the internal assonance (*see / reach*), with 'I long to see you' reaching across to 'I

> long to reach for you'. The couplet is for a couple and a coupling, and it reaches back (we should see and hear) to two earlier parallel lines:
>
> Why wait any longer for the world to begin
> Why wait any longer for the one you love
>
> It is as though 'longer' were a longer form of the word 'long', and so it is, but not of this yearning meaning of the word. (155)

Those who are familiar with Ricks's criticism will recognize this as a characteristic example of his method and style, whether he is commenting on John Milton or David Ferry. He succeeds in pointing out a number of facts about the two lines by Dylan: (1) they are parallel in syntax, (2) they rhyme (light/night), (3) they have internal assonance (see/reach), (4) they contain, in the word 'long', an echo of two earlier lines which use the word 'longer'. The question I want to ask is: does this demonstration also prove that the lines are highly effective as poetry, that they evince skill and produce pleasure by their subtle handling of language? (I'm ignoring, as Ricks does, the fact that they are written to be sung, and are normally encountered, not on the pages of a book of literary criticism, but in the ear.[1] I have no qualms in agreeing that 'Lay, Lady, Lay' is a terrific song—but that isn't what is at stake here.)

One test would be: how easy is it to construct lines that have the same features as the ones that Ricks points out? The answer is, very easy.

> I stand and read this paper here to you,
> I stand and keep on reading though I'm blue.

This couplet evinces syntactic parallelism, rhyme, and internal assonance; and it's not difficult to imagine an echo with an earlier line containing, say, the word 'standard'. One could produce hundreds of

[1] This is not to say that Ricks never alludes to Dylan's singing of the songs he discusses; but his aim in the book is to show the brilliance of Dylan's poetic language.

such examples in an hour or two, though it would be a pretty mind-numbing exercise. If Dylan's lines are exceptional as poetry, it can't be for the reasons Ricks gives. My own feeling is that they are—in their spoken form—little more than workmanlike. Perhaps their most interesting feature is one on which Ricks makes no comment: the regular iambic pentameter of the first line isn't repeated in the second, which breaks down rhythmically in its second half. This is clear if you compare an imaginary alternative, 'I long to reach for you across the night'. It's hard to keep the melody out of one's head, of course, encouraging a stress on 'in' that saves the rhythm: 'I long to reach for you—in the night.' It's also interesting that the temporal sequence is reversed, suggesting that waking together, blissful though it is, is secondary to what happens before going to sleep.

Why, then, is it possible, momentarily at least, to find Ricks's commentary convincing, to feel that he has indeed shown that the poetry truly teems, that the rabbits he pulls out were really there? His most effective trick is to draw upon the language of the poem in his own description, creating the illusion of an extraordinarily close relationship between his words and Dylan's. For Ricks, 'I long to see you' doesn't merely echo 'I long to reach for you', it 'reaches across' to it. The two lines also 'reach back' to the earlier lines. Then Ricks sets up his own echoing sequence by seeming to suggest that Dylan's having written a couplet is particularly appropriate when the subject is a couple who are coupling. These rhetorical devices are immense fun, but they don't actually *say* anything more about Dylan's poetic achievement than a plainer version would. Ricks observes earlier in the book that the fact that writing about literature exists in the same medium as the art it explores 'can give to literary criticism a delicacy and an inwardness that are harder to achieve elsewhere' (7); this may be so, one might respond, but it also constitutes a temptation to the critic to create an *effect* of delicacy and inwardness by recycling the very words being commented on.

The short passage I've focused on here may not contribute very much to an evaluation of Dylan's poetry, but what is undeniable is that the cumulative power achieved by the multiplication of such examples over the several pages devoted to a single poem (which is how, for the most part, 'Lay Lady Lay' is treated), and over the several hundred pages of the book.

This device of what we might call 'verbal incorporation' is to be found everywhere in Ricks's criticism. After the citation of Keats's lines in *Endymion* about Adonis's mouth being opened 'By tenderest pressure' we read 'The tenderest pressure of the lines themselves...' (*Keats and Embarrassment*, 12). Stevie Smith's rhyming of 'diffident' and 'accident' is called a 'diffident accident' (*The Force of Poetry*, 252), while Byron's rhyming of 'resource' and 'recourse' is said to be 'itself both a resource and a recourse'—and Byron having used the words 'hide' and 'betrayed' earlier in the stanza, Ricks can't resist telling us that 'There is something the lines wish both to hide and to betray' (*Essays in Appreciation*, 150). It is, of course, only one tool in Ricks's well-stocked chest, but it will have to stand for all the ways in which his immense skill as a writer is deployed to move, delight, and persuade the reader. Another critic, without this rhetorical flair, might point out the same features of a poem and fail to convince. And one has to ask, in spite of Ricks's own insistence that the rabbits must really be there for such criticism to work, if there is *any* verse, however limp or leaden, that he could not bring to illusory life.[2]

A second technique of which Ricks is master is the detection of *allusion*—he's written a book on the topic (*Allusion to the Poets*)—and sure enough, Dylan is shown to be a master too. It's not the overt allusions that bring out Ricks's peculiar talents; it's the slight echoes that reveal, he argues, Dylan's unconscious absorption of literary masterpieces. Thus Dylan's 'Not Dark Yet' is shown to have no less

[2] Ricks often praises the awkwardnesses in Dylan's writing that many listeners have simply been prepared to overlook. Thus in 'The Lonesome Death of Hattie Carroll', the line 'With rich wealthy parents who provide and protect him' is found to be a marvel of suggestiveness: neither the repetitiveness of 'rich wealthy' nor the solecism of 'provide...him' is allowed to be a weakness; on the contrary, Ricks declares them to be poetic subtleties (*Dylan's Visions of Sin*, 230).

than 28 words or phrases in common with Keats's 'Ode to a Nightingale' (361–7); 'too many likenesses', writes Ricks, 'for it to be likely that they are coincidences' (367). And 'One Too Many Mornings' shares the following words with a five line speech from Act III scene I of *The Comedy of Errors*: 'down', 'the street', 'get' [gettin'], 'came' [comes], 'in', 'from', 'my', 'door', 'for', 'whence' [where], 'walk', 'one', 'when', and—the phrase Ricks looked up in the *OED* where he found this citation from Shakespeare—'one too many'. Having introduced the paragraph by saying 'It cannot be more than a coincidence', Ricks ends it by asking, with his familiar stylistic tic or trick, 'Is this one too many to be coincidental'? (426). But what is really being demonstrated in such examples, something important about Dylan's writing or Ricks's extraordinary sharpness of eye and ear?

What I'm trying to argue can be summed up in a maxim, oversimplified as all maxims are: *The more powerful the critic's technique, the less reliable the critical judgements it is used to make.* Of course, there is a great deal more to Ricks's authority as a critic—I've made no mention of his erudition, his editorial skill, the breadth of his reading, and so on—but I suspect his other strengths would have counted for far less (especially outside the academy) had they not been allied to verbal dexterity and a fine eye for intertextual connections. My maxim leads to a rule of thumb, this time borrowed from scientific discourse, a version, in fact, of Occam's razor: *A critical method should be no more powerful than is absolutely necessary for the task it is called upon to carry out.* Any excess of power will only serve to distort what is supposedly being described.

We need to read criticism with a critical eye: if we find it persuasive, is it because it has identified a feature of the literary work that genuinely contributes to our enjoyment, or is it because of its own literary flair? And if we produce our own commentary on a literary work, in the classroom or on the page, we need to do so in a sceptical spirit, continually asking, 'Does what I'm pointing out really matter in my experience of the work?'

Critical power: the poet

It would be very satisfying to have Christopher Ricks's reading of the lyrics of another song, entitled 'My Ride's Here', recorded by a popular performer. Here's one of the verses:

The Houston sky was changeless
We galloped through bluebonnets
I was wrestling with an angel
You were working on a sonnet
You said I believe the seraphim
Will gather up my pinto
And carry us away Jim
Across the San Jacinto
My ride's here

Anyone familiar with the poems of Paul Muldoon will spot the affinities—the Wild West setting, the precision of the references (the bluebonnet is the state flower of Texas; the San Jacinto River runs from Lake Houston to Galveston Bay), the leaps of narrative logic, the specialized terminology (seraphim, pinto), the ingenious off-rhymes (changeless/angel; seraphim/away Jim). And, indeed, these lyrics were written by Muldoon, in collaboration with the performer, the late Warren Zevon.[3] Muldoon himself plays in a rock band for which he writes the lyrics.

But for the moment, it's Muldoon as critic I want to spend some time with. In 1998, Muldoon gave the Clarendon Lectures in English Literature at Oxford. Published as *To Ireland, I* (Donalbain's words to Malcolm after Macbeth's murder of Duncan), the book presents a remarkable tapestry of Irish writers, arranged in alphabetical order, and knotted together by a series of deftly-handled allusions. Let me cite an instance of Muldoon's characteristic mode of proceeding:

[3] Published in Muldoon, *General Admission*, 101.

> Samuel Beckett . . . was so much taken by resonances of his own name that he would surely have delighted in that phrase in the anonymous ninth-century poem . . . :
>
> Berait beich
> (becc a nert)
>
> While the word *beich* means 'bees' in this context, it is cognate with a number of sharp-ended or pointed things, including *boc*, a 'he-goat' and *bac*, . . . meaning, in Modern Irish, 'a quirk; an angular space, hollow or object; a river turn; a crozier, a mattock, a billhook, a prop, a pin, a crook, a peg, a thole-pin; a joint, a hook; a shackle, a hindrance, a stop; a fire-hop, a fire-prop, corner of hob; act of supporting, holding back, hindering'. The word *becc* means 'little, small, tiny or few'. In other words, *Beich becc* is a version of the 'diminutive beaked thing' of Beckett's own name. I'd like to suggest that Beckett was familiar not only with this poem but with that other ninth-century poem about 'The Blackbird Over Belfast Lough' . . . The first line of 'The Blackbird' . . . reads *'Int en bec'*. Here *bec* refers quite specifically to the 'beak' or 'bill' of the blackbird. I'm reminded, though, of that passage in *Malone Dies* . . . . (12–13)

And Muldoon goes on to quote the wonderful passage in which Mr and Mrs Saposcat discuss the fountain pen they plan to give their son, following it with the remark that the word 'pen' is cognate with *binn*, a 'peak' in Irish, and *le bec*, a 'nib' in French, and suggesting that the picture of the bird on the pen's box, 'its yellow beak agape', to use Beckett's words, is the same bird referred to in the Irish poem about the blackbird (13).

It's dizzying stuff, and in spite of the great show of scholarship the reader is bound to ask: is he serious? The reader who knows Muldoon's poetry, above all, will wonder where to draw the line between scholarly identification carried out in all earnestness and free association indulged in with wicked glee. The book is studded with phrases like 'would surely have' and 'I'd like to suggest', as in the passage I've quoted—perhaps enough to keep Muldoon on the windy side of the laws of scholarship—but nowhere does the mask of sober seriousness slip. The point, surely, is that the line can't be drawn: the cultural arena is thronged with a million echoes and reflections, and who can say that any particular one is a matter merely of chance? So it would not be accurate to say that *To Ireland, I* is simply a parody of scholarly allusion-hunting of the type Ricks is so good at; it's in fact full of captivating connections and hints of unexpected links. But it would not be accurate, either, to say that it's entirely trustworthy, that Muldoon isn't chuckling as he knits together his intricate interlacings. And the pleasure in reading the book lies in being aware of both of these—and of the fact that such commentary has a life of its own, which often leaves the text under consideration far behind.

The lectures that Muldoon gave as Professor of Poetry in Oxford, published as *The End of the Poem*, have more of the literary critic and less of the literary trickster than the Clarendon Lectures, but there are passages that seem to operate in the same zone as the earlier series. Discussing Marianne Moore's 'The Fish', for instance, Muldoon quotes the phrase 'A fritillary zigzags...' and goes on to note that the zigzag is a familiar element in Moorish art and architecture. Moorish and Moore-ish are linked (as with 'Beckett' and 'beak'), and related to the Andalusian pansy mentioned in another poem, and to the line further on in 'The Fish' that contains a 'gold horse-shoe', the horse-shoe arch being another feature of Moorish buildings. There follows a rare moment of reflection on this method of commentary:

> Now, I know that this kind of reading may sometimes seem a little fritillarian (in the *dicey* sense which underlies both the butterfly and the flower so familiar to this audience), perhaps a little fiddle-headed [this is a word he's going to make much of later in the essay], but what can I do? I'm sitting at a desk I acquired from the gentleman who looks after surplus furniture at Princeton. His name is Sam Formica. On the desk are two books. One is *The Botany of Desire: A Plant's-Eye View of the World* by Michael Pollan. The other is Archie G. Walls's *Geometry and Architecture in Islamic Jerusalem*. (249)

The echoes, the coincidences, the interlacings are there in the world, says Muldoon, as real as anything else. He seems to imply the irrelevance of intention: there is no suggestion that Archie G. Walls set out, because of his name, to dedicate his scholarly efforts to arches and walls. Ricks, by contrast, tends to agonize over the question of intention, settling for 'unconscious or subconscious intentions' to get him out of the problems his allusion-tracing has got him into (*Allusion to the Poets*, 4).

Ricks and Muldoon, then, practice two styles of commentary that are, on the surface at least, very similar in their procedures. (Like Ricks, Muldoon is given to using words lifted from the texts on which he is commenting, as with his use of 'fritillarian' in the passage I quoted—though unlike Ricks, he can make fun of himself as he does so.) To my mind, the great usefulness of the second example is that it opens our eyes to the dangers of the first. Both of these critics demonstrate the immense power of the method of close reading developed in the first half of the twentieth century, but only one of them is aware that it's in that very power that its limitations, as well as its potential for humour, lie.

Muldoon's *The Loaf* and the limits of commentary

What kind of commentary, then, can best *serve* the poem it deals with, not coming between the poem and the reader with a dazzling display of erudition and keen observation that all too easily substitutes for the experience of the poem, but allowing it to be re-read with enhanced insight and enjoyment? I don't believe there's a recipe for such commentary; different audiences have different needs at different times, different critics have different strengths, and, perhaps most importantly, different poems call for different kinds of response. Perhaps it's more a question of attitude, or, as I've been arguing, of ethics: a sense of responsibility towards the work (with that useful word 'work' standing for the linguistic object one is engaging with and the labour put into it by the poet) or, more specifically, responsibility towards what is singularly inventive in the work. The critic who astonishes with the brilliance of his close reading—whether it be in the Richards–Empson–Brooks tradition in which we can situate Ricks, or the deconstructive tradition of Paul de Man or Barbara Johnson, or the minute stylistic analyses of Roman Jakobson and his successors—will always have an audience, both because it's pleasurable to watch the skilful conjurer at work and because they often do achieve the kind of responsible response I'm advocating. My point is just that when the poem becomes a textual object on which critics feel they have free reign to deploy whatever techniques they are skilled in, there is always the possibility that it, and its writer, and the potentially rewarding experience being offered by them, will not be at the heart of the reading.

I'm not, of course, talking about critical approaches that take as their goal the exposure of a poem's ideological flaws or dubious complicities; such approaches owe allegiance to a set of values entirely separate from the poem. Nor am I concerned with commentary whose task is primarily to situate a work historically or biographically, or to provide the information necessary to understand its language and its references: such commentary is important—indeed, essential—but it doesn't pose the problems that evaluative and interpretative responses do. My interest is in criticism whose aim is to do justice to the value of a poem as a source of pleasure and insight.

At the risk of over-simplifying, I will set out some straightforward principles to complement my remarks in chapter 2. These principles may be obvious, but I don't believe their consequences are always followed through. (I'm concentrating on poetry here, but they could be modified to apply to literature more broadly.) A poem, like all literary works, is not an object but an event: it happens in time, and it has the power to produce change when it happens. (Two of the most influential books of New Criticism were entitled *The Well-wrought Urn* and *The Verbal Icon*: wrong from the start, one might say.) Furthermore, a poem doesn't happen in neutral space; it's the human *experience* of an event. The words printed on the page have no life of their own, nor does a sounded reading or recording if there is no listener to hear it. It's an experience of language, or more strictly, of language's powers—to move, to terrify, to enlighten, to argue, to charm. And it's an experience that differs from reader to reader, time to time, place to place; we read as individuals with particular histories, particular psyches, particular expectations, not as abstractions. Criticism of the kind I'm endorsing doesn't claim to rise above these particularities, but to take account of them as far as it's possible to do so. A commentary that does justice to a poem is a report on a particular individual's experience, but not from a safe distance: it's an attempt to convey to another reader of the poem how it moves (in both senses), how it pleases, sometimes how it teaches, in such a way that the other reader can test, and perhaps share, the reading.[4]

My argument thus far has been that the event of the literary work—to the extent that it's experienced as *literary*—is an event whereby otherness enters the life of the reader or hearer, a singular, inventive otherness that asks the reader to adjust, however minutely, her grasp on the world. The power of poetry, then, lies above all in its moments of risk, of danger; those moments, perhaps, where the poet is least able to say what was intended, where the critic is most likely to veer off into displays of learning or theoretical sophistication.

To provide exemplification of these general principles, I could quote examples of critical readings I've found working in this way—including, I must stress, readings by Ricks and Muldoon—but instead I'll offer some comments of my own on a poem of Muldoon's. His poetry shows the same alertness as his criticism to the possibilities of interconnection and echo, of figure and trope, of sound pattern and sense deviation, and the reader often feels—as with Muldoon's great precursor, Joyce—that however great the quantity of ore extracted, the poem's veins hold a good deal more. It's not, in other words, a question of hats and rabbits; Muldoon's poems do, indeed, truly teem. A reading of a Muldoon poem alert to the hazards entailed

[4] Miller's 'implicative criticism' shares these goals: it is 'not a (retrospective) report of thought but a (present) performance or display of thinking, an event not an end'; its features 'make the time and occasion of reading an essential element of it; which is to say further that other occasions may make for other readings; and to say that some of the benefits of the reading are left behind when the reading stops' (351).

in the powerful techniques of modern criticism would be one that takes full account of, and full pleasure in, all the ingenuity, but is constantly alert to (or in quest of) the purposes that ingenuity is serving. It would also be one that eschews the rhetoric characteristic of the powerful critic, the weaving of the poem's words back into the commentary, the ostentatious use of devices like alliteration and rhyme, the impressive display of knowledge in the detection of allusions. Rhetoric can't be avoided, of course; any commentary is an attempt to persuade by means of well-crafted language, but what I wish to challenge is the implicit notion that the more intricate and witty the critical response, the better the poem.

I've chosen 'The Loaf', from Muldoon's collection *Moy Sand and Gravel,* both because it has a particular resonance for me (I first read it when living not far from Muldoon's house outside Princeton) and because it is, by Muldoon's standards, a relatively simple poem, which will make it possible to keep my commentary brief. I first read it as I worked my enjoyable, though sometimes bemused, way through the collection, and of course it triggered associations with many other poems, by Muldoon and others; but for the purposes of this exercise I'll leave these echoes and allusions out of consideration—and thus read in a very unMuldoonian, as well as unRicksian, manner. I must stress that this is not meant to be a blueprint for poetic commentary, just my way—for the present moment—of trying to convey what happens when I read, and enjoy, and find myself moved by, this poem.

'The Loaf': the title doesn't give much away—I hold it suspended, to be filled out with meaning as the poem proceeds. The poem starts off with an immediate sense of a straightforward, personal voice:

> When I put my finger to the hole they've cut for a dimmer switch

There's nothing poetic about this language, nothing tricksy or exhibitionist. The anonymous 'they' is immediately understandable as a modern colloquial reference to the workpeople, those whose job it is to do things like cutting holes for switches. (The dimmer switch is a sure sign of contemporary living; a home is being upgraded). The line is a rhythmic whole: stresses spaced out by one, two, or three unstressed syllables. It's a calm beginning; the curiosity implicit in the movement described isn't agitated or anxious but a natural response when seeing, for the first time perhaps, the material inside the walls of one's house.

The second line has the same matter-of-fact tone and evenly spaced rhythm:

> in a wall of plaster stiffened with horsehair

However, I take in the information quite greedily, since I'm still trying to get my bearings: 'stiffened with horsehair'—how long ago were houses built with horsehair in the walls? The sentence still hasn't reached its verb, but now it arrives to provide an answer:

> it seems I've scratched a two-hundred-year-old itch.

So horsehair-stiffened plaster might be found in a 200-year old house. Does it matter that I know that part of Paul Muldoon's house is over 200 years old? It's not knowledge I can erase from my consciousness, though I wouldn't claim it to be essential to reading the poem. The rhythm stutters a little on the hyphenated adjective, putting additional weight on the final stressed word: 'two-hundred-year-old itch'. But why does touching the ancient exposed plaster seem like scratching an itch? Is the rhyme already calling the shots at this point (a worry that Muldoon sometimes courts in his verse)? It presents an enigma, as Barthes would say, that I read on to solve.

The resolution is not, however, immediately forthcoming. Instead I encounter something quite unexpected:

> *with a pink and a pink and a pinkie-pick.*

It's here that the poem—hitherto an intriguing but not particularly remarkable personal anecdote, matter-of-factly related—carries me into unfamiliar territory: otherness confronts me and obliges me to respond. The first-person intimacy is gone; language itself, or the tradition of popular verse, or the archaic domain of the child, seems to be speaking, or even singing, the words. Suddenly sound—which had not been particularly foregrounded in the previous lines—becomes central to my experience: a regular anapaestic rhythm up to the final word, where the triple movement gives way to duple and at the same time a consonant is dropped to transform 'pink' to 'pick'. I recognize the signs of a traditional refrain—of, say, a work song or a children's chant—in the beginning on 'with a', the tendency towards nonsense, and the repetitions; and these signs are confirmed in print by the use of italics. It's as if history is speaking through this archaic form: we seem to have moved two hundred years back in *poetic* time as well. Usually in nonsense refrains, however—'With a hey and a ho and a hey nonny no'—there's no point in looking for meaning, but in this refrain some sense pushes through the opacity of the line. A pinkie is a finger—the little one, usually—so that takes me back to the first line: a 'pinkie-pick' could be the action described there. But *pink*? A colour? A flower? Though no doubt an ingenious enough critic could find justifications for these meanings, I think it's important to resist them if they are no more than the products of ingenuity. The only relevant association that comes to my mind is with the verb 'to pink', to make holes. The meanings hover indistinctly around the line. I read on.

The opening of the next stanza tells me immediately that a pattern is being set up; finger is replaced by ear, touch by hearing:

> When I put my ear to the hole I'm suddenly aware
> of spades and shovels turning up the gain

Another pattern is making itself known in the rhyme: 'aware' remembers 'horsehair'. 'Spades and shovels' retroactively invites me to find another meaning in 'pick'. And then I reach 'turning up the gain' and

I'm stumped, and will have to move on. (Being willing to move on is crucial to making the most of Muldoon, who provides far more than any one reading requires—cheerfully skipping uninterpretable words is a strategy I learned in first coping with *Finnegans Wake*). Later, I use the *OED* to discover that a gain is, among other things, a transverse channel made in the side of an underground roadway. Well, that's something that would be made by spades and shovels; but it still seems a stretch. So I Google the phrase, and at once all is clear: when adjusting an electric guitar, you 'turn up the gain' until the amplification is correct. Here my knowledge—which many readers would not share—that Muldoon is a keen player of the electric guitar comes irresistibly to confirm the rightness of this interpretation.

Putting his ear to the hole—let's assume the speaker is male—he hears spades and shovels increasing the volume of sound

> all the way from Raritan to the Delaware

Again my own history comes to my aid: I lived for many years not far from the Raritan River and Raritan Township, and walked along parts of the Raritan and Delaware canal. Otherwise I might have had to have recourse to Google again. I also know that Muldoon's house overlooks the canal. Other readers might have to move on without making anything of these proper names. The rhyme on 'Delaware' brings the three-line unit once more to a close, as did 'itch' (though this time it's *rime riche*, traditionally frowned on in English though valued in French and Muldoonian).

A canal, then; and the sound of the labourers who dug it. But why does a hole in the wall trigger this particular hallucination or mental leap? Once more, the question remains unanswered as the refrain, in a new form, takes over:

> *with a clink and a clink and a clinky-click.*

It's not an exact duplication, but all the words either repeat or rhyme with the first version of the refrain. This time a conventional onomatopoeia helps to make sound dominant, and it's easy to connect 'clink' with spades and shovels. Once again, the 'n' disappears in the final word. One can read 'click' in many ways, and there is a temptation to suggest smart interpretations—the sort that the bright freshman will come up with in class. But what actually *happens* in reading the word? The parallel with the first refrain is confirmed, and the resonance of the nasal element in 'clink' disappears, giving the line something like a diminished close. 'Click', of course, is another traditional onomatopoeic word, but with a different range of suggestiveness than 'clink'. Perhaps that's all that matters, not the possible reference to cameras or misfiring guns or light switches that might be proposed by a reader scrutinizing the poem as an object to be exhaustively analysed.

I'm now able to predict much of what remains—seeing the poem on the page I notice that there are five stanzas, and I can guess at the reason, since we now have a third sense organ:

> When I put my nose to the hole I smell the flood-plain
> of the canal after a hurricane

The reader who was puzzled by 'Raritan' and 'Delaware' now gets an explanation, as violence enters the poem with the storm and the flooded canal. But it's the next line that brings me to the emotional centre of the poem:

> and the spots of green grass where thousands of Irish have lain

A reader who didn't know that Muldoon was himself an Irish immigrant to New Jersey would miss the personal charge here, but would understand the point that the canal was the product of Irish immigrant labour. Here is the two-hundred-year old itch waiting to be scratched: the story of the Irish workers in the early nineteenth century giving their lives to the commercial interests of American industrialists. I say 'giving their lives' because the greenness of the spots of grass and the word 'lain' irresistibly suggest the many deaths such workers suffered, even if 'thousands' seems an exaggeration. (But why shouldn't the poem at this point expand to take in *all* the Irish labourers who died in the United States on such projects?) If I decide to take advantage of Google, I quickly find out that in the 1830s four thousand Irish immigrants were hired to dig the Raritan and Delaware canal with picks and shovels, and that during the construction an epidemic of cholera broke out, as a result of which dozens of men were buried along the banks.[5] Another account mentions the many deaths from 'exertion and poor hygiene' as well.[6] This is the smell that carries across two hundred years, mingled with the stench of the flood.

As I read this stanza, I register the three rhyme-words: not only do 'plain' and 'lain' echo 'gain' from the previous stanza—I've realized by now that the non-refrain part of the poem is in terza rima—but 'hurricane' makes it a triplet, a kind of central sonic clustering before the rhyme returns to its alternating pattern. Recognizing the terza rima makes me think, of course, of Dante's *Commedia,* of the imaginative leaps involved in writing that poem, of the lamentable scenes described there... but I'm not convinced that these connections, pleasing as they are, are part of the experience of the poem that makes it powerful and memorable. In a different kind of poem—say, one by Hart Crane—an association of this type might be an integral element of my experience.

The refrain almost writes itself now, as though it were the product less of a human intention than some non-human power. (Rhyme's combination of the arbitrary and the meaningful has been extended to a whole line.) It would be enough to be given the letters 'st' to be able to generate the entire refrain:

> *with a stink and a stink and a stinky-stick.*

[5] <http://www.nps.gov/upde/historyculture/dhcanal.htm> accessed 4th November 2014.

[6] <http://www.trails.com/tcatalog_trail.aspx?trailid=HGN066-056>, <http://en.wikipedia.org/wiki/Lambertville,_New_Jersey> accessed 4th November 2014.

Although the rhythm of the cheerful jingle is still there, the content moves in another direction, towards rotting flotsam and decomposing corpses. Again the last compound enacts a transition, and again the meanings of the last word are potentially wide-ranging though not necessarily all relevant. The suggestion I find I can't banish is the stickiness of putrefaction.

Thinking I've understood the logic of the poem, I expect the fourth sense to be taste, making possible a climax on vision. I'm wrong, though: what comes next is an invitation to *look* across two centuries to a scene of painful poverty:

> When I put my eye to the hole I see one holding horse dung to the rain
> in the hope, indeed, indeed,
> of washing out a few whole ears of grain

It's a scene that's hard to believe—were men really driven to this extreme? That 'indeed, indeed' insists that they did, and I have to trust the poet. Were I examining the poem for things to say about it in the vocabulary of practical criticism, I might draw attention to the alliteration and assonance in the series 'hole', 'holding', 'horse', and 'hope', and the exact puns on 'hole' and 'whole', 'I' and 'eye'. Listening to the poem as it unfolds, however, these seem to me important only as part of the natural repetitiveness of speech, a sign not of carefully-fashioned language but of spontaneous utterance.

Then the refrain: it's appropriate to the sense organ of the stanza, but takes the poem even further into the realms of nonsense, of children's rhymes, of rhythm and repetition as a bodily phenomenon, of language dissolving into chanted sound:

> *with a wink and a wink and a winkie-wick.*

This is, perhaps, the riskiest moment in the poem, the furthest departure from the inseparability of language from mature human feeling many of us were taught to value by Leavis and his followers. It's as if the machinery of the poem has taken over entirely, for what meaning can 'winkie-wick' have? Reading the poem on the page I notice the –ie ending of 'winkie', which suggests a noun like 'pinkie' rather than an adjective like 'clinky' or 'stinky'. But *winkie* is not to be found in the *OED*, and Google, though it throws up some fascinating material (some of it rather dubious), is no help. Yet the sound-pattern remains compelling, that stark plosive shutting down the line after the repeated nasalized endings of all the previous stressed syllables. (Here I can't avoid an aural memory of Muldoon's own performance of the poem, with its slow, deliberate emphasis on both 'winkie' and 'wick', as if defying anyone to find the words silly and embarrassing.)

Now I move expectantly to the resolution: even if I'm listening to the poem, I'm well aware that this is the final stanza, the fifth sense, and surely the least likely as a way of making contact with ancient masonry. 'When' gives way to 'And when' to mark the incipient conclusion:

> And when I do at last succeed
> In putting my mouth to the horsehair-fringed niche

Tasting the ancient plaster requires, not surprisingly, considerable will-power ('at last succeed'), but the poem, and the Irishmen it commemorates, demand this act of communication and communion, this culminating kiss. The successive stresses and clotted consonants of the phrase 'horsehair-fringed niche' slow down the line; and I wonder if it's an example of the over-ingenuity of which I've been critical when I feel that the reader is being made conscious of his own mouth at this point. The terza rima pattern circles back to the rhyme of the first stanza, 'niche' containing within itself the historic itch we began with.

The next line finally solves the puzzle of the title:

> I can taste the small loaf of bread he baked from that whole seed

A fairy-tale ending, perhaps, a tiny triumph in the face of adversity, starvation fended off for another day; but also a painful close-up from a chapter in the linked history of Ireland and America, conveyed by linking the past and the present through a quotidian object and compelling poetry. And now I've fallen into the trap myself, using in my own discourse a word from the poem, almost its last word:

with a link and a link and a linky-lick.

Not quite the last, because of that dropped 'n' which we've seen coming from the start of the line. Up to now, this last syllable of the refrain has always produced a diminution of sense, but this time it comes as a climax: closing the poem, it closes the physical gap between the speaker and the material substance he's exploring through the senses. By putting his tongue to crumbling plaster he seals a bond between himself and those other Irishmen who made a home (of sorts) in this place.

I've been writing as if the experience of the poem was a single, continuous, linear event, followed, perhaps, by a little bit of research; but of course it doesn't happen like that. Any reading is characterized by discontinuities, reversals, interruptions, repetitions: I read over lines I don't grasp or that I want to savour; I come back to the poem in a different mood or with different knowledge; I keep bits of it in my head that I can revisit without needing a text in front of me. Empson gives a good description of this aspect of the temporality of reading: 'What often happens when a piece of writing is felt to offer hidden riches is that one phrase after another lights up and appears as the heart of it; one part after another catches fire, so that you walk about with the thing for several days.' (*Seven Types of Ambiguity*, xi).

And the poem I've read itself changes as I read more; for instance, it takes on sharper meanings when I reach the end of the collection's last poem, 'At the Sign of the Black Horse, September 1999', a poem set on the bank of the Raritan and Delaware canal in flood after a hurricane. Having referred to the Irish navvies and to the 'hole cut for a dimmer switch', having used the phrase, 'with a dink and a dink / and a dinky-dick', the poem ends with a starving Irishman washing 'an endosperm / of wheat . . . from a pile of horse keek / held to the rain, one of thousands of Irish schmucks who still loll, still loll and lollygag, / between the preposterous towpath and the preposterous berm'.

All I've tried to do here is imagine, in simplified form, the event of the poem as it might take place for me; and to convey something of that experience to my reader. Weak criticism, perhaps, but it may get closer than the most powerful criticism to what is truly valuable in extraordinary poems like this one.

Postscript

I shared my reading of 'The Loaf' with Paul Muldoon, and his response included the following:

> You remember Wee Willie *Winkie* 'crying through the lock'? And you might recall Emerson, one of my heroes, in 'The Conduct of Life', writing of how 'the German and Irish millions, like the Negro, have a great deal of guano in their destiny. They are ferried over the Atlantic, and carted over America, to ditch and to drudge, to make corn cheap, and then to lie down prematurely to make *a spot of green grass* on the prairie.'

What was I to do with this information? One view would be that these allusions, authorized as they are by the poet himself, must now form part of my reading. Another would be that they have no special standing, but must be judged in the same way as any other suggestion about interpretation. My position is somewhere between the two: authorial comments can't be automatically accepted since they may be wide of the mark, but they should be treated with particular care because of the likelihood that they have something to offer. In this case, Muldoon's reference to 'Wee Willie Winkie' confirms my own first response, since the nursery rhyme was the only thing that the word 'winkie' brought to my mind (though I wasn't able to see any connection with the events of the poem and so rejected it); and his singling out of the phrase 'crying through the lock' provides the missing link with the action of peering through the hole in the wall. The identification of a quotation from Emerson is less helpful. To know a poet has consciously incorporated a phrase from an author doesn't make it an allusion; that requires the phrase to have a distinctiveness that makes it memorable, and the text in question to be one a reasonable number of readers can be expected to know. 'A spot of green grass' is not particularly distinctive, and 'The Conduct of Life' not something readers are likely to carry in their heads. And yet...now that I do know the Emerson passage, it will come to me every time I read that line. I am, after Muldoon's comments, like it or not, a different reader.

CHAPTER 5

Context

In discussing how the reading of a literary work achieves a responsible response to singularity, I've touched on, but not developed, questions of context. It's time to scrutinize the term more carefully. Taking it to mean, in an admittedly imprecise way, the material and ideological conditions within which the acts of writing and reading occur,[1] there are three different, but related, moments to consider:

(1) In the creation of a work of literature, there is the question of the relation between the writer and her context;
(2) In the reading of a work of literature, there is the question of the relation between the reader and her immediate context;
(3) In the reading of a work of literature, there is the question of the relation between the reader and the original context of the writer.

We can explore these three moments separately. There is also the question of the various contexts within which the work has been read

[1] By 'ideology' I simply mean non-material conditions such as patterns of thought, accumulations of knowledge and emotional proclivities, whether these are acknowledged or, as in classical Marxist accounts of ideology or in Freudian accounts of the operations of the unconscious, unacknowledged. I'm using 'reading' to include all the modes in which literary works are received, including hearing and watching. And I'm sidestepping the obvious fact that there's no easy way to distinguish between 'text' and 'context', inside and outside, and the related fact that context is inexhaustible. Derrida's 'Signature Event Context' remains the most important exploration of these aspects of context.

between the moment of its original creation and the moment of its reading. I shall touch on this issue at the end of this essay.[2]

The context of creation

I argued in *The Singularity of Literature* that artistic creation (in contrast to mere production) takes place when an artist succeeds in exploiting the tensions, contradictions or fissures in the cultural environment within which she is working in such a way that something—an object or a practice or a conceptual paradigm—hitherto nonexistent and apparently unthinkable comes into being. (Creation understood in this way is not limited to artworks, but for the purposes of this chapter I shall confine myself to the domain of art, as it's generally understood, and more particularly to literature.) It's evident that this new entity must have some relation to what already exists in the cultural field, since if it did not it would be entirely unperceivable, or perceivable only as an absurdity; the question to be asked, therefore, is: What is the nature of this relationship between, on the one hand, the acknowledged and, on the other, the apparently unacknowledgeable to which the artist succeeds in gaining access? It cannot be one of reproduction or imitation or representation: even if a large part of what comes into being repeats or imitates or represents that which already exists, some element or principle must have been outside the realm of what can be known or felt for creation in the full sense to occur. To be outside that realm, but to have a relationship with it, the new—or the other, to use the language of *The Singularity of Literature*, borrowed from Levinas and Derrida—must be *excluded* in some way by the existing habits and norms that constitute the familiar or the same; that is to say, its nonexistence is not due to

[2] A related question arises from the different contexts constituted by different cultures around the globe, whether simultaneously or with a historical gap; for a discussion of this issue, see chapter 6.

chance, to the contingent fact that no-one has happened to bring it into being, but to its impossibility within those existing habits and norms.[3]

This exclusion should not be understood as something that has happened as a historical event: it is rather that the relatively settled existence and degree of coherence of the cultural fabric depends on certain possibilities being kept outside the domain of the same. In order to bring the other into that domain, the artist has to find a way of escaping the hold of those norms, in search of what we might call (unavoidably echoing Donald Rumsfeld) the unknown unknowns—unknown because the culture operates not only to exclude them but to exclude awareness of their exclusion. In order to achieve this, the artist takes advantage of the fact that culture is never seamless and monolithic: the result of a variety of historical forces often operating in conflict, it pulls in more than one direction at a time, it's constantly under pressure from alternative cultural formations arising from differences in class, gender, generation, nation, and so on, and its efforts to occlude that which threatens it never wholly succeed. It's this fractured and turbulent character of culture that the artist exploits, heightening conflicts, prising apart chinks in the fabric, pushing disruptive tendencies to the limit.

In this description, I've used 'culture' as if it were an unproblematic concept. It is not, of course. To say that an artist works within, and upon, a particular culture, and that the reader reads within a particular culture, is to simplify a highly complex situation: any individual participates in a variety of overlapping cultures, none of which is stable, all of which are themselves internally divided. And 'culture' here stands for many different kinds of entity, preference and

[3] An interesting version of this distinction between the contingently absent and the necessarily absent is given by Margaret A. Boden, writing in the framework of computational psychology. In 'What is Creativity?' she distinguishes between 'first-time novelty' and 'radical creativity', the second of which involves the emergence of an idea that 'is not just improbable, but *impossible*' (79). She explains this impossibility by positing a 'conceptual space' that may be merely explored or may be transformed by the alteration of its 'generative rules'.

behaviour, including habitual practices, mental frameworks, affective predispositions, and material conditions. Since the operation of the cultural context in the creation of an artwork initially takes place in the mind and body of an individual, whether working alone or with others in a group, what is relevant to our discussion is what I've called the 'idioculture' of the artist: the singular, and constantly changing, combination of cultural materials and proclivities that constitutes any individual subject, the product of a specific history of exposure to a variety of cultural phenomena. An idioculture is the internal, singular manifestation of the broader cultural field, registered as a complex of particular preferences, capabilities, memories, desires, physical habits, and emotional tendencies.[4] An important aspect of the artist's idioculture is the absorption of the appropriate techne governing, and providing resources for, the art form in question.[5]

This unique idioculture, in conjunction with the physical matter specific to the particular art form, constitutes the material out which the artist creates the work. (It might be argued that the prospective audience's expectations and habits of mind are also part of this material, but in the creative process these are only hypotheses and thus part of the artist's idioculture.) Whatever degree of coherence an idioculture possesses at any given moment is the product of limitations on what can be thought and felt; and it's in challenging these limitations that creation occurs. Although it's tempting to think of the relation between artist and context as one that exists between a human individual on the one hand and an external field of objects and behaviours on the other, it's in fact the *internalized* context that provides the materials with which, and within (or against) which, creation occurs. While no-one would deny that Yeats, for instance, engaged

[4] For a fuller account of the concept of idioculture, see Part I.

[5] Henry Staten, in 'The Wrong Turn of Aesthetics' and 'The Origin of the Work of Art in Material Practice', gives an account of the importance of techne. Institutional theories of art also stress the importance of the 'artworld' within which the artist works and within which artworks are received. See, for example, Arthur Danto's influential essay 'The Artworld' and George Dickie's arguments in *The Art Circle*.

tirelessly with the external context of Irish politics, British publishing, existing poems, natural objects, human individuals, and so on, the creation of a poem was for him, as the creation of a literary work is for every writer, a matter of exploring and shaping the impress of that multifaceted and far from seamless external context upon his mind and body.

For the literary artist, the physical materials are usually of less importance than is the case in the other arts. Obvious exceptions are drama and, if we're including it among the literary arts, film. The history of poetry also provides examples of the creative exploitation of external materials, in this case the technologies of writing—for instance one could cite the part played by the typewriter in opening up new possibilities in the development of modernist poetry.[6] Here, as in all the arts, the material possibilities and limitations are significant only to the extent that the artist understands—or, more often, perhaps, discovers in practice—what can be done with them; and this understanding forms part of the artist's idioculture. The most obvious material with which the writer works, language, is primarily a mental faculty, though some verbal arts—poetry and drama in particular—may treat the voice itself as a medium.[7]

Creativity in the domain of language is usually manifested at the level of verbal collocations, syntax, or discursive connections, rather than at the level of the word—Lewis Carroll and James Joyce being among the obvious exceptions. Generic conventions constitute another important set of contextual cultural materials, and beyond these are the conventions that govern the literary enterprise more generally. Beyond these

[6] There have been numerous studies of the effects of the changing technologies available to writers and readers; particularly influential has been the work of Friedrich Kittler (*Discourse Networks, 1800/1900* and *Gramophone, Film, Typewriter*). See also Hugh Kenner, *A Homemade World*; Steven Connor, 'Modernism and the Writing Hand'; and Darren Wershler-Henry, *The Iron Whim*.

[7] Strictly speaking, the material the writer is working with in these cases is only his *own* voice—or, occasionally, that of an assistant reading back the words. Apart from this, the material being explored is once more an internalized representation, in this case a representation of other possible voices.

again are broader conventions determining what may be said or written at a particular time in a particular place, what may be represented, even what may be thought. Then there is the field of what is known: historical knowledge, practical knowledge, scientific knowledge, and many more knowledges. Emotions, too, have a cultural dimension which the artist is likely to have absorbed. And one should not overlook the bodily dimension: rhythms, for instance, are learned at an early stage of life, and are lodged in the musculature as well as the brain. (Some aspects of rhythm are undoubtedly universal, but others are culture-specific, and are closely linked to the phonetic character of particular languages.)[8] In all these domains, opportunities for creativity lie in the operation of limits, the existence of boundaries to what may be thought, said, or felt; the creative writer uses what is allowable against itself in order to open up new areas, or exposes the existence of hitherto unrecognized boundaries in order to transcend them, or finds in the incommensurability of one domain with another the possibility of a fresh relationship between them. If the work has social consequences arising from its operation as literature (and it must always be remembered that literary texts can also function as historical documents, ethical examples, autobiographical revelations, psychological studies, and in many other non-literary ways), this is the mechanism by means of which it happens.

Because the context within which a work of literature is created is largely a set of internalized materials, a large proportion of which are unconscious, and because creation is something different from the reorganization of what already exists (one might be reminded here of the Coleridgean distinction between imagination and fancy), the phenomenon of creation is often portrayed as mysterious. Artists frequently describe the process as one in which the new configuration of language, sound, space, or colour comes to them unexpectedly, from a source they cannot name. (The ancient idea of the Muse is no doubt a

[8] See Attridge, *The Rhythms of English Poetry*, 59–75; 80–2.

reflection of this experience.) This does not happen out of the blue, of course, but as the outcome of an intense engagement with existing materials; creation can therefore be described neither as wholly an act nor wholly an event, neither wholly something the artist does, nor something that happens to the artist. I've introduced the compound term 'act–event' to refer to this hard-to-describe phenomenon, and discussed it most fully in Part I. The artist's manipulation of the cultural materials constituting his idioculture, that is to say, is not done with a definite end in view—if the completed work could be known ahead of the process of creation it would not be creation of the new or the other but simply a production within the framework of the old or the same.

Creation, then, is something an artist, or a group of artists working in conjunction, brings about, but also something that happens to the artist. It could also be said that creation happens to a culture: here we would be talking about the difference made by the new work of art to the culture at large. We need a new term for this event, however, as there is no guarantee that an individual's creation—which can only be the bringing into being of something new for that individual—will also bring something new into the culture. Two possible terms present themselves: we can say that the artist has produced an *original* work or, deploying a term more common outside the domain of art, that the new work is an *invention* (and, accordingly, that the artist has demonstrated either originality or inventiveness). Originality, in its most general sense, refers to the introduction into the culture of anything new, whether fruitful or fruitless. The originality that is of importance in cultural history, however, is what Kant called 'exemplary originality', and it's this that I'm equating with invention. In the third part of this essay, I shall make a distinction between the two terms, but for the moment, I want to keep both in play, as both are possible ways of referring to the relation of the historical event to its context that we're interested in. An invention or an exemplarily original work, then, is an individual's creation that introduces into a culture a hitherto excluded possibility that will in turn open the door for further acts-events of creation, and these may themselves prove to be inventions. Clement Greenberg, in discussing the sculpture of Anthony Caro, sees this:

> It ought to be unnecessary to say that Caro's originality is more than a question of stylistic or formal ingenuity. Were it that it would amount to no more than novelty, and taste would not, in the event, find itself so challenged by it. Caro's art is original because it changes and expands taste in order to make room for itself. And it is able to do this only because it is the product of a necessity; only because it is compelled by a vision that is unable to make itself known except by changing art. (*Collected Essays and Criticism*, IV, 208)

The creative manipulation of the cultural context as embodied in an artist's idioculture, that is, can modify the external context when the work of art is made public, and thus make possible shifts in the idiocultures of others that may bear fruit in further inventiveness. This will only happen, of course, when the new disposition of cultural materials brings with it new tensions and fractures that may be exploited in turn. Another indication that an invention has occurred is that it gives rise to imitations, its reconfiguration of cultural materials making possible further uncreative productions along the same lines. Although such works rank lower in the general estimation of art—we say that a novel is formulaic, we talk of genre films—they are an important contribution to the culture, helping to consolidate fertile new movements, often increasing the range of their influence and, not least, bringing pleasure to many.

To instantiate this argument by means of examples would require the detailed examination of moments in the history of literature, involving an account of both the cultural context and the individual artist's relation to it, as well as a detailed analysis of the work of art in question. There is space only to offer some hints in the field of literature. Originality can be a matter of what content is imaginable in a fictional work: thus the appearance of La Fayette's *La Princesse de Clèves* in 1678 challenged the existing models of subject-matter of the *roman* (i.e. the romance) and the *nouvelle* (the novella)—in the former, unrealistic, often supernatural, events set in distant places and times; in the latter, plots involving accepted conventions of conduct in more familiar settings—by creating a heroine whose psychological interiority and challenge to moral codes opened a hugely fruitful new area for fictional exploration. To bring this new subject matter to light it was necessary to be inventive generically as well as in content: La Fayette combined the strangeness and length of the romance with the real-world setting of the novella (so that strangeness becomes not a matter of the supernatural but of unconventional behaviour) in a genre that had never been imagined, or imaginable, before. Initial readers were, inevitably, perplexed by the new form.

In fact, inventive subject-matter usually requires formal inventiveness, and it's impossible to say whether the formal breakthrough makes possible the incorporation of new subject-matter, or the demands of the new subject-matter produce formal inventiveness. Marlowe, in order to go beyond the boundaries of existing drama in the grand spectacle of *Tamburlaine,* needed a hitherto undiscovered flexible metre, and transformed Surrey's invention of blank verse into a heroic medium—or, alternatively, experimented with blank verse until he found he had at his fingertips a medium whose capabilities prompted him to imagine a new kind of drama. The development of the English theatre—both as an institution and as a building—provides a good example of material changes that facilitated literary inventiveness; the point again is that it was Marlowe's—and later Shakespeare's—understanding of the potential of the new material developments that led to the Elizabethan revolution in the writing of drama; at the same time, the new, expansive drama demanded an appropriate theatrical setting. Wordsworth, reacting against the limitations on content that characterized the poetry of his predecessors, invented a new vehicle for his poems: the 'lyrical ballad' utilizing a verse-form hitherto excluded from serious poetry and a concreteness of language deemed unfit for it. At the same time, the possibilities of this form enabled him to appreciate how he could embrace hitherto untapped subject-matter. In every instance of originality, the otherness of the new creation can be seen to be related to what was dominant in literary culture, both building on it and overcoming its exclusions. Had a poet written lyrical ballads a hundred years earlier (and one might doubt whether this would even have been possible), it's likely that they would have made no impression on the reading public or on other poets.

Hindsight makes it difficult to appreciate the way in which certain cultural norms have dominated previous periods; and our own lack of creativity prevents us from recognizing that similar limits operate just as strongly today. Until Chaucer, at some time in the 1370s, wrote a poem using a five-beat, duple metre that came to be known as iambic pentameter and to seem one of the most natural metrical forms in English, it was beyond the aural imagination of speakers of the language. Until Defoe, at some time before 1719, embarked on a fictional account of a castaway that mimicked authentic first-person narratives, the idea of such a work was unavailable to writers. Until Eliot wrote a poem that he published in 1922 as *The Waste Land*, it was difficult to conceive of a radical discontinuity of voice, subject, metre, and style in a single, highly effective work. We feel today that we are in an age in which there are few limits on what a writer can do; but it's unlikely that we are the first generation to feel this, and no doubt posterity will be able to discern—thanks to the work of future inventive artists—the very real exclusions on which our current artistic production (and reception) depends.

The context of reading

Discussions of literary context pay much less attention to the context within which reading takes place than they do to the context of writing. Yet the reading process is just as dependent on the context within which it occurs, a context that, once again, can be thought of as the impress of the external culture upon an individual subjectivity—conscious and unconscious—that I'm calling an idioculture. How I go about reading—my choices of what to read, my assumptions about the purpose of reading, the habits I draw on when I read—are all imbibed from the culture, or cultures, that have formed me. And reading a literary work, like creating a literary work, is, as I've emphasized, both an act and an event: something I do and something that happens to me. On the one hand, to the extent that it is an *act*, I can control many aspects of my reading, including the pace, the scrupulousness of attention (taking in every word, skipping occasional passages, skimming briskly), and the degree of concentration on the words I read. Different genres allow different possibilities: listening to an audiobook or watching a play, I can't control pace but I can, to a large extent, control concentration; reading poetry I can choose to read aloud, frame the words silently as if spoken, or read rapidly as I would do for extended prose. On the other hand, to the extent that reading is an *event*, I'm affected by what I read, intellectually, emotionally, and sometimes physically, without having any control over this process. Matters are not quite so simple, however; just as a writer can manipulate existing cultural materials to allow that which is other—that which is excluded—to emerge, although there is never any guarantee that this will happen, so a reader can go some way toward achieving an openness to whatever the work may offer. This involves an effort to clear the mind of preconceptions, thus to some degree resisting the pressure of context, and, somewhat paradoxically, a willingness to be surprised, plus a willingness to treat surprise as a reason for fresh engagement rather than for a mental closing down.[9] That this description could be equally applied to the act–event of creation is not fortuitous.

This account may sound like a prescription for a mode of reading found only in small and specialized pockets of the population such as university literature departments; but it shouldn't be taken to imply a

[9] This resistance to the pressure of context toward conformity with existing habits of mind is foregrounded, under the term 'self-binding', in Dorothy J. Hale's account in 'Fiction as Restriction' of recent theoretical arguments that stress the alterity of the literary work. I would prefer to emphasize the self-*opening*, the readiness to be changed, the hospitality toward the other, involved in a responsible reading.

highly conscious strategy that has to be learned in the classroom. There are plenty of good readers among the general populace, just as there are plenty of bad readers in literature departments. Nor is the matter of better and worse readings a question of a linear scale of value; context plays a part here too, in that one reads a particular type of work at a particular time for a particular purpose. A good reading of *Paradise Lost* obeys very different protocols from a good reading of *Doctor No*; reading a Herbert poem for the sheer pleasure of it demands different kinds of attention from reading it in order to write a critical article, neither of which is 'better' than the other.

One can, however, arrive at a general account of what the best reading in ideal circumstances would be, one that could be said to do justice to the work in question, or, more particularly, to its singularity, alterity and inventiveness (if it possesses these qualities) and, at the same time, to the specificity of the time and place of reading. (In fact, whether or not a work is found to have these attributes will be in part dependent upon the time and place of reading.) Such a reading would be one that brings to bear on the work all the relevant cultural resources available to the reader, but at the same time does not allow those resources to limit what the work may do. A reading along these lines can be called *creative*, in the sense that it brings into being something hitherto excluded by the reader's idioculture, as well as *responsible*, in the sense that it welcomes the otherness of the other, and does justice to the inventiveness of the author. The idea of a creative reading as a response to alterity is not opposed to the experience of recognition, which may be part of the pleasurable response to a work of literature: the sense that one has gained an insight into oneself, or that a writer's words have captured what one thought was an entirely private concern or feeling. Here too there is an element of surprise, a sense of unexpected intimacy with something experienced as other in the literary work.[10]

[10] Rita Felski, in a chapter entitled 'Recognition', describes this fusion of familiarity and strangeness well; first, recognition: 'I feel myself addressed, summoned, called to

A creative reading may lead to an *inventive* reading: one that, as with an inventive creation, has an impact that is not just individual and internal; this will usually be either a reading enshrined in a new piece of writing or one that forms part of a pedagogical activity, formal or informal. In these cases, the question of context arises in a different way, which again may be understood in relation to a notion of responsibility. For a responsible reading, in the sense of a verbal response to a literary work, is one that takes into account not just the work being read but the context within which the new writing in response to it is undertaken and the context within which it will be received. Under these circumstances, the choice of the work to be read is not just a matter of personal preference but possesses wider cultural importance: it serves to endorse the work (unless it's being dismissed as worthless) and contribute to its continuing life within the culture. A responsible choice is one that is based not just on an estimation of the work's quality—'this work deserves to be better known', for example—but on its importance to one's place and time—'this work is particularly appropriate given current conditions and demands'. And the reading offered, to be responsible as well as creative, will not only do justice to the singularity of the work but also be aware of the context within which it, and the work to which it is responding, will have effects.

Let me take just one example. I've written a little about the fiction of the South African-Scottish novelist Zoë Wicomb, and hope to write more in future. In choosing her work to engage with in print I'm

account: I cannot help seeing traces of myself in the pages I am reading'; but at the same time, alterity: 'Indisputably, something has changed; my perspective has shifted; I see something that I did not see before' (*Uses of Literature*, 23). She stresses that recognition does not imply a simple affirmation of the subject's self-understanding; it can 'confound [readers'] sense of who and what they are' (23), produce both a 'powerful cognitive readjustment' (35) and a 'heightened awareness of the instabilities and opacities of personhood' (42), and be 'discomfiting, even unpleasant, requiring a reckoning with one's own less appealing motivations and desires' (47). Given these and other similar descriptions, it is somewhat surprising that Felski sets up her discussion in opposition to theorists of 'literary alterity'.

motivated by a sense both that it's worthy of greater notice than it has achieved up to now, and that it's of particular value at this moment in this culture (broadly speaking, 'Western culture', and within it, Anglophone culture—although my idioculture is, of course, a particular inflection of these very general entities). Wicomb's ambitious and superbly-written work *David's Story*, for instance, makes an important contribution to the genre of the novel, exploring notions of novelistic truth that are highly relevant to literary culture today, and at the same time invites a fresh understanding of national liberation struggles, and of the place of gender and racial equality within the movements engaged in such struggles. To say this is not to take an instrumental view of the work: while it may be true that Wicomb's novel, if widely read, could have an effect on the criticism of the novel or on the historiography of liberation movements, and a critical response devoted to these ends would not be unjustified, to respond in words to the novel as a work of literature is, in some sense, to report on an experience, on the act-event of reading (and re-reading), as something valuable in itself—or, to be more precise, valuable in the changes it may effect in readers' attitudes and capacities, whether or not these are consciously registered, and whether or not they lead to action.

Wicomb's novel is important today, I would argue, because it offers readers a pleasurable journey into a terrain with which they will be unfamiliar, a journey during which they will encounter surprising representations of places, events and people, unexpected turns of plot, and verbal originality. Through these and other inventive manipulations of literary resources, the novel has the capacity to effect change, however slight, in its readers, quite apart from any historical knowledge that might be absorbed. By braiding together the chequered history of the Griqua people of South Africa and the difficult social reintegration of the guerrilla army in the wake of apartheid, the novel crystallizes for the reader historical realities registered on the minds and—quite literally—the bodies of vividly imagined characters. By posing the question of the truth of historical and political narrative through an account given unwillingly by a former guerrilla to a female narrator it keeps that question alive in the very process of reading. By including scenes of immense power, such as the nightly torture of a woman member of the ANC's fighting force—scenes whose referential basis remains mysterious, and which would find no place in a history of the movement—it produces an affective response more telling and more memorable than any factual representation. Different readers—different idiocultures—will, of course, experience the novel differently; or, to put it another way, will read a different novel, since the novel, as a work of literature, is nothing other than its readings. Yet it remains the same novel to which all these readings respond, the same string of English (and a few Afrikaans) words: the same only because it's constantly open to change in new contexts, according to the principle that Derrida terms 'iterability'.

Present reading and historical context

Reading a literary work with an openness to its singularity, and an attentiveness to the singularity of the time and place in which it is being read, is not, clearly, an exercise in historical reconstruction. The experience is not one of appreciating the originality of the work in the context within which it was created, but a pleasurable sense of moving, here and now, beyond the familiar and the habitual—provided that the work responds to this kind of reading, in this particular place and time. Many different ingredients may contribute to this sense: a new understanding of aspects of the familiar world, an enjoyment of the surprising conjunctions of sounds and meanings, a satisfaction at the working out of an unexpected pattern, a pleasure (which may be mixed with darker responses) at the arousal of unfamiliar shades of emotion, a delight in the unexpected power of language to capture perceptions and emotions. The reader who has an experience of this kind may or may not be familiar with the facts surrounding the creation of the work; we need a different language from that of 'historical context', therefore, to talk about the encounter at the heart of the literary institution. The term I take from Derrida is 'invention':[11] the experience of new horizons, fresh perceptions, unexpected patterns, surprising linguistic power and precision that I've been describing is an experience of the inventiveness of the literary work.

In the first section of this chapter, I made no distinction between the inventiveness and the (exemplary) originality of a work of art at the moment of its creation: both terms are appropriate for the effect of the work on its immediate context, registered culturally as a result of the experiences of contemporary readers. In changing the focus to readings taking place at some temporal remove from the moment of creation, it becomes necessary to distinguish between a historical fact accessed through scholarship—originality—and the experience here and now of a certain kind of newness—inventiveness. How is it, we need to ask, that following generations can continue to find a work inventive? If the range of possibilities opened up by the inventive work becomes part of the cultural landscape to be exploited by later artists, why do we still find that work conveying a sense of new opportunities for thought and feeling decades or centuries later? It's not sufficient to say that through an act of historical imagination we are able to reconstitute the original moment of creation, reliving the artistic breakthrough as if we shared the cultural field which it challenged, including its limitations and internal tensions, and thus can re-experience the inventiveness of the past moment. Such a feat might be possible for the scholar who has absorbed the particularities of a former culture to a high degree, though it remains unlikely that anyone could reinstate with sufficient completeness the mental world of, say, a Regency gentleman in order to be able to experience Byron's *Don Juan* as one of its first readers would have done—and, in any case, it could never be proved that this had been achieved. Historical investigation of this sort is valuable in documenting originality, which is matter of comparing artistic works with their forerunners. But originality does

[11] See Jacques Derrida, 'Psyche: Invention of the Other'.

not necessarily translate into inventiveness in the sense in which I'm using it: the former is a historical fact, the latter a quality that remains important in current reception. In any case, this kind of historical re-imagining remains well beyond the capacities of most readers. Yet readers—and I should stress again that my interest is not limited to academics or students—continue to testify to the freshness, the surprisingness, the eye-opening novelty, the breathtaking emotional power, of many works of the past, including the distant past of the ancient world.

It's necessary, then, to distinguish between the experience of inventiveness in a present reading and an appreciation, based on historical awareness, of a work's originality. There is certainly pleasure to be gained from the latter if one possesses the appropriate historical knowledge. This knowledge is always subject, of course, to revision; what we think of as an original intervention in a cultural context can always turn out to be an imitation of an earlier, hitherto unacknowledged, work. In a strict sense, therefore, the original context remains irretrievable: what we have to go on are the best efforts of historians to reconstruct the past, and the best efforts of literary historians to judge which elements of that past are relevant to the work or the writer in question.

To acknowledge that that original context is irretrievable in any final and comprehensive manner is not to argue, however, that awareness of it can never be relevant. For one thing, a reader cannot banish whatever knowledge she possesses about the original context, which may include 'knowledge' that is in fact inaccurate, and can't prevent this knowledge from colouring her reading.[12] A reader who knows nothing about the context of *The Autobiography of Alice B. Toklas* will

[12] The degree to which other texts or utterances will colour one's reading depends on the degree of authority one accords them, which is not a matter of conscious decision but depends on a host of institutional and psychological factors, as yet insufficiently studied.

have a very different experience from one who does.[13] Genette is one theorist who has the good sense to see this: 'As long as the receiver knows, or thinks he knows, the "genetic" circumstances of the production of the work, they influence, for better or worse, the reception and, especially, appreciation of that work' (*The Aesthetic Relation*, 144).

But there is no simple correlation between the amount of contextual knowledge and the quality of the reading: good readers are not necessarily those who are in possession of the greatest amount of information, though the ignorance of particular facts may in certain cases produce an inadequate reading, one that fails to register the work's potential inventiveness in the present. Once again, it's important to stress that different situations and different texts demand different kinds of reading: the particular context (composing the introduction to a scholarly edition, for instance) may require detailed historical knowledge, whereas another context (lying on the lawn on a sunny afternoon with an anthology of recent poems, say) will require very little.

The question of the original context is often discussed as though the reader accesses—or fails to access—something external to the internal reading process.[14] To clarify this question, we need to return to the notion of idioculture. That the identity of a work is the result of a

[13] One area of debate in which this issue is particularly salient is that of fakes and forgeries: a reader who thought *Ossian* was a genuine medieval work and then discovered its real provenance would find it, on re-reading, to be a different work. It might still give pleasure, but of a distinct kind, because it would be read in terms of a different context. Kant alludes to the effect upon aesthetic enjoyment of beliefs, accurate or not, about the object when he notes that listeners to a nightingale's song, on being told it is a 'roguish youngster' imitating the bird, will cease to enjoy it (*Critique of Judgment*, 169 [*Akademie* edition, 304]). The forged painting or statue that is an exact replica of an original raises the question in an even more extreme form. See Denis Dutton, ed., *The Forger's Art*, and K. K. Ruthven, *Faking Literature*.

[14] Thus Peter Lamarque, in *The Philosophy of Literature*, argues against the theory that limits the meaning of a work to its original historical and institutional context but continues to hold that 'work-identity is bounded by historical conditions of production (and institutional conventions)' (80)—rather than by the reader's conception of those conditions.

process of creation within a historical and institutional context is indisputable; but our only access to that process, and the context within which it occurred, is in the present, and in the course of reading the work, even if we turn to the notes and then back to the text, our only resource is the knowledge we bring to it. That is to say, awareness of the original context forms a possible part of one's idioculture, whether well- or ill-informed; and this awareness can contribute to our sense of the work's inventiveness. But the experience of the literary work's inventiveness involves far more than a sense of its originality in its original context: it is inventive in relation to the present context, as manifested in the complex cultural intersection that is the reader's idioculture. Just as the work at the time of its birth found possibilities for otherness within an apparently coherent cultural fabric, embodied in the artist's idioculture, so the work at the time of its reception can exploit the possibilities for otherness in the apparent coherence of the culture embodied in the reader's idioculture.

The puzzle remains, however. Why should the work that is inventive in a historical moment and cultural context long past and very different from our own still speak today in an inventive manner? Why does it often feel as if I'm sharing, as I read, an earlier writer's breakthrough into new territory by means of the shaping of language and the testing of generic limits when I'm the product of a cultural history so distinct from the cultural histories of her contemporaries?[15]

[15] Accounts of literature which celebrate the changes wrought by the passage of time and by the cultural differences between the contexts of creation and of reception tend to overlook this experience of temporal transcendence. Thus Wai Chee Dimock, in 'A Theory of Resonance', argues for a 'diachronic historicism' without acknowledging that synchronic historicism is an experiential feature of reading literary works—a feature that is part of the distinctiveness of literature. The special power of literature, or art, in relation to the passage of time has been the subject of a number of important interventions by, among many others, T. S. Eliot, Gadamer, Benjamin, Kermode, and Coetzee. A recent acknowledgment of this dimension of the experience of literature is Felski's use of the Freudian notion of *Nachträglichkeit* to comment on the 'transtemporal movement of texts' (*Uses of Literature*, 119–20); by including this discussion in the chapter on 'Shock', however, she implicitly limits what is a much wider phenomenon in literary reception.

(Gadamer's discussion of the fusion of the horizon of the writer with the horizon of the reader offers one approach, but is concerned with interpretation rather than invention.) It doesn't always work this way, of course: works that are highly original in their time can fall prey to cultural change and lose their inventiveness, appreciated only by cultural historians who are aware of their earlier importance. Klopstock's *Messias* took the German literary world by storm in 1748, but few readers now can experience the excitement it provided its audiences in the middle of the eighteenth century. And inventiveness can remain latent, until a later cultural moment provides the context within which it can exercise its estranging, clarifying, or intensifying powers. One of many examples of writers barely recognized in their lifetimes is Fernando Pessoa, whose constant self-reinvention (including the use of over seventy heteronyms) speaks to early twenty-first culture with a potency not only unappreciated by but in many respects unavailable to early twentieth-century readers, or potential readers. In spite of such counter-examples, however, it remains true that there is a significant correspondence between works which entered their original cultural contexts with the force of invention and works which provide the experience of inventiveness in today's contexts; the current roll-call of the most rewarding writers in the history of literature is not very different from the list of those who introduced influential innovations into literary writing.

The traditional explanation for this fact is that certain writers explore universal human themes with consummate skill, so that their works are timeless, available to anyone who can appreciate good art. The question of context falls away, on the assumption that such works transcend both the conditions of their creation and the conditions of particular readings. What is wrong with this view is not that there are no human universals—it's surely correct that many literary works deal with fundamental human concerns as relevant to Aeschylus as they are to Ayckbourn—but that a much larger body of works dealing just as directly with such topics from across the centuries have little to offer today. Inventiveness lies in the handling of these topics, not in the fact of choosing them. And the question of what 'good' writing is, as a slight acquaintance with literary history shows, very much a matter of context. My discussion of inventiveness is an attempt to articulate an evaluative category which acknowledges the context-boundedness of both creation and reception.

Part of the answer must lie in the contingencies of cultural history. The present cultural moment may echo an earlier one in certain respects without there being any historical connection between the two, so that what was inventive then seems inventive once again. (Fortuitous similarities can work in a similar way when an artefact from a different culture speaks to our own.) Or a work that was inventive in one way may, through the operation of pure chance, be inventive in a different way now. The work that we find inventive may even have been highly imitative when produced, but for some reason having nothing to do with its original contextual relation now has the power to engage fruitfully with the current context. A related phenomenon is the effect of sheer cultural difference: a work of the past, or of another culture, can in its very strangeness push at the limits of contemporary culture. The potency of *Sir Gawain and the Green Knight* stems more, perhaps, from the weirdness of its narrative when seen from a modern perspective than from any sharing of cultural values or ethical norms.

Chance effects probably account for only a small part of the continuing liveliness of works of the past, however. We need to examine the possibility that the explanation lies in cultural continuities that bridge temporal distance. Although it's obvious that the idioculture of a Greek spectator in Athens witnessing the first performance of *Antigone* is vastly different from that of a reader engaging with a modern English translation today, the power of the work—even for a reader who has very little acquaintance with the cultural history of Ancient Greece—suggests that there are sufficient similarities between the two for something of the play's inventiveness to survive today. While many of the features of the play that would have been inventive to that original audience now have very little purchase—the unprecedented use of a third actor, for example, is not a device that packs much of a punch today—but Sophocles' handling of the languages of politics, of personal dilemma, and of religious commitment, his evocation of character, and his treatment of narrative have remained both powerful and challenging, as numerous commentaries on the play over the centuries have testified.

It's one of the characteristics of inventiveness, experienced in the act–event of reading, that the passage of time has been neutralized, that we feel that we are directly in touch with the author's creative activity and that we are sharing the thoughts and emotions of the original readers. Though this is inevitably an illusion for much of the time, it's not one we're likely to be able to test: there is no infallible way of distinguishing between chance effects and historical continuity. What seems like pure fortuitousness to the critical mind may in fact be a hidden connection across the centuries. Historical knowledge can be a corrective here, though it may be at the expense of a certain amount of pleasure. To learn that Marvell's 'vegetable love' would have had no suggestion of edible plants to his first readers might take away the possibility of enjoying an inventive metaphor. More often, historical knowledge (which includes familiarity with other works of literature), absorbed into the idioculture of the reader, is likely to increase the potential for enjoyment. If I read a Victorian pot-boiler before I've read Dickens, Eliot, and Thackeray I might find it inventive; to read it after them would be a different, and less pleasurable experience—but my engagement with the great novelists would have been all the more rewarding.

There is, then, no single answer to the question I've posed. The fact of art's ability to produce the experience of invention as an immediate, present unfolding of new possibilities depends on a combination of historical continuities, charted or obscure, and contextual coincidences. Furthermore, we should not overlook the role of the institutions of art, as they currently operate, in encouraging readers, listeners and viewers to open themselves to this experience; this, too, is an important aspect of context. In a different cultural space, the reader of the literary work might be encouraged to approach it as a hermeneutic or historical puzzle, a guide to living, or a manifestation of the author's approach to the divine. In these cases, however, there would be grounds for withholding the appellations 'literature' and 'art'.

We may end with the persistent question that comes up whenever there are competing interpretations of a work or passage: what counts as a relevant context? Differences in interpretation and evaluation are often the result of different answers to this question. By shifting attention to the act–event of creation and the act–event of reception, I've implied that the question needs to be rethought as a matter of idioculture. If our concern is the experience of literature (rather than, say, the external history of an institution) we need to phrase the question slightly differently: what kind of contextual information is it valuable to have absorbed, when engaging with a literary work, in order to maximize the experience of invention—and along with invention the closely-related qualities of alterity and singularity? It will be clear, I hope, that there is no single answer; a reader who is responding fully to a literary work lives through it and sometimes lives with it, and he comes to the work, on each encounter, as a different idioculture, experiencing different aspects of its inventiveness at different times. The absorption of contextual information, the acquisition of a feeling for particular historical contexts, and the recognition of the pressures and predilections of the present ideological context will change the work's surprises and satisfactions, usually for the better—though there is always the possibility that an excess of contextual information may drown out the work's singularity. The critic and the teacher can enhance the capacity of others to experience and enjoy the inventiveness of a work by drawing attention to features of its original context and by pointing out its relevance to the present context; it can also be illuminating to consider the various contexts within which a work has been read since its creation, as a way of bringing to light otherwise occluded features. But much contextual information will turn out to be irrelevant to the best reading of the work. Where the line is to be drawn, however, cannot be predicted and is not fixed for all readers, for all texts, or for all time. Because, in the reading of the literary work, context (past and present) is always put into play via a singular idioculture, general rules governing what is valuable in terms of contextual information are always subject to revision in the light of specific instances. And specific instances of responsible and creative reading, in response to specific instances of inventive writing, play a major role in determining the course of literary culture, constituting in themselves part of the context within which literary works continually come freshly into being.

CHAPTER 6

Culture

The previous chapter raised the question of context primarily as a matter of historical distance; very similar issues arise when we consider the effect of spatial distance between cultures, each the product of different historical pasts and geopolitical presents. In what follows, I use a particular example to explore these issues further.

Inventiveness and cultural distance

When Alaa al-Aswany's Arabic novel *Imarat Ya'qubyan* was published in 2002, it quickly established itself as a runaway popular success. It was the Arab world's best-selling work of fiction for 2002 and 2003, and listeners to the Middle East Broadcasting Service voted it the best novel of 2003.[1] A highly successful Egyptian film and mini-series followed. By 2007 the work was in its ninth edition.

In 2006 in the U.S.A. and 2007 in the U.K., an English translation by Humphrey Davies with the title *The Yacoubian Building* appeared, to great critical acclaim—the British paperback includes two pages of glowing tributes from the country's leading newspapers and magazines—and achieved substantial sales. The novel has been translated into at least eighteen other languages, and in 2010 al-Aswany responded angrily when the Israel-Palestine Centre for Research and Information made an unauthorized Hebrew translation freely available. Samia Mehrez, in her 2008 study of cultural conflict in the Egypt of the Mubarak era, calls the novel's global triumph 'mind-boggling

[1] Translator's note, Al Aswany, *The Yacoubian Building*, xi.

and overwhelming', and cites nearly 200,000 sales worldwide at the time of writing (*Egypt's Culture Wars*, 56). This figure has undoubtedly risen considerably since then.

The questions I want to ask in this chapter are: What is the relation between these two sets of facts? To what degree do the reasons for the success of the Arabic original overlap with the reasons for the success of the various translations—and the English translation in particular? And, to raise an ethical question, what would constitute a responsive and responsible reading of one of the translated versions by a reader without Arabic, a reading that could be said to 'do justice' to al-Aswany's work? Finally, what difference do the momentous changes in Egypt since 2011 make to these questions?

I'm using this very specific example to raise the much broader issue of *cultural distance* as a factor in reading. Inevitably, when a work crosses geographical, linguistic and/or temporal boundaries the cultural context within which it was produced and within which it was first read (for simplicity's sake, I shall assume for the time being that these are the same) differs from the cultural contexts within which it is received. If, then, the work that I encounter strikes me as excellent, how do I know whether that excellence is a direct response to the author's achievement in his own milieu, or is generated by the cultural difference between that milieu and my own? And how much does it matter which of these it is?

To get to grips with these questions, it's necessary to consider what 'excellence' might mean when used in this way. I've been arguing that literary works that achieve high status in Western culture are characterized by their *singularity*; those that are seen as merely following out a formula, and are thus barely distinguishable from other examples of the genre in question, are accorded low standing and may not, in fact, be dignified with the title 'literature'. The same is probably true of most of the cultures that now rub shoulders in the global arena. This singularity is the result of *inventiveness*: the inventiveness of the work, reflecting the inventiveness of its creator, though not necessarily in any straightforward way. And the singular, inventive work can be thought of as one that introduces into the field of the same—the habitual, the taken-for-granted, the normal—something *other*, something that can't be exhaustively explained within existing norms of thinking and feeling. While the uninventively formulaic work can achieve a degree of popularity, global and enduring success is more likely to spring from an author's capacity to invent new forms and discover new subject-matter, particularly when what is offered to the reader is glimpses of ideas, emotional complexes, or factual realities upon whose occlusion the persistence of the status quo has depended. It can be no accident that the canonical works in the European literary tradition are those that have broken new ground in form or content, or, very often, both. A reading that can be said to do justice to such a work is one that responds to its singularity, inventiveness and alterity with an active, creative reading, bringing to bear on it the reader's own singular existence as the product of a variety of cultural and other forces—the individual subject's idioculture. At the same time, a creative reading of this kind involves a certain kind of passivity, a capacity to be hospitably open to the otherness of the work and to be ready to be changed by what it has to offer.

Using these terms to rephrase our question, we can ask how to account for the experience of inventiveness, singularity and alterity that a reader may have when encountering a work that arises from, and on its initial publication spoke to, a significantly different cultural context from her own. To what extent does the responsible reading of such a work imply an attempt to ignore any sense of inventiveness (from now on I'll use just one of the three interlocking terms to imply all of them) that arises *solely* from the cultural distance between the contexts of production and of reception? If so, how can this be achieved? How can we know if it has been achieved? If, on the other hand, it's legitimate to capitalize on effects of inventiveness that arise from cultural difference, how can we avoid reducing the work to an example of pleasurable exoticism?

The first point to make in tackling these questions is that this problem is not unique to the situation in which a work is read in a different part of the world, and thus a different cultural context, from that in which it was created. Exactly the same question arises when the work being engaged with was written in the same place but at an earlier period; here too there are likely to be significant differences between the two contexts that in themselves could account for an experience of inventiveness, and here too it's not easy to say just what a responsible reading would consist of. Is the best reading the one that most successfully shears off modern assumptions and utilizes historical knowledge to approach the work with the habits and predispositions of the earlier period? Or is it legitimate to allow the effects of historical change to enhance the experience of inventiveness?[2] If a work is *both* historically and geographically distant, of course, these questions—which have been mulled over repeatedly in many different literary theoretical discourses—become even more acute.

To begin to suggest answers, we need to banish any notion that there's a real possibility that a literary work could be read without *any* cultural distance between reader and work, the idea that there exist instances of the perfect matching of context of production and context of reception against which we can measure other, necessarily inferior, kinds of reading. Cultural difference is not a matter of black and white, but of degree: there can never be total accord between the moment of creation and the moment of reading. Even a work written by someone very like myself and published recently in my own country will speak from a different place: variations in class, dialect, experience, personality, background, profession, family, and more will always have an impact. Here we can see the inadequacy of my earlier working assumption that the cultural contexts within which a work is produced and within which it is first read are identical; they can be very similar, but some differences will always necessarily make themselves felt. This complicates any attempt to measure the effects of cultural distance between 'the work' and the situation of the reader, as

[2] Some of these issues are discussed in chapter 5.

it's not clear whether we're referring to the author's own context or that of its first readers. There may be later readers, or readers in other places, who, in terms of their situation and assumptions, actually come closer to the author than those original readers. Moreover, the 'first readers' don't constitute a homogeneous and clearly-defined group any more than 'later readers'. Another problem is that it's never a simple matter to say what the author's cultural context actually *is*; it remains a matter of interpretation, as does the cultural context of those 'first readers'. Our access to them is largely a mediated one, through other texts.

A second, complementary, point that equally deserves attention is that there will nearly always be *some* degree of overlap between the context of production and the context of reception, stemming from shared historical and cultural conditions or, sometimes, arising out of sheer coincidence. If there were no such overlap, the work in question would be incomprehensible, a complete blank to the reader. The only case in which this would not be so is where chance factors grant the work an intelligibility in its new context that has absolutely nothing to do with its original meanings, a situation that's hard to imagine. A museum-goer in twenty-first century Britain may enjoy many features of a seventh-century Mayan figurine that would have possessed no value to the original viewers (or users) of the object; nevertheless, the fact that the figurine implies a certain valorization of the human body provides a minimal degree of overlap. We are almost always, then, operating in a realm of *relative* cultural distance, somewhere between complete coincidence and total difference.

Given this inevitable in-betweenness, what constitutes a responsible reading? One extreme position is that the ideal reading situation is an encounter, as Raymond Williams sarcastically puts it, of 'naked reader with naked text' (Foreword to Jordanova, *Languages of Nature*, 11): the question of the original context and readership is held to be irrelevant, as is the question of the reader's own formation and the biases and blind spots that have resulted from it. This argument would be valid only if it were possible to encounter works of art in a vacuum, having jettisoned everything one has absorbed about one's own culture and that from which the work has sprung. But it's out of one's own cultural inheritance, one's idioculture, that one responds to art, and that inheritance includes knowledge, accurate or otherwise, about the work being engaged with and about the place and time of its production. If I'm familiar with Yoruba religion I will read Ben Okri's *The Famished Road* differently from someone who is not; and if I do possess that knowledge I'm not able to discard it while reading. It's not only part of the book's formation, it's part of my own. There is no such thing as a pure reading of the words on the page: even if I know nothing about the text's origins, I'm seeing through the refracting lenses bestowed upon me by my particular background, and these will lead me to infer an origin, whether or not I'm conscious of this deductive process. This is why even an argument that one should take into account one's own formation, as far as possible, but not that of the work, is implausible: there is no way of separating the two. The context of the work is something I bring to my reading, not something out there to which I have unmediated access and can choose to ignore if I wish; it's part of my mental world as the product of my earlier reading and other experiences I've lived through.

The argument at the other extreme is analogous to the demand for a wholly historicized engagement I alluded to earlier: it would allow a reading to be responsible only if it wholly eradicated the effects of the context of reception and was entirely absorbed into a reconstructed context of production. According to this view, I would be able to do justice to Satyajit Ray's *Pather Panchali* only if my idioculture was transformed, for the duration of the film, into a simulation of that of a moviegoer in West Bengal in the 1950s. Put like this, the argument is clearly fallacious; no amount of research would enable me to achieve this transformation. But it's implicitly present in any claim that the closer one gets to the original matrix of a work—and by the same token, the more one sheds one's own cultural assumptions—the better one's reading. Perhaps a responsible reading is one that, *as far as possible*, invokes the original context of the work? We've already seen that 'the original context' is a problematic notion, and it's equally difficult to know what 'as far as possible' means. Does responsible reading hinge on the time and money one has available to carry out the research needed to establish that context? The elitist implications of this conclusion are unsatisfactory in themselves; fortunately, there is little theoretical justification for such a position, which would discredit most of the actual reading that takes place.

If we are to abandon both the idea that a pure engagement with the text 'itself' offers the best reading and the idea that the paradigm toward which one should be striving is complete recovery of the original context, we find ourselves occupying a rather messy, but perhaps more realistic, middle position. One possible stance that suggests itself would be that as long as the reader experiences the work as inventive it *is* inventive, and that there's no need to worry about whether this experience is the result of the reader's distance from the original cultural matrix or is really a response to the author's inventive act; it will, in any case, *feel* like the latter if no thoughts about the original context are allowed to interfere. Yet most of us, I think, would be unhappy with this position. One's readings are, surely, usually improved by increasing one's knowledge about the cultural context of the work and at the same time scrutinizing one's own assumptions for cultural biases. What needs to be rejected is the notion that there is one ideal reading towards which all empirical readings strive, or even that—since our readings are all mediated by our own specific cultural histories and situations—there is one ideal reading for a particular reader at a particular time.

If we return the verbal noun 'reading' to the verb, and remember that the literary work has its existence as an event rather than an object, as I've been arguing throughout this book, we can come closer to an understanding of the multiple possibilities that a concept of responsible reading encompasses. I'm reading responsibly if I'm simultaneously referring the words back to what I know about the various contexts that are relevant—the literary traditions out of which the work emerges, the conditions under which it was written, the aims of the writer and those of her peers, the social, historical, economic, and political backgrounds to the act of writing and the earliest readings, the discussions of the work that may have taken place in print or other media since publication—*and* referring my own responses to what I'm able to access of my own culturally-derived ways of thinking and feeling. Certainly, if I carry out some detailed research I may be able to improve my knowledge of the relevant contexts, and there may be some payoff in my reading (though this can never be guaranteed), but I should not be under the illusion that I will eventually be able to read in just the same way as those 'first readers'.

Reading *The Yacoubian Building*

Let us return now to *The Yacoubian Building* and our question about the variety of readerships, and let us simplify that question as one about Egyptian readers, or perhaps even urban Egyptian readers, for whom the depicted events would have had a highly familiar ring, and British or American readers, for the large majority of whom they would not be at all familiar. Al-Aswany's novel uses the building named in the title—a grand apartment block in downtown Cairo that has seen better days—as a microcosm of Egyptian society, following the interlinked stories of several of its occupants as they deal with the challenges of their personal lives and those thrown at them by Egypt's social, economic and political systems and processes. It is set in the late 1980s and early 1990s, though readers of the English translation are told in a translator's note not to pay too much attention to this fact as 'the novel reflects the Egypt of the present', thus providing them with some extra-textual information which readers of the original version presumably did not need. Humphrey Davies's 'present' must be around 2006–7, when the translation was published, whereas al-Aswany started the novel in 1998, much closer to the period in which it is set, and the initial publication was in 2002; we're left to conclude that nothing much changed between 1990 and 2006—and the novel certainly conveys the impression that the Egypt it reflects is not in any imminent danger of being transformed.

The picture of urban Egyptian life painted in the novel is a far from pretty one: the gap between rich and poor is vast, symbolized by the contrast between the lives of the wealthy occupants of the largest apartments in the building and those of the indigent group who inhabit the small rooms on the roof originally built for storage; corruption flourishes at all levels; advancement is dependent not only on being able to afford the necessary bribes but on having the right family background; women are routinely abused; the democratic machinery is a sham; torture is an accepted part of police methods; prejudice against homosexuality is widespread. As a result, every character is engaged in a struggle to achieve fulfilment, whether it be sexual, financial, political, or professional; and most fail.

As one indication of the type of critical response to *Imarat Ya'qubyan* that has emerged from the Arab literary world we can take Samia Mehrez's 2008 comment: 'Within the Egyptian literary field, al-Aswany, a dentist by profession, is perceived as a writer of "popular" and not avant-garde fiction; his first novel, *Imarat Ya'qubyan*, is considered "scandal literature" that appeals to the literate masses but not the literary elite' (*Egypt's Culture Wars*, 56). Mehrez clearly speaks for the 'literary elite' to which she refers: she has served as a member of the Naguib Mahfouz Award, a rough equivalent of the Booker Prize for Arab writing, which conspicuously failed to honour *Imarat Ya'qubyan* when it was published. Her comments hint that a dentist writing his first novel could hardly be expected to produce important literature (hence her words about its 'mind-boggling and overwhelming global success' that I cited earlier). But she's well aware that the translated version was treated with much more respect by the 'literary elite' in the West: she notes that *Le Monde* referred to it as a 'masterpiece of the contemporary Arab novel', and adds, now distancing herself somewhat from the elite, 'Much to the venerable scribes' dismay, al-Aswany's spectacular success came to confirm that the way into the international republic of letters may depend not on the scribes' local status in the alley but rather on the global village and what *it* deems to be a 'classic' (56).

No doubt Mehrez is correct when she says that one explanation for the success of al-Aswany's novel compared to others regarded more highly by the so-called 'venerable scribes' is its relatively conventional form; whereas a novel like *Dhat* by Sonallah Ibrahim 'requires, in fact demands, the active creative participation of its readers... *Imarat Ya'qubyan* navigates within the boundaries of classical realism that appeals to a much wider spectrum of uninitiated readers in the global village' (57). But this, of course, does not explain why many another novel written in a traditionally realist style has had nothing like the success of al-Aswany's novel. We will need to revisit the question of the novel's form in due course.

It is Mehrez's epithet 'scandal literature' that points to another, perhaps more important, aspect of the novel's appeal to its readers in the Arab world. It was shocking in two different ways: in its frank portrayal of sex, including homosexual encounters, and in its unflinching depiction of the endemic corruption of Egyptian society. Pamela Nice, interviewing people in Cairo in 2006 about the novel and the film, which had just been released, found both of these being given as reasons for reading the book. 'Few could deny', she comments, 'that both the book and the film created a phenomenon in Cairene culture because of the many taboos broken in the name of freedom of artistic expression', and she goes on to list both torture, exploitation and bribery on the one hand and sexual explicitness on the other (Nice, 'A Conversation'). The director of the film, Marwan Hamed, focuses on the same qualities: 'The book is very, very bold.... It addresses some of the issues people don't even dare to talk about. The amount of realism in the book and the amount of honesty Alaa Al-Aswany had for the characters is something I admired very much' (Salama, 'As *Yacoubian Building* Sets').

Imarat Ya'qubyan, then, struck Egyptian readers, and perhaps readers more widely in the Arab world, with the force of truth: it exposed realities which both officialdom and most media kept hidden. Al-Aswany himself seems less than happy that this aspect of his work is the one that readers in his own country repeatedly focused on; Nice records him as saying, 'People say "Yacoubian Building" was popular because of the sex, exposed corruption, police brutality, etc. but won't acknowledge that, perhaps, it was a good piece of literature.' In a 2007 interview, 'Egypt is in a State of Reserve and Backwardness', he said, 'I seek to create literature... not to liberate people or to call for equal rights for women. I tackle issues such as these in my columns or articles.'

The sympathetic portrayal of homosexuality was clearly an important element in the book's shock-value in the Arab world. No doubt for many readers this aspect was hard to accept, given the extent of anti-gay prejudice in Arab culture; for others, it must have been a positive expansion of mental and emotional horizons; for yet others, a welcome endorsement of their own attitudes and convictions. One of the novel's central characters, Hatim Rashid, the gay editor of a French-language newspaper in Cairo, falls passionately in love with a young police officer from northern Egypt, and the novel tracks the highs and lows of the relationship with the same attention as it does the heterosexual exploits of the aging playboy Zaki Bey or the secret second marriage of the businessman and drug-dealer Hagg Azzam. Sex is also prominent in the story of Busayna, the beautiful roof-dweller who finds that she can't keep a job in a store without granting sexual favours to the proprietor, but who finally catches the eye of Zaki Bey and agrees to a marriage that gives the novel a conventional happy ending of sorts.

To most Western readers of the translation until 2011, the power of the book could not be said to lie in its revelation of unspoken truths. Some readers would have already been aware of Egypt's rampant corruption, heavy-handed political rule, and gross disparity between the rich and the poor; others would have been surprised to learn of these problems; in neither case would the content have come over with the shock of unspoken but widely known truth frankly revealed.[3] The book's depiction of sex is tame in comparison with much Western fiction, and its willingness to include gay relationships hardly startling to a Western reader. We need to look elsewhere, then, for an explanation for its success in the West in this period. Perhaps al-Aswany's faith in his own work as 'a good piece of literature' has something to do with it.

The *Daily Telegraph* reviewer, Tash Aw, notes the 'rich mixture of characters', the 'wry delivery', and the way in which the narrator refrains from making judgements, in 'this superbly crafted feat of storytelling' ('Upstairs, Downstairs'). Rachel Aspden, in the *Observer*, while describing al-Aswany's prose as 'resolutely affectless' (another way, perhaps, of describing its reluctance to offer judgements), praises his treatment of religious extremism as 'without sensationalism or irony' and admires his eye for details ('Sex and the City'). For Alev Adil, in the *Independent*, this 'addictively readable' novel combines 'the humanist realism of Balzac with the hyperbolic momentum of Egyptian soap opera' ('Home Truths'). The *San Francisco Chronicle*'s John Freeman likes the fact that *The Yacoubian Building* doesn't close neatly: 'Some plotlines end abruptly, in tragedy, while others simply vanish into the noise of the street' ('A Window'). Lorraine Adams, in the *New York Times Sunday Book Review*, comments that 'Aswany's empathy combines with perceptive narrative detail' ('Those Who Dwell Therein', 2006).

In their various ways, these reviewers, and others, praise not just the boldness with which al-Aswany portrays the injustices and injuries inflicted on his characters and describes practices usually concealed, but the skill with which the stories are told—a creative achievement which is part and parcel of the enjoyment readers experience. Al-Aswany's inventiveness, to which these readers are responding, lies partly in his continuous interweaving of the various plots—there are

[3] For a survey of Egypt's political, social and economic conditions before the popular uprising of February 2011, see Rodenbeck, 'The Long Wait'.

no chapters, just a series of short episodes, sometimes continuous, sometimes jumping in time and place—and in the use of a style capable of dealing with a great range of behaviours without judging or moralizing. This is not to say there are no villains, for there are plenty; but they are minor players, and the main characters, whatever their weaknesses, are treated with understanding and frequently with generous humour. The handling of Taha, the roof-dweller who dreams of becoming a policeman and who turns his anger at rejection into radical Muslim activism, is particularly deft; while there is no suggestion that his faith-inspired violence is to be lauded, its origins are convincingly detailed, and the blame is laid as much on the secular establishment as on the Islamic fundamentalists who indoctrinate him.

Al-Aswany's handling of sex is an area where Arab and Western responses are visibly distinct. Whereas in the Egyptian context, what seems most striking to readers is the openness with which sexual, especially gay, relations are described, Western reviewers often found al-Aswany's treatment of the subject wanting. Adil's view is that 'the depiction [of male homosexuality] is often uncomfortable because it seems prejudiced rather than permissive.... At times, the voice is culturally as well as sexually conservative'; while Aw extends his critique to the depiction of heterosexual relations as well, citing clichés—homosexuals bear a 'sad, mysterious, gloomy look', for instance—that 'create a sense of bathos and risk puncturing the believability of the novel'. Cultural distance is clearly at work to produce two different novels here.

Responsible reading across cultures

If Arabic-speaking and English-speaking readers were not reading the same novel—beyond the fact that translation inevitably introduces differences—what are the implications for the question of responsible reading? If I, as a member of the latter group, find the novel inventive for its handling of narrative, its tonal subtlety, its reworking of the canonical nineteenth-century realist novel, its moral stance, and its sheer informativeness, how concerned should I be to learn that these are *not* central to responses by the former group?

My answer is that I should not be concerned, just as I should not withdraw a negative judgment of some of al-Aswany's (or his narrator's) sweeping generalizations about women and homosexuals if I become convinced that Egyptian readers don't share my view. I cannot *not* read the novel in the context of the tradition of the European novel, to which it in part belongs, through translation but also through its evident affinities with that tradition; and to do so is to be alerted to some of the details of its technique that might seem unimportant to someone at home in the traditions of Arabic literature. In other words, *The Yacoubian Building*, entering the space of Western literature, offers itself to readers in a new context, one which downgrades certain aspects but heightens others. This doesn't represent a betrayal of the novel, but a new exploitation of its potential. Exoticism does, inevitably, play a role, and the strangeness of some of the scenes depicted in the novel provides Western readers with certain pleasures not granted those who are familiar with them; but if this strangeness is understood as part of the novel's subtle challenge to our habitual ways of thinking, although not part of the novel's original effectiveness, there is no reason for it to be dismissed.

I started writing about *The Yacoubian Building* in 2010, little thinking that the oppression and corruption of the Mubarak era would, a few months later, become a familiar story around the globe, and that the apparent permanence of his regime would be exposed as illusory. For someone picking up the novel, whether in the original or the translation, after the fall of Mubarak, it had become a different book: a tale of the bad old days, one more account of the evils that made revolution necessary, and a warning about the dangers of a return to authoritarian rule, wholesale corruption, and sexual oppression. For Arab readers, it no longer boldly made public what few people dared speak openly about; for readers in the West, it confirmed what they had recently heard about from many non-literary sources. For a while, it looked as if a Egypt was being reborn, free of the shackles that weigh so heavily upon the characters in *The Yacoubian Building*. When al-Aswany was asked in an interview if he saw himself taking on a role in the new Egypt, perhaps as Minister of Culture; he replied, 'It is much better to be a good novelist' ('Like Being in Love'). Now that the authoritarianism of the Mubarak era appears to be back (I'm writing this in 2014), novelists like al-Aswany are needed all the more.

Let me end this chapter by summarizing my argument. The ethics of reading literary works from other cultures is not, it turns out, significantly different from the ethics of reading works from one's own culture, which are always distanced to some degree or other. That distance is part of what makes the work valuable, and a responsible reading is one that will take full account of it rather than one that attempts the impossible task of abolishing it. I'm not speaking here of the value of such works when treated as documents that may convey important information about other cultures, a valid function but one which literary texts share with other kinds of document; I'm speaking of the value of a certain kind of *experience*, a pleasurable opening up to new possibilities that only art can produce. There's no guarantee that this opening up will be beneficial, though it usually is; it's the opening itself that is valuable. *The Yacoubian Building* is a useful repository of knowledge, and thanks to its popularity it no doubt helped to spread awareness of the problems the people of Egypt faced—and perhaps played a small part in emboldening them to rise against their totalitarian ruler. But its value as a *literary* work lies in the multiple readings through which it has come to life over and over again, dislodging old attitudes and shifting old configurations of feeling by means of its subtly interlaced tracings of imagined lives and passions, achieving this differently in its Arabic original from the way it does in its translations, but memorably and productively in all of them.

CHAPTER 7

Metaphor

Performing literature

The proposal at the heart of this account of literary practice is that the work of literature as a feature of Western culture (indeed, as one of the ways in which that culture has for a long time defined itself) can be usefully understood by means of a trinity of terms, each of which is implicated in the other two: *alterity*, *invention*, and *singularity*. It may be helpful to give a brief reiteration of the way in which I've been using these terms in discussing the distinctiveness of the literature.

Alterity (or *otherness*) refers to the work of art's challenge to existing frameworks of knowledge, feeling, and behaviour. This is not a matter of simply *opposing* accepted norms, since opposition occurs within a shared horizon; rather, it's the introduction into the known of that which it excludes in constituting itself as the known. (When I say 'known', I'm letting the word do duty for a much wider array of habits, expectations, prejudices, beliefs, and traditions than it normally suggests). Because the known depends on this exclusion, the introduction of that which is excluded requires a shift in the norms and habits on which we normally rely for our dealings with the inner and outer worlds we inhabit. Although novelty has been more valued in certain periods than in others, the artists we regard as significant have always sought to bring into being works that in some way go beyond the familiar—even if they do so only by presenting the familiar in a slightly unfamiliar light. The power of the work of art lies in the shifting of habitual ways of thinking and feeling that enables both the artist and the respondent (using this rather inadequate word to cover the reader, the viewer, and the listener) to acknowledge alterity. What is peculiar about works of art, however, in contrast to other irruptions of alterity into the cultural field (we might think of philosophical arguments, scientific discoveries, mechanical inventions), is that they can sustain their alterity across time, both the time of generations and the time from one reading, viewing, or listening to another.

The coming-into-being of the work of art is, I've been arguing, both an *act* and an *event*; it's something the artist does (or a number of artists do in a collaborative process) and something that happens to the artist (or artists). The name I give to this act–event is (and this is the second item in my trinity) *invention*, a useful term since it refers also to the product of the act–event. And it brings together the artist who creates the work and the person who experiences it: in responding to a painting or a poem as an invention, in other words, I'm responding both to the object and to the act–event that produced it (even if I know nothing, in historical or biographical terms, about that act–event). It's for this reason that the alterity of the artwork does not, in some cases at least, disappear as the culture learns to accommodate itself to it. Unlike the mechanical invention, which effects a change and then ceases to be surprising, the artwork can remain inventive, never wholly assimilated—or it can become inventive in new ways as the culture alters. The inventiveness to which we respond is unlikely to be identical with what a contemporary of the artist would have regarded as its inventiveness; in fact, it's the work's openness to new contexts that enables its inventiveness to persist. (By contrast, the work's *originality* is a historical fact about it, always open to reassessment as we gain more information, which may or may not be part of our enjoyment of it.)

Invention, to use Derrida's phrase, is always *the invention of the other* (and it will be evident that the ambiguity of that phrase encapsulates the doubleness of the act–event). And what is invented is always—this is the third of the three interrelated terms—*singular*. That is, the alterity of a work of art is not some quality or property that may be present to a greater or lesser degree; it's indissociable from the work's identity as a recognizable work (through all its mutations). The long-held view that the work of art is, or should be, unique is a reflection of this aspect, although to stress uniqueness is to imply that the work has an unchanging and circumscribed core, whereas singularity, in the sense in which I'm using it, depends on openness to change and porousness in new contexts.

How, then, do we respond to the work of art *as* a work of art, and not as any of the large number of other things that it may also be (a historical document, a biographical utterance, a psychological betrayal, a social marker, a political intervention, and so on)? Clearly, we respond to its inventiveness, alterity and singularity as a challenge of some sort to our expectations and habits. But this must mean more than enumerating its qualities or analysing its elements: we have to do justice to it as an event, and to the eventness of that event. It must happen anew in our response, each time we read it. Putting it in a different metaphoric register, we must *perform* it; or more accurately, and preserving the undecidability between act and event, when we read a literary work as a literary work *we find ourselves performing it*. (I'm willing to leave the ambiguity of that phrase unresolved too.)

This is the part of my argument to which I would like to devote a little more attention. Performance, like most of the terms I'm using, has a multiplicity of meanings, but I hope my use of it will be clear. In performing the work of art, which may be a sculpture I'm looking at or a piece of music I'm listening to, I'm making it happen, as a singular, inventive other impinging on my culturally and historically specific situation as a subject. In doing so, what I'm making happen is the work's *own* singular performance—of the effects of light, say, of the dynamics of narrative, of the emotive possibilities of sound, and so on. I am, if you like, living through its performance, not simply observing it.

To make this discussion more precise, I need to limit myself to literature; there are too many different kinds of performance involved in the different art forms for a general account to get us very far.

A work of literature can perform—or stage, or enact—anything that language can do. By using these theatrical terms, I mean to bring out the element of self-distancing that is involved, what Derrida calls the 'suspension' of the normal properties of language[1]: the language of a literary work may function in exactly the same way as the language of daily life, *except* that as long as we're reading it as literary language its operations are on show, its powers operative yet not quite closed down onto a non-linguistic world. Thus, to take an example, one of language's most useful properties is referentiality, its capacity to send the hearer or reader to something outside itself. The literary work *stages* referentiality, so that while it continues to propel the hearer or reader in this manner it simultaneously interrupts the process by making the very process of referral part of the point: we're affected not just by what is being referred to but by the power of language to refer, and of *this* language to refer in *this* way.

The category of literature thus differs from the category of *fiction*, the distinguishing feature of which is that the objects and events referred to are imaginary.[2] The literary work may refer to real as well as to imaginary events; it's the *staging* of referentiality that marks it as literary—in a literary reading, that is. It's perfectly possible for a work of history to be open to (and to yield fruitfully to) a literary reading. And it's perfectly possible to read a single work in more than one manner at once; in fact, it's probably impossible not to. If I enjoy E. P. Thompson's *Making of the English Working Class* as literature, this does not mean I cease to enjoy it, and learn from it, as history.

[1] See '"This Strange Institution"', 44–50. Paul Ricoeur also uses this term in analysing the operation of metaphor, though in the service of a more conventional account of the two levels of sense, the literal and the metaphorical; see *The Rule of Metaphor*, 221.

[2] This apparently straightforward statement conceals, of course, a complex set of much-debated issues. To elaborate a little: we call something fictional when there is no *necessary* relation between its assertions and assumptions and the world we inhabit. If the sun rises in the east in a fictional work, this is not because it has to. I've discussed this topic in the chapter entitled 'Deconstruction and Fiction' in *Reading and Responsibility*.

Let me be clear, though. My argument is *not* that we become necessarily conscious of the process of referring in reading a literary work: that is something we're likely to experience only occasionally, predominantly in modernist or postmodern texts. It's that the very process itself works differently, because we are reading for the event, not for the outcome. We take pleasure in the events of referring, and in the power of language thus exemplified—the power to bring before us in an instant the lushness of a garden or the gait of a tramp or the pain of a bee-sting. Description, to take a slightly different category, is not itself a literary device—it functions in many kinds of language to convey information, and once the information is conveyed its job is done; the reader of a novel, however, may well enjoy the process of describing that goes on in it, the staging of what we might call *descriptivity* in all its potency, and may want to read it again to re-experience the enjoyment. Something similar may be said of the *themes* we detect in literary works: the discovery of a theme is not peculiar to the reading of literature, but to be taken through the experience of thematizing is. Literary works don't offer knowledge, but they may stage the knowability—or the unknowability—of the world by staging the procedures whereby knowledge is articulated, or whereby its articulation is resisted.[3] Nor do they offer moral guidance, read as literature; language's power, however, to evoke guilt, to crystallize ethical goals, to convey the difficulty of choice, is something many literary works enact.

Any linguistic process or capability can be staged in literature: there is nothing distinctively literary about using language to cajole, promise, frighten, endear, arouse, or anger, but the literary comes to the fore when we experience these speech acts as linguistic events. Even communication, so basic to the functions of language, is not central to literature. However, it's not a matter, as Roman Jakobson argued in his well-known 'Closing Statement', of communication becoming

[3] See the following chapter for a discussion of 'knowing' in literature.

displaced from its centrality by a different function when language is used in a literary way; rather, we experience the communicativeness of language *while it is communicating*, and it's this that displaces the communicative function from its dominant position.

Metaphor and metaphoricity

I want to take as an example for further exploration a feature of language use often held to be highly characteristic of literature: metaphor.[4] It might seem that in metaphor we have a literary property that is not staged or performed, but that simply occurs. When used in works not conventionally classified as literature, we are often told, those works are drawing on a literary device. I want to argue, however, that when metaphors are used *without* being staged, *without* the slight sense of self-distance I've been talking about, they are not functioning in a literary way, and it makes no sense to call them literary devices.

It will help to look at a couple of passages that employ metaphorical figuration. Here is Hume, in *A Treatise of Human Nature*, on the challenge of scepticism to reason:

> Reason first appears in possession of the throne, prescribing laws, and imposing maxims, with an absolute sway and authority. Her enemy, therefore, is obliged to take shelter under her protection, and by making use of rational arguments to prove the fallaciousness and imbecility of reason, produces, in a manner, a patent under her hand and seal. (Volume 1, 182)

[4] I'm using the term 'metaphor' in a fairly general sense to refer to the creative use of language whereby a fresh semantic alignment—one that is not already coded in the language—is achieved, whether on the basis of similarity (metaphor in the strict sense), contiguity and association (metonymy), or part-whole relations (synecdoche). To place metaphor and metonymy in opposition, as Jakobson famously did (and Lacan equally famously after him), seems to me to obscure their similarity as tools for the enlargement of the semantic, and perhaps emotive, range of the language. For a valuable rethinking of the operation of metaphoric and metonymic relations, see Don Paterson's two essays entitled 'The Domain of the Poem' and my discussion of these essays in 'Don Paterson's *Ars Poetica*'.

Now in the terms of my own argument it would be possible to say that, for a moment, Hume invites us to read his philosophical prose as literature (while not ceasing to read it as philosophy). This would mean enjoying not just the clarity of the argumentation—a *philosophical* pleasure—but the exhibition of language's power to represent such intangible entities as reason and scepticism in the guise of concrete images through the use of metaphor. And perhaps a certain kind of reader would do just that, with perfect legitimacy; it's not a question of texts having inherent properties that require them to be read in certain ways, but of how they may be read and how they respond to different kinds of reading. It seems more likely, however, that the reader working her way through *A Treatise of Human Nature* will respond only to the argument and will treat the metaphor in a purely instrumental way, as adding to the perspicuity of Hume's own reasoning at this moment when he is questioning the operations of reason. Having got the point, she can move on to the next stage of the argument.

Here, by contrast, is the first stanza of Robert Graves's 'The Dangerous Gift':

> Were I to cut my hand
> 	On that sharp knife you gave me
> 	(That dangerous knife, your beauty),
> I should know what to do:
> 	Bandage the wound myself
> And hide the blood from you.
> 	*Collected Poems*, 280

Here, as in the passage by Hume, the metaphor invites us to understand more clearly an intangible quality, in this case a kind of beauty, by giving it a concrete form: but what makes this happen *as literature* is its invitation to participate in the unfolding of the metaphor itself, its staging of the potency of what we can call 'metaphoricity'—and, of course, the inventiveness with which this is done, to produce a singular poem and to surprise the reader with its otherness. We take pleasure in the occurring of the metaphor as we read: the sharp knife that seems a real object in the first two lines is transformed into a way of specifying, or perhaps, more accurately, *feeling*, the perilous power of sexual beauty, but we remain aware that it's the potential of metaphoricity that's being exploited, that language is being made to exhibit its power to conflate categories and generate new compounds of meaning and emotion. (Unless, that is, the reader is not moved by the poem, and finds the lines predictable and uninventive...)

Another contrast that we can draw is between literary metaphor and the metaphors of the casual spoken language. The recent development of cognitive poetics has arisen in part out of the growing awareness that many of the features that have traditionally been taken as marking the literary use of language are in fact intrinsic to language use in its most common forms.[5] The employment of figurative language is one of these features. As Ronald Carter puts it in his study *Language and Creativity*, summarizing recent work in cognitive linguistics and echoing, perhaps unconsciously, many earlier writers, including Vico, Herder, Rousseau, and Nietzsche:

> The starting point and continuing emphasis of this research are that human language and the human mind are not *inherently* literal. In writings by cognitive linguists figurative language is seen not so much as deviant or ornamental but rather as ubiquitous in everyday language, especially spoken language. Discussions of figurative language proceed on the assumption that the fundamental roots of language are figurative. (*Language and Creativity*, 70)

Here is one of the examples Carter has culled from the CANCODE corpus of spoken English, uttered by a retired male schoolteacher: 'The second year I had, I started off with 37 in the class I know that, of what you call dead wood the real dregs had been taken off the bottom and the cream the sour cream in our case up there had been creamed off the top and I just had this dead wood' (129). Again, we can say that

[5] See, for example, Lakoff and Johnson, *Metaphors We Live By*; Gibbs, *The Poetics of Mind*; and Turner, *The Literary Mind*.

metaphor is being used in a literary manner here: that the speaker is sharing with his hearer a pleasure in the metaphorical power of language—in particular, the way in which dead metaphors can be brought to life by mixing them (*dead wood—dregs—cream*) or by developing them (*dregs—taken off the bottom; cream—sour cream—creamed off the top*). And certainly the reader of this speech in Carter's book will find the attraction of giving it a literary reading almost irresistible. But in the context of the give-and-take of conversation it seems more likely that the metaphorical potential of language is being used here in a purely instrumental way, to make the speaker's point as vividly as possible.

The most common account of metaphor goes something like this: we encounter, in speech or writing, a word or phrase that does not make sense if understood literally, for instance, 'This house has been far out at sea all night'.[6] So we engage a different interpretative gear, which enables us to make sense of the statement through metaphor: for 'far out at sea' we understand something like 'so subject to the wind that the occupants have felt as if they were in a boat far from land, at the mercy of the elements'. Such an account makes no distinction between literary and non-literary uses of metaphor; it is as appropriate for Hume as it is for Graves. We can move it towards a more properly literary account if we stress the *activity* involved: the registering of an anomaly, the searching for a sense that would fit with the literal context, the experience of strangeness that is produced, the richness of the meanings made possible by the indeterminacy of the metaphor. All this is correct, but it still sounds like a recipe for the domestication of metaphor, even if we are responding to the act–event of domestication rather than to the meaning arrived at. And it rests on the somewhat wobbly foundation of the notion of *deviation*, which tends to get us into trouble because of the problem of defining the norm from which deviation occurs.

Two interesting accounts of metaphor play down the idea that our ability to interpret metaphor depends on a special linguistic ability and

[6] This is the first line of Ted Hughes's poem 'Wind', *Collected Poems*, 36.

procedure. Dan Sperber and Deirdre Wilson present one of these in *Relevance* (231–7), as part of a general theory about communication that has been immensely influential in cognitive poetics. They insist that metaphor 'requires no special interpretive abilities or procedures' (237), regarding metaphorical utterances, like all utterances, as interpretations of the speaker's *thought*. The literal utterance is only the limiting case, in which the utterance is identical to the thought; other utterances vary in some way or other from the thought they represent. The utterance can be a loose version of the thought (as when I say it's midnight when the clock I've just looked at shows 12.08), or a hyperbolic version, or a metaphoric version. This analysis has the advantage of placing metaphor in the context of a range of non-literal uses of language, and of stressing the variety within metaphoric uses themselves; the emphasis on the processing of metaphor (as part of a wider exploration of speakers' and hearers' processing activity) is also useful. However, the notion that the linguistic utterance translates a 'thought', either literally or non-literally, assumes a binary structure that is hard to justify and that reintroduces, with all its problems, the old model of a norm from which figurative utterances deviate. Thus the speaker, we're told, will 'adopt, on different occasions, a more or less faithful interpretation of her thoughts' (237): the literal is faithful, the metaphoric faithless. We are asked to accept that there is an inner realm of thought (and, presumably, feeling) that is without deception or self-deception, and an outer realm of language which may or may not falsify that inner, pure, realm; it's not hard to see that this is another version of the traditional valorization of speech (or the language of the heart) over writing from Plato onwards that Derrida deconstructed a long time ago.

A more radical account of the processing of metaphors is Donald Davidson's well-known essay, 'What Metaphors Mean'.[7] Davidson's thesis is the apparently simple one that 'metaphors mean what the

[7] First published in *Critical Inquiry* in 1978, reprinted in Sheldon Sacks, ed., *On Metaphor*, from which I'm quoting, and included in Davidson's *Inquiries into Truth and Interpretation*. Davidson further developed his argument in 'Locating Literary Language'.

words, in their most literal interpretation, mean, and nothing more' (30). This may sound like a claim that metaphors have no existence, but Davidson is in fact moving us to a domain other than that of *meaning* in which the force of metaphors is profoundly felt. As he explains, 'I depend on the distinction between what words mean and what they are used to do. I think metaphor belongs entirely to the domain of use' (31). In other words, the effectiveness of metaphoric uses of language derives from what *happens* when we hear or read them, and this is not a process of translating them back into a literal meaning or a prior 'thought' but of treating them—with whatever imaginative capacities we possess—as words with their usual meanings. The result, Davidson tells us, is that the metaphor makes us notice things that we hadn't noticed before: connections and likenesses that, if we tried to paraphrase them, would have no clear limit.

Davidson doesn't make any distinction between literary and nonliterary uses of metaphor; 'Metaphor,' he says, 'is a legitimate device not only in literature but in science, philosophy, and the law' (31). This is quite true, of course, but it doesn't follow that the reader of a scientific treatise encountering a metaphor will treat it, or be treated by it, in the same way as the reader of a poem would. In the former, the reader will seek to close down the potentially endless implications to produce something clear and firm; in the latter, the reader will allow the metaphor to do its work relatively unhindered by such expectations. Nor does Davidson escape the 'deviation' model, basing it on the patent *falsity* of the sentence containing a metaphor: 'Generally it is only when a sentence is taken to be false that we accept it as a metaphor and start to hunt out the hidden implication.... Absurdity or contradiction in a metaphorical sentence guarantees we won't believe it and invites us, under proper circumstances, to take the sentence metaphorically' (40). This is a somewhat disappointing conclusion after the promising idea that the words in metaphorical sentences mean what they normally mean; the relation between sentences and the world they refer to has now become the key to the movement into a metaphoric register. But patently false statements are not hard to find in literary works—Davidson clearly doesn't mean the kind of false statement that is the norm in *all* fictional language; we could turn not only to folk and fairy tales, romance and fantasy, but also to the genre of 'magic realism', whose effectiveness relies on our *not* taking the patently absurd goings-on as merely metaphorical.

A better sense of how metaphors impress themselves on the reader comes from a passing comment Davidson makes on novelty. 'What we call the element of novelty or surprise in a metaphor is a built-in aesthetic feature we can experience again and again, like the surprise in Haydn's Symphony no. 94 or a familiar deceptive cadence' (36). Leaving aside the problems Davidson introduces by using the word 'aesthetic', this statement points to the *sequentiality* which is a necessary part of the experience of metaphor. If, as I'm arguing, metaphor in literary works, when read as literature, is performed, the opening up of semantic (and thence emotive and even somatic) possibilities is a product of the relation between one word and the next, one phrase or sentence and the next. There is, it seems to me, a continuum along which sequences of words invite greater or lesser inventiveness on the part of the reader because they conform more or less fully to the expectations encoded in the language. Davidson's model may work for the passage by Hume, where we register immediately that the philosopher can't possibly be talking about kings and their enemies and so allow their metaphoric implications to come into play; but in literary works we are constantly alert to resonances that take us away, perhaps only a very short distance, perhaps very far indeed, from the most straightforward meanings and uses of language.[8] I want to hold on to Davidson's idea that the words in metaphors mean what they usually mean, and Sperber and Wilson's insistence that metaphors require no special interpretative procedures; but I want to add that our

[8] I've made use of Davidson's 'What Metaphors Mean' in discussing J. M. Coetzee's use of allegory; see chapter 2 of *J. M. Coetzee and the Ethics of Reading*.

experience of literary metaphors involves an enjoyment of the powers of metaphoricity as it expands the possibilities of language.

Metaphor and the reader

My insistence on an ethical dimension to our responses to works of art may seem inconsistent with what I'm arguing in this chapter, given that I'm stressing art's staging of the processes whereby we engage with the world, each other, and ourselves, as distinct from the direct engagement that occurs outside art, and that one might assume was the domain of the ethical. However, what I've said about art's capacity to introduce alterity into the settled framework of our lives should indicate that I'm not proposing to re-introduce the notion of art-for-art's sake or championing the autonomy of the art object. The point I would stress about the ethical—and political—significance of art is that although it has profound effects in the world, these can never be predicted in advance, and that this is a constitutive impossibility. If the effect of the other could be known in advance, it would not be other. So art, in the strict sense, is ineffectual as a political tool—which is not to say that the objects we call artworks haven't been and won't continue to be immensely valuable in political struggles, just that this value depends on their capacity to be used in ways other than the artistic.

My focus here, however, is on the reader. I asked earlier in this book what it means to 'do justice' to a work of literature, and answered that it means doing justice to the work's singularity, inventiveness, and alterity in a singular, creative response. In thus responding both to what has been created and the process of creation itself, we're responding to the work, again in both senses, of another person. (For simplicity's sake, I shall stay with the assumption of a single writer, though everything I'm saying could apply to a group or a series of writers). And the impulse to do justice to the work, which means to make it happen anew—and always differently—in one's reading of it, is an ethical impulse: in Levinasian terms, to respond to the other not as a generalizable set of features or a statistic but as a singularity. Levinas's term for the singular other, appearing before me and obliging me to take responsibility for it, is the *face*—and his use of the term is not metaphorical, although it's not simply literal either.[9] We might extend the notion of the face, and the obligation it imposes, to the concrete, specific, ungeneralizable, work of art.

Now let us pose the question with regard to the specific phenomenon of literary metaphor. I've chosen a well-known passage by Shakespeare, because I want to keep alive the dual question of inventiveness, alterity, and singularity over time and over many readings. The passage was written some four hundred years ago, and most readers will already have encountered it several times: under these twin conditions, can it still be said to introduce the other into the same, to surprise by its inventiveness and alterity? And if so, how does one do justice to it as a literary work? More specifically, how does one do justice to its metaphors? How do we perform metaphors, or the figurative potential of language, in a passage such as this? (Of course, in concentrating on the working of metaphors I'm leaving out a great deal more that could be said: for example, I'm not making any attempt to see the passage in its historical context, which would be an important part of a full reading.)

Enter JULIET above at her window
But soft, what light through yonder window breaks?
It is the east, and Juliet is the sun.
Arise, fair sun, and kill the envious moon,
Who is already sick and pale with grief
That thou, her maid, art far more fair than she.
Be not her maid, since she is envious;
Her vestal livery is but sick and green,
And none but fools do wear it; cast it off.
It is my lady, O, it is my love!
O that she knew she were!

[9] See, in particular, Levinas's discussion of the face in *Totality and Infinity*.

She speaks, yet she says nothing; what of that?
Her eye discourses, I will answer it.
I am too bold, 'tis not to me she speaks.
Two of the fairest stars in all the heaven,
Having some business, do entreat her eyes
To twinkle in their spheres till they return.
What if her eyes were there, they in her head?
The brightness of her cheek would shame those stars,
As daylight doth a lamp; her eyes in heaven
Would through the airy region stream so bright
That birds would sing and think it were not night.
(Act II, scene ii, 2–22).

A literary work may be performed in many ways. It may be read silently or aloud, or experienced in someone else's performance—and in the case of a play-text, that can range from a straightforward reading to a full theatrical production or a film. If someone else is performing it, and we are responding to that performance in a way that brings to bear on it our own creativity, we can still be said to be performing it ourselves, in the extended sense in which I'm using the word in this book. We're not simply interpreting it, discarding the husk of form for the kernel of meaning. For the purposes of this discussion, let's imagine that we're reading *Romeo and Juliet* aloud, and have reached the moment when Romeo looks up at Juliet's window not long before dawn.

When I, as a literary critic, comment in writing on a literary work I've read or heard I may offer an interpretation or a description, or I may go further and attempt to convey the work's singularity, inventiveness, and alterity in my particular time and place by taking my readers through the experience of performing, and being performed by, the work. Such a commentary will only work if it finds readers who, in their turn, will read it responsively and creatively, in conjunction with a similar reading of the original. And by responding creatively I don't mean freely associating; I mean affirming inventiveness by an answering inventiveness, whether enunciated or unarticulated, that is prompted by the specificity and special value of the work. In this sense, a full response to a literary work is a responsible one.[10]

The first line of the speech appears to be unmetaphorical: Romeo observes a lighted window in the darkness. However, the word 'breaks' seems to me (I won't hide behind a generalized 'we' or 'the reader') charged with a degree of metaphorical suggestiveness: this light not only breaks through the window—the *OED* allows the meaning 'penetrates', continuing its definition with nice appropriateness, 'as light breaks the darkness'—but also conjures up the idea of *daybreak*. What also suggests some expansion beyond the literal is the grammatical form of the line: one would think that there is no mystery about a light in an upper room at night, yet this light seems to be, for this viewer, unusual enough to provoke a question. This slight enigma impels me onto the next line, where the answer to the question reveals that, although one could hardly call the unorthodox use of a question a metaphor, something like a metaphoric understanding of the light was already stirring in the previous line—what we took there to be the shining of a candle or a lamp (with perhaps overtones of the onset of dawn) is to be retrospectively understood as the radiance of a girl's beauty.

To comment in this manner is to imply that in reading line one I don't know what will come in line two; this is of course not true after my first encounter with the speech, but it captures the fact that the lines *stage* enigmas and resolutions, metaphorical expansions, and so on: these events are still effective on the hundredth reading precisely because they are not simply using these linguistic capabilities but showing them off in a sequential process. (If I wanted to complicate the reading further, I could discuss the interplay between knowing what lies ahead and performing a certain ignorance of it.)

The metaphor, when it comes, is as plain as any metaphor could be, expressed in the simplest diction and syntax (contrasting with the

[10] I've given a fuller account of responsible reading in chapter 2; and see also Attridge, *Reading and Responsibility*.

inversion of the previous line): 'It is the east, and Juliet is the sun'. If the words mean what they usually mean, as Davidson encourages us to think, they invite me to imagine, and share, a frame of mind in which a window can also be a horizon, and a woman can also be the rising sun: the frame of mind of a man suddenly, desperately, in love. And at the same time, because I'm not overhearing a scene taking place next door but reading a literary work, I take pleasure in the operation of the metaphor, in its surprisingness, its directness, its charge of satisfaction as it helps to make sense of the previous line. Another way of putting this is that I'm aware of a source of this language that is not Romeo (though it's an awareness that I don't bring into full consciousness most of the time); there is an author, about whom it would be possible for me to know nothing except that this line is his invention, and that in responding to the line I'm responding to the act–event whereby he invented it. My responsibility as a reader is to this author, not as flesh-and-blood man but as he is to be found in the line, as well as to the singularity and alterity of his invention.

A further dimension to the metaphor is the range of other metaphors it calls up, that panoply of literary figurations in which the beloved, human or divine, is the sun. It's no ordinary metaphor: Derrida devotes careful attention to the solar metaphor in 'White Mythology', calling it the 'paradigm of the sensory *and* of metaphor' (250). Yet what is so surprising about this particular manifestation of the metaphor is its elementariness, elementalness even, as if all those elaborate comparisons were falsifications and unnecessary hyperbole: quite simply, 'Juliet is the sun'.

Although the line seems to close in on itself in its simplicity and directness, the following lines open up and develop the metaphor (and thus increase the force of its metaphoricity): 'Arise, fair sun, and kill the envious moon, / Who is already sick and pale with grief.' I find myself taken on a strange semantic journey, in which an image of a lovely girl looking out of a window at the night sky fuses with an image of the rising sun diminishing the brightness of the moon. 'Arise' belongs to the first of these images, but suggests 'rise', belonging to the second; 'fair' belongs to the first (we wouldn't normally call the sun 'fair'), but 'sun' to the second. 'Kill' then comes as a particular surprise, a metaphor *within* a metaphor, a human action being used of an astronomical body itself standing for a person, but in its murderous suggestion taking me into a new semantic domain rather than back to the girl standing at the window. That domain continues to govern 'envious', as human attributes now spread to the moon—presumably not only a metaphorical moon to match the metaphorical sun, but the real moon, that both Romeo (and perhaps Juliet) can see in the sky above. The oddness of 'envious' is then given some justification in a new conceit: the specific quality of the moon's light, 'sick and pale', is ascribed to its envy—its envy of the sun (within the metaphor of sunrise) and of Juliet's sun-like radiance (within the half-metaphoric, half-literal representation of the scene itself).

The emotional tonality of the speech is further complicated by the wish on Romeo's part that the real sun should *not* rise (not many lines later Juliet is saying, ''Tis almost morning, I would have thee gone,' and Romeo is observing how 'The grey-ey'd morn smiles on the frowning night'). If only Juliet were the sole sun, the joy of the moment would not be darkened by an awareness of the literal sun, about to rise. The unexpected violence of 'kill', and the imputation of envy to the moon, feed into this sense of hostile forces all around—for of course daylight implies discovery by the Capulets.

In the next line, the metaphorical sun turns back into something closer to the literal Juliet, now not a sun-like beauty but a virgin devoted to chastity: the moon's envy, it turns out, as the conceit is given a further unanticipated turn, is that of the mistress outdone by a follower—'That thou her maid art far more fair than she.' Yet some lingering sense that the girl remains sun-like is provided by the repetition of the word 'fair', now yoked in memory with 'sun'. Romeo is beginning to play with his metaphorical scheme now, as is Shakespeare; and the reader who is enjoying the lines (rather than finding them an inaccurate representation of what a love-struck youth might actually say to himself) is enjoying the sport as well.

But if Romeo's verbal games seem unrealistic, that aura of courtly rhetoric is shattered by the note of sexual urgency in the next line: although the metaphor is further extended, it's now used to express unambiguous desire for physical union: 'Be not her maid, since she is envious'. Of course, the second half of that line is completely spurious as argument, because the moon's envy is something Romeo has just invented; but desire does not necessarily appeal to logic to justify itself. It's as if the metaphor he has been developing as an expression of his delight has suddenly struck him as having some potential as a tool of seduction, though there's no denying the joke (and the joke itself is partly a joke about the power of metaphor). The metaphor is then further extended—'her vestal livery is but sick and green'—with the moon now standing for the ideal of virginity, and virginity itself troped as an ill-coloured outfit (with hints of the maid's traditional green-sickness and the jester's motley). Romeo's urgent appeal that gives the extended conceit its climax—'cast it off'—is a metaphor that threatens to become literal, as the young man looks at the girl dressed, no doubt, for bed.

My experience of that final injunction is of the metaphoric urge exhausting itself as the very literal fact of desire takes over, and the three lines that follow are all the more powerful in their resistance of metaphoricity, as critics have often noted and actors recognized. But soon the metaphors reappear, this time in a more fanciful guise as Romeo indulges in a little narrative. I'm now made aware not so much of the power of language to express emotion through metaphor, but of the extraordinary capacity of metaphorical language to take leave of the observed world. I find myself enjoying the excessive elaboration of the 'eyes as stars' metaphor ('having some business' is a wonderfully down-to-earth note to strike in connection with astral imagery) just as much as the representation of ocular beauty that is to be enjoyed. This is metaphor revelling in metaphoricity.

I've tried to give some sense of how I participate in this passage's inventive metaphors as I read it, performing, and enjoying, the metaphors as metaphors while responding to their evocation of human emotion. Although I've read it dozens of times, I find as I re-read it in order to write about it, it remains surprising, not quite the familiar passage I had remembered. I don't make any great claims for this reading, except to the extent that it's motivated by a desire to affirm the inventiveness and singularity of the passage, to bring it into the realm of the familiar—the discourse of literary criticism, for instance—while preserving its otherness. This is what I take to be the aim of a responsible, and hence ethical, reading; an attempt to do justice to the work, the work that has survived four centuries (by not remaining the same) and the work that someone called William Shakespeare undertook, or found himself undertaking.

CHAPTER 8

Knowing

What do literary works know?

Do literary works think? Can works of art know?

Several theoretical discussions of literature over the past quarter-century have tried to capture some specific quality of the literary work by ascribing to it these capacities. Pierre Macherey's *A quoi pense la littérature?* was published in 1990, and although the 1995 English translation preferred the title *The Object of Literature,* the introductory chapter preserved the original question, 'What is literature thinking about?' In 1992, a large conference was sponsored by *Le Monde,* the University of Maine, and the town of Le Mans, to consider the question 'L'art est-il une connaissance?'; one of the speakers was Alain Badiou, who entitled his talk, 'Que pense le poème?'[1] And in 2003 Stathis Gourgouris published a book entitled *Does Literature Think?* (It's quite striking that this string of titles associating literature with thinking returns again and again to the form of the *question*—perhaps echoing Heidegger's questioning title about thinking itself, *Was Heisst Denken?*)[2]

[1] Droit, ed. *L'art est-il une connaissance?*, 214–24. In spite of the similar title, Badiou's article 'Qu'est-ce que la littérature pense?' bears no resemblance to this essay; in it he claims—to my mind unhelpfully—that 'what literature thinks is both a real marked in language with the seal of the One, and the conditions governing the way that real is marked' (38).

[2] Heidegger's text, which has been translated into English both as *What is Called Thinking?* and as 'What Calls for Thinking?', is a set of lectures given in 1951 and 1952 in which Heidegger closely associates thinking—in the sense he wishes to promote—and poetry. Although one can imagine all these titles as statements, their interrogative form suggests that the question of literature and thinking *is* a question, and perhaps too that thinking as it happens in literature is never far from questioning.

What I'm interested in is the implicit personification in these titles: rather than describing the work as the product or embodiment of thought, or as a spur to thought, something about the experience of reading leads the theorist or critic to ascribe to the work *itself* the capacity to think. Although the personification in the title is not always carried through consistently in the discussion that follows (Macherey, for instance, is interested in literature as a mode of philosophy; Gourgouris in literature as a mode of what he calls 'mythic thought'), it suggests that, at least for the duration of the reading, we may respond to a series of words as if they had something like human consciousness. Gourgouris elaborates on the question he wishes to address in his book as follows: 'The more challenging point is not to determine *what* literature thinks (what is its cognitive object), but *how* literature thinks—what is the process by which literature might provide us with access to knowledge and what sort of knowledge this might be' (1–2).

Clearly, the notion that the work of literature thinks is related to the idea that it *knows*. The question of art and knowledge, and its close relative, the question of art and truth, of course go back a long way—even further back than the time of Plato's Socrates, who refers to the *ancient* quarrel between poetry and philosophy, perhaps even further back than Hesiod, whose Muses (in the *Theogony*) describe themselves as tellers of lies that have the appearance of truths as well as purveyors of real truths. But the more specific notion of the artwork as itself the knower, rather than merely the bearer of knowledge, is perhaps a more recent one, and raises rather different questions.[3]

[3] An interesting version of the idea that literature 'thinks' and 'knows' is Simon Jarvis's argument in 'What Does Art Know?' Taking Adorno's insight that the truth-content of a work of art is not a matter of propositional truth but produced in its engagement with form (broadly understood), he gives a fine description of the creative process: 'The really new work of art is . . . that which makes a precise and decisive technical intervention in traditions of thinking-through-making which have already itself shaped the artist who is now to shape them' (66). Because the artist is thinking through making, and in so doing is in part the servant of those inherited traditions, Jarvis can say the thinking takes place in the work as much as—or more than—in the

Someone who engagingly teases out a number of the implications of such a conception of the work of literature is Michael Wood, in his 2005 study *Literature and the Taste of Knowledge*. At the outset of his book, Wood offers what he calls a rather 'schematic' frame for his enterprise: 'Thinking of Proust and asthma, say, we could ask, not what Proust knew about the condition or what doctors know now or knew in Proust's time, but what *A la recherche du temps perdu* knows about asthma—what it knows and perhaps will not tell us directly, or what it knows that only novels know, or only this novel knows' (8). Wood goes on, 'Many see dangers in such a personification—the novel is not a person and can't know anything, only novelists and readers can' (and one might perhaps add to this pair narrators and characters within novels), but he wants 'this form of the question . . . just to hang in the air' (8–9). When, later in the book, he mentions again those who have resisted the notion that literature can know—'a number of friends and colleagues with whom I've discussed the subject of this book have objected strenuously to my use of personification'—he offers a justification for its use. To sketch his argument baldly: it reminds us that literature can mean something quite different from what the author meant; that its form is what makes it literature; and that reading literature is an act of creation (110–12)—all of which I warmly endorse, as the chapters of this book will have made clear. And he sums up: 'What literature knows, what a novel or poem or play knows, is strictly, unfiguratively, what I now know that I didn't know before I read the text' (112). Here I part company with Wood, as will become evident as we go on.

Wood is able to use the manifold suggestiveness of his primary metaphor to provide some acute readings of literary works, and to set going a number of intriguing trains of thought. But does his justification of the metaphor fully explain the temptation it seems to hold out

mind of the artist. What he leaves out, however, is the role of the reader in activating any thinking (or accessing any knowledge), whatever its source.

to literary theorists and critics?[4] Since we can't take these formulations literally, we have to ask what work the anthropomorphism is doing in these accounts. What is it about one's experience of a work of literature that might lead one to consider—if only through the suspension of disbelief—that the verbal object before one is capable of thinking and knowing? And is it a defining characteristic of the literary work or a property of certain works only? Are there literary works that seem to think or know nothing, or to lack the capacity to think or know?

It's clear that the issue here is not one of *agency*: there seems to be no problem about ascribing to works of literature (or the other arts) a whole series of purposive acts. Flicking through F. R. Leavis's critical works, for example, one discovers that a poem can *offer, register, convey, impose, demand, pull itself up, recognize, settle into,* and *pick up.*[5] In Paul de Man's *Allegories of Reading,* the text can *try, confront, disguise, seize, deconstruct, seduce, deny, behave, take for granted,* and *feel a need.* We're quite happy to say that a novel *resists* interpretation, or *reinforces* conventions, or *undermines* beliefs. A sculpture can *intimidate,* or *entertain,* or *shock.* Yet there are acts that we would hesitate to associate with a work of art. Would we not raise an eyebrow if a colleague said, 'This stanza feels profound grief'? (This would be different from observing that it feels *overloaded* with emotion, say, where it is the reader who is doing the feeling). Could we accept assertions that artworks *imagine,* or *consider,* or *remember*? All such terms imply a metaphorical leap that, at the very least, makes us pause.[6] The difference seems to be that in these cases, unlike *register, resist,* and so on, the metaphor implies consciousness and mental effort rather than just agency: the work is

4 As an example of a fine critic of poetry who is drawn to the trope, here is a comment by Angela Leighton: 'For all their powers of memory and invocation . . . these elegies know that there is nothing else' (*On Form,* 226).

5 I found these verbs in Leavis's *New Bearings in English Poetry* and his edited volume *A Selection from Scrutiny.*

6 Jarvis, in 'What Does Art Know?', claims that he is not employing a metaphor when he states that works of art 'think' and 'know', since we can't say what it would be *literally* to think or know something (69). Following this logic, one could apply a host of other verbs to works of art.

deemed to possess a subjectivity enabling it to do things of which only humans (or in some cases humans and animals) are normally capable. After all, a desk can resist my efforts to move it, a car can demand attention, an argument can undermine one's assumptions. (A borderline case, perhaps, is Leavis's 'recognise': poets may recognize, but can poems?) Of course writers themselves, and the characters or speakers in their works, may do all these things with impunity, and some critics take care to restrict their use of words suggestive of human subjectivity to these individuals, real or fictional; but my interest is in the ascription of such terms—and in particular words suggestive of thought and knowledge—to the works themselves.

Let's take a poem that we might be tempted to say 'knows'. This short work is by John Wilkinson:

Mount Disk

Scamp hope lips the cart. Remember
those were client days, posting high profits
before storms came straggling. Took
a dive then we were affluent
despite mounting terror. Time accumulates
where it was wont to slip off. Every
line cross-hatches, don't
exaggerate, grappling with crimson
in its uptick, you can't ignore that now,
it won't do, it superimposes, it ghosts
ever more thickly, the waves
pile onto each other, the silage suffocates,
the nimbus furs. Suffering
wads strings round a shoreline lunch party.
Rest well-covered. Underneath our
lavishment the fern chorus straps.[7]

Not only might we say, were we given to this kind of personification, that this poem knows, we might want to call it a 'knowing' poem: by

[7] *Blackbox Manifold* Issue 9 (2012); <http://www.manifold.group.shef.ac.uk/issue9/JohnWilkinson9.html>.

which we would mean it seems to harbour some hidden knowledge, revealing only that it, and not the reader, is privy to the secret. Only the poem knows, we might want to say, what sort of cart is lipped, who is being told not to exaggerate, what superimposes, whether 'straps' is a verb or a noun. It's not a matter of trying to fathom an authorial meaning: it seems pretty certain that if we cornered John Wilkinson and demanded answers to our questions, he would not be willing or able to give them—or if he did, that his answers would need further interpretation on our part. If the poem gives pleasure to us, it's in its refusal to answer these questions, in the activity of guessing and testing and shaping we are encouraged to engage in.

The idea of the art work having the capacity to know is not limited to accounts of literature. Michael Wood's inspiration, in *Literature and the Taste of Knowledge*, comes in part from an earlier book, Peter de Bolla's *Art Matters*, a study in which de Bolla takes up the challenge of finding words to articulate the experience of a powerful work of art. He concentrates on three such works: Wordsworth's poem 'We Are Seven', Glenn Gould's 1981 performance of Bach's *Goldberg Variations*, and Barnett Newman's painting in the New York Museum of Modern Art, entitled *Vir Heroicus Sublimis*. It's in relation to the last of these that de Bolla asks what Wood calls 'the truly haunting question': 'What does this painting know?'[8]

It may seem a surprising way to describe an abstract work of art, but one must respect the honesty with which de Bolla attempts to capture his own experience of standing in front of this painting. Figure 8.1 shows the painting, though it gives no sense of its size. Figure 8.2 is a photograph of Newman, with Jackson Pollock and Tony Smith, sitting next to *Vir Heroicus Sublimis* at Newman's exhibition at the Betty Parsons Gallery, 1951; some sense of the huge scale of the painting comes across from this image.

[8] De Bolla's question in on p. 31; Wood quotes him on p. 8 of his work.

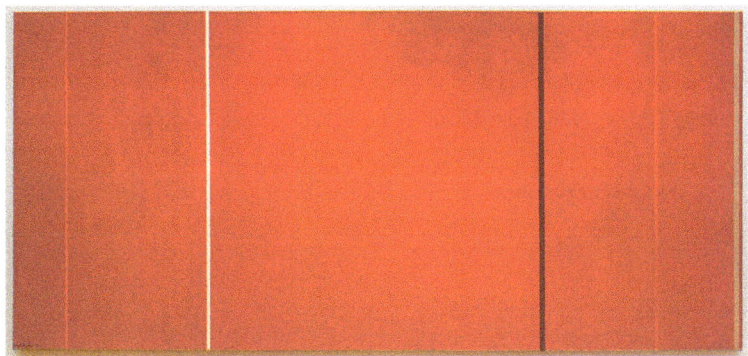

Figure 8.1. Barnett Newman, *Vir Heroicus Sublimis*
(© 2008 SCALA, Florence; ARS, NY, and DACS, London)

Figure 8.2. Barnett Newman, Jackson Pollock, and Tony Smith, sitting next to *Vir Heroicus Sublimis* at Newman's exhibition at the Betty Parsons Gallery, 1951
(Photograph by Hans Namuth © 1991 Hans Namuth Estate, used with the permission of the Center for Creative Photography, University of Arizona).

De Bolla gives a lengthy and subtle account of his response to this work; I'll focus, however, on his summary of the issue of knowing:

> Once again I am prompted to ask: What does this artwork know? I phrase this question in full light of the fact that it is virtually unintelligible—it might be slightly better to recast the question as, 'What is its way of knowing?'—but this does not detract from the very powerful sense I have of getting closer to the work, closer yet still not close enough. This leaves me with the virtual impression of a depth to the work, of something contained within it that I have yet to fathom, a space I may, perhaps, never inhabit. (52)

Again, then, we have the impression of a secret being guarded by the work, a secret that resists any amount of looking, and one to which the artist cannot be expected to have privileged access. It is, in every sense, for de Bolla, a knowing work of art.

Some works of art, then, might be called 'knowing' in that they convey a sense of meaningfulness without that meaning being entirely graspable. (This is very different from the work of art in which we sense a knowing mind behind the mind we're presented with—as in the case of Browning's dramatic monologues: in such examples, and related examples of irony, we're invited to share in the creator's knowingness. We are knowing; the unfortunate narrator is ignorant.) We can all think of many works of art—at least visual and verbal works—that would qualify for the adjective; most of them probably modern or postmodern examples, though not necessarily so: earlier examples might include Shakespeare's strange poem 'The Phoenix and the Turtle' or Goya's baffling *Los Caprichos*. (I'm not sure I can come up with any wordless musical works that deserve the adjective; de Bolla doesn't endow Bach's Goldberg Variations themselves with the capacity to know, although he does say that Gould's performance recorded in 1981 'can be understood as a philosophical argument' [90]). How justifiable is it to say that these works 'know' something they are refusing to reveal? Or that they have the capacity to 'think'?

Ways of knowing and thinking

I'd like to approach these questions obliquely by looking in a different way at thinking and knowing in works of art. I've been arguing throughout this book for a conceptualization of the work of literature as an *event* rather than an *object*. And, as I noted in Part I, theorizations of the event crop up in a number of philosophical oeuvres, including those of Heidegger, Lyotard, Derrida, Deleuze, and Badiou. (Although elsewhere Badiou elevates the event to something that takes place rarely and with profound historical effects, in 'Que pense le poème?' he states that 'the poem offers itself as a thing of language that one meets each time as an event' [215]—which seems to me quite correct.)

In *The Singularity of Literature* I drew on a number of these sources in arguing that the work of art exists, as art, only in the event of its reception, and I've elaborated on this position in earlier chapters of this book. I've made the point that although artworks function in a number of ways—they convey information, they offer moral lessons, they comfort and console with familiar wisdom and memorable language, and so on—my interest is in their operation *as art*, as engaged in a practice that differs from other practices an individual or a culture might engage in. However, to use the word 'event' alone is to miss the important part played by the reader, viewer, or listener: the artwork doesn't just happen, it arises out of an active engagement. I've already signalled my agreement with Wood's claim that reading a literary work is an act of *creation*, and I use the term 'act–event' in order to capture the strange duality of this process, in which active and passive are not clearly separable—whether we're talking about the work or the person responding to it. In this way, the work is remade each time it is read, including its handling of knowledge. Gourgouris comes close to my position in stating, 'Each text posits its own object of knowledge, each time anew, by means of its form, its horizon of possibility...and the conditions under which it is read....Reading can be considered part of its conditions of production' (*Does Literature Think?*, 11).

In order to elaborate on the active aspect of the reading process, I relate it to the notion of *performance*. My argument is that the work of art *stages* the intersubjective practices, emotional shifts, intellectual developments, physical urges, and so on, that occur 'for real' outside art. It does this by using the same materials—colours, images, textures, tones, words, narratives, and many more—that we use for these real-life practices, but deploying them as if in the theatre or between quotation marks. So, for instance, a string trio may stage agitation without agitating the listener; a painting may stage grief without arousing grief in the viewer; a novel may stage ethical choice without making the reader choose. They can do these things because, outside art, sound has the power to agitate, sights can cause grief, words may be used to pose ethical dilemmas. We can say, therefore, that a poem, for instance, performs the powers of language (to move, to calm, to enrage, to bless, and so on), and that the reader, in performing the poem, performs these powers. This is the sense in which I'm happy to grant agency to the work of art.

In asking about the role of thinking and knowing in works of art from this perspective, the most obvious question is whether we find these activities being staged or performed in the event that constitutes the art work. (This has nothing to do with the thought and knowledge that went into the creation of the work, of course.) The answer is, at least as far as literature is concerned, clearly yes. Macherey, who sustains the notion that literary works are a form of philosophical thought throughout his book, uses a metaphor that seems to point to this rather different way of understanding art's relation to thought: 'Literary texts are the home of a form of thought which speaks its name without displaying the marks of its legitimacy, because its exposition is a form of *theatricality*' (232, my emphasis).

There's a long tradition in Western literature of writers finding linguistic means to stage the processes of thought, something made possible by the close connection between language and thinking. In fact it would be hard to find a literary work that doesn't to some degree do this, though the genre most closely identified with the mimesis of thinking is the lyric poem. (I prefer to say 'thinking', where it's not too clumsy to do so, as the noun 'thought' freezes and reifies a continuous movement.) Keats's *Odes*, for example, stage the evolution of the poet's thinking in relation to an object or imagined object. The poems are about thought, yes, but any factual information they may provide about the workings of the human brain is irrelevant to their functioning as poems.[9] What matters is that the reader participates in the to-and-fro of thinking, and the feelings, memories, and hopes that arise to complicate the process, while never being under the illusion that this is anything other than a performance of the movements and proclivities of the human mind.

The twentieth century was, of course, the time of the great flowering of fictional modes designed to engage the reader in the minutiae of unfolding thought processes: Joyce, Woolf, and Richardson all developed techniques for bringing the language of prose closer to the language of thinking, and bequeathed to their successors a set of rich new literary resources. Among those successors, I'll mention only Beckett, who in the three novels we know as the Trilogy and some of the later prose made wonderful comedy out of the rambling, self-correcting, currents of thought of his narrators. And there is the poetry of David Antin, who performs a kind of thinking-aloud in front of audiences and then publishes edited transcriptions of these events as highly engaging poems.

In the non-verbal arts, however, the staging of thinking is less easy to detect. Could one say that the transitions and juxtapositions in the Eroica symphony present themselves to the listener as an echo of the movement of thought?[10] Does the viewer of Manet's *Déjeuner sur l'herbe*

[9] At times, the poem's involvement with thought is thematized: in the 'Ode to Psyche' the poet promises to 'build a fane / In some untrodden region of my mind, / Where branchèd thoughts... shall murmur in the wind'; in the 'Ode to a Nightingale' 'the dull brain perplexes and retards' the poet's attempt to escape the world where 'but to think is to be full of sorrow'; and the Grecian urn 'dost tease us out of thought'.

[10] One way in which non-verbal music enacts something like thinking is in the use of leitmotifs or allusions to other works. Peter Maxwell Davies's music theatre piece, 'Mr

move around the visual space in a process akin to thinking? To make such claims, one would have to show that we can think with sounds and with visual images. The latter is the more likely, though one needs to distinguish between a static image and the essentially mobile character of thought. The moving images of film are a much more likely place to find the staging of thought processes—or their breakdown, as in Christopher Nolan's *Memento* and Michel Gondry's *Eternal Sunshine of the Spotless Mind.*

One series of artworks that evoke some of the qualities of thought are William Kentridge's 'drawings for projection', where the technique of repeatedly altering a charcoal drawing, photographing each stage, and putting the sequence together enables the artist to produce a shifting, self-transforming work of art that stages the processes involved in thinking. Ed Halter makes the connection with the fictional techniques I've referred to in a *Village Voice* review of a showing of nine of Kentridge's animated films: 'The evocative, allegorical narratives smudge and coalesce in a visual stream of consciousness punctuated by recurring motifs: mid-twentieth century office gear like rotary phones and adding machines, which morph into the forgotten black bodies of company workers'. And Kentridge himself has made the same literary association: 'Since James Joyce there has always been in modernist writing the notion of a stream of consciousness—floating connections rather than a programmed, clear progression. What I'm interested in is a kind of multi-layered highway of consciousness, where one lane has one thought but driving up behind and overtaking it is a completely different thought'.[11]

Thinking, then, can be staged in art. What about *knowing*? Badiou, in 'Que pense le poème?', argues that a poem presents thought without

Emmet Takes a Walk', for instance, represents the thought processes of a suburban everyman—a Leopold Bloom *de nos jours*—walking to a railway line to throw himself beneath a train, and although voices are used, mental associations and sequences are also signalled by purely musical quotations.

[11] Cameron, Christov-Bakargiev, and Coetzee, *William Kentridge*, 30.

knowledge (223), thought as act, and although this seems correct, it doesn't mean that poems—or art—have nothing to do with knowing. Do we use language, sounds, colours, images to know? Or to strive for knowledge? The answer is surely yes, but it's somewhat harder to find art works that exploit this fact in order to perform knowing, or trying to know, or failing to know. The prime modern literary example here would probably be *What Maisie Knew*, a novel in which Henry James limits the perspective on the events of the plot to the understanding of a growing girl and allows us to share with her her increasing knowledge of the world and its (mostly wicked) ways. So we get passages like the following:

> I so despair of courting her noiseless mental footsteps here that I must crudely give you my word for its being from this time forward a picture literally present to her.... I am not sure that Maisie had not even a dim discernment of the queer law of her own life that made her educate to that sort of proficiency those elders with whom she was concerned.... She judged that if her whole history, for Mrs. Wix, had been the successive stages of her knowledge, so the very climax of the concatenation would, in the same view, be the stage at which the knowledge should overflow. (208)

James's syntactic labyrinth, his almost obsessive self-qualification, succeeds in involving the reader in the gradually expanding realm of Maisie's knowledge. And we might note the narrator's 'I so despair of courting her mental footsteps' and 'I am not sure that Maisie had not even a dim discernment...': the language also enacts the question of knowing, or not being able to know, just how much Maisie knows.

With the other arts, we're again on trickier ground. It's hard to relate absolute music to the act of knowing, and programme music usually relies on a verbal narrative. (Opera, of course, is a different matter: *The Magic Flute*, *Parsifal*, *The Midsummer Marriage*—to go no further—could all be said to involve the audience in the activity of knowing as well as desiring to know.) In the visual arts, too, it might be difficult to find convincing examples of the staging of knowing. Could one say that in order to give oneself fully to Masaccio's representation of the expulsion of Adam and Eve one has to share in the enactment of a terrible knowing? Or that the great paintings of the Annunciation, such those by Fra Angelico or Jan van Eyck, invite the reader to participate in the offering and accepting of knowledge (knowledge that undoes that which Adam and Eve acquired)? I leave these questions open. Just let me note that there are plenty of visual representations that convey *knowledge,* just as there are verbal ones; but this capacity to provide information is something art shares with many other cultural products (the illustrated encyclopaedia, for instance).

To sum up: if we conceptualize the work of art as an act–event, rather than an object, and as coming into being in the performance of a viewer or reader, thinking and knowing can be seen to be central to many verbal or visual texts. Works of art, engaged with in a creative manner that is at once passive and active, can produce an intense experience of the mind's workings, an experience that is not quite the same as simply thinking and knowing. In such cases, however, the thinker or knower can often be understood as a character, even if only in the sense of the persona conjured up by a lyric poem; and so we're not likely to say that the work *itself* 'knows' or 'thinks'. Nor are the examples I've been discussing necessarily what we would call 'knowing' works of art: they don't convey that sense of secrets deliberately and overtly withheld that we associate with knowingness.

Literature's secrets

I want now to return to my earlier examples of knowing art in the sense of works that seem to guard a secret, to which we will never gain access, and which the artist is not in a position to divulge. If these works are only artworks in so far as they happen, over and over, as events, when performed by the responsive and creative reader or viewer, is there a way of redescribing these qualities without personifying the artefacts in question? I've argued that what we respond to can be described in terms of an interdependent trio of properties, *singularity, alterity* or *otherness,* and *invention*: that the work that comes into being in our performance of it strikes us with its difference from all other works, its singularity; by its challenge—great or small—to the norms and habits by which we comprehend the world, its otherness; and by a sense that its coming into being as we experience is an opening onto new possibilities of creativity in thinking, feeling, and knowing, its inventiveness. In responding fully to the work, therefore, we are changed—perhaps only momentarily, perhaps permanently—as we adjust our own frames of understanding, our own habits of feeling, our own ways of knowing to allow us to perceive what is before us in its singularity.

When a work seems to be possessed of its own capacity to think, to question, to harbour knowledge, so much so that we call on metaphors that supply it with a brain, a will, a consciousness, it's a sign of both its otherness and its inventiveness. It is other to the world of assumptions, connections, narratives, habits that the artist and the audience share; it operates according to a different set of norms and conventions. We can shift our own frames of understanding to find in it some meaning, but in that very shifting we experience the alterity of the work, and a feeling of its resistance remains. And that sense of a different world with different norms is also—if we're able to find in the work something we register cognitively and emotionally as art and not just as an ineffectual rearrangement or rejection of convention—a sense of inventiveness, of the creation of fresh possibilities for thinking, feeling, knowing.

Crucial to the work's power to open onto new worlds is its *form*; but form, even in the visual and plastic arts, must be understood as taking place in the viewer's or listener's experience, not as a static set of properties or relationships. Wood reminds us of the power of form, using his favoured personification: 'My hunch is that the villanelle'—he is discussing Elizabeth Bishop's 'One Art'—'may well know quite a lot about things like love, loss, repetition, design, language, memory, longing' (136). Putting this in terms that avoid personification, we might say that the form of the villanelle, as it unfolds its repetitions and variations, is an effective vehicle for the staging of love and loss, memory and longing.

Let us look again at the Barnett Newman painting. Standing in front of the painting, de Bolla finds himself prompted to ask 'What does this artwork know?' I shall attempt to rephrase the question without the personification: how, in confronting this work as it hangs on the wall of the Museum of Modern Art in New York, in scanning across its great width and height, in moving closer and further away, in absorbing its colours, in registering the relative sizes of the different bands created by the 'zips', in allowing remembered paintings and sights to be recalled, in testing the title against the painting's forms and colours, in bringing to mind the discourses that might bear upon it, how, in doing all this, do I find myself adjusting, for the moment at least, my familiar grip on the world? Does the scale of the work, along with its comparative simplicity, require recalibration of my sense of the relation between a painting and the human body? Does the title, *Vir Heroicus Sublimis*, encourage me to rethink notions of heroism and sublimity, and the tradition of heroic painting? Responding to the tripartite structure produced by the two more central zips, do I find myself reinterpreting the many religious triptychs I've seen, busy with figures, but here repeated as three blocks of sheer colour? Does the remarkable confidence of the work inspire a new acknowledgement of human energies?

I could go on; but the point is that a full engagement with a work of art involves such processes of thought and feeling; and if the work seems to know things that we don't, it's because it brings us to the limits of our own understanding, raising questions and making connections that have not hitherto been part of our mental—or physical—universe. Wilkinson's poem does not simply hug its secrets to its chest; it invites the reader to become intimate with the workings of words, with the mutual interference of different registers—of the lyric poet, the financial expert, the engraver, the health professional, and more—as they rub up against one another, with the capacity of syntax to branch in numerous directions. And in so doing it induces us to reassess the logical and referential functions of language. Were the poem simply nonsense, its power in this respect would be very limited: we would remain outside it, and note how easily words lose their coherence and referential power. It's the moving towards and away from sense that engages the reader, the invocation of a poetic tradition—the patterns of echoing sound, the play of monosyllables against polysyllables, the conventional four-line stanzas, the exploitation of line-breaks—and its undermining, the restless refusal to settle on a coherent image or assertion. The event of the poem is the reader's performance of these echoes and disjunctions. It's not so much a knowing poem as a poem that tests the relation between sentences of English and the activity of knowing.

Works of art don't 'know' or 'think', then, though they can involve the viewer, reader, or auditor in a performance of knowing or thinking. If they appear to have these human capacities, it's because in responding to their alterity, singularity, and inventiveness we find our cognitive faculties engaged and tested; our familiar maps prove inadequate, and we move into new and strange territory. When Wood says, as I noted earlier, 'What literature knows, what a novel or poem or play knows, is strictly, unfiguratively, what I now know that I didn't know before I read the text', I'm tempted to correct him: what makes us want to say that literature knows is the experience of challenge and discovery that makes us different after reading the text—though this difference is not simply a matter of knowledge acquired. I prefer Gourgouris's formulation: 'One gains a sense of knowing something other than the knowledge that comes from the words one has read, a knowledge that alters not only one's relation to those words but also the relation to one's sense of self as a "knowing subject"' (13). John Dewey, too, articulates the difference between the two kinds of relation to knowledge:

> The sense of increase of understanding, of a deepened intelligibility on the part of objects and nature and man, resulting from esthetic experience, has led philosophic theorists to treat art as a mode of knowledge.... But there is a great difference between the transformation of knowledge that

> is effected in imaginative and emotional vision.... In both production and enjoyed perception of works of art, knowledge is transformed; it becomes something more than knowledge because it is merged with non-intellectual elements to form an experience worth while as an experience. (*Art as Experience*, 288–90)

This capacity to reconfigure one's grip on the world and on oneself is a power that all art possesses: it's not limited to those works we might call 'knowing'. But there's a way in which we could consider such works as paradigmatic rather than exceptional. Derrida has linked the literary itself with the notion of the *secret*; to summarize briefly, the work of literature—and we can extend this observation to all works of art—retains its secret because it is a secret without hidden depths, without concealment.[12] A work of art states what it states, presents what it presents, no more, no less; and it refuses to say anything further, no matter how hard we press it. Discussing Baudelaire's short narrative 'Counterfeit Money', Derrida points out that we can never know whether the beggar in the story is given a genuine or a counterfeit coin by the narrator's friend:

> Baudelaire does not know, cannot know, and does not have to know, any more than we do, what can be going 'through the mind' of the friend, and whether the latter finally wanted to give true or counterfeit money, or even wanted to give anything at all.... As these fictional characters have no consistency, no depth beyond their literary phenomenon, the absolute inviolability of the secret they carry depends first of all on the essential superficiality of their phenomenality, on the *too-obvious* of that which they present to view. (152–3)

J. Hillis Miller underscores Derrida's point in an essay entitled 'Derrida's Topographies': 'There is nowhere to go behind the smilingly enigmatic words on the page, no authority to whom to appeal, not even to the author, in order to decide this question, even though the

[12] See 'Passions', 20–4 and 33–5 n. 14, and 'Literature in Secret: An Impossible Filiation', especially 156–7.

decision is essential to our reading of Baudelaire's text' (309).[13] Here's a new personification to add to the list: for Miller, it appears, a text can smile. It's the same quality of the work of art that leads commentators to use words like 'know' and 'think'; and what could be a better synonym for the adjective 'knowing' than 'smilingly enigmatic'?

If a work of art advertises its possession of secrets in a flagrant manner, we may want to call it 'knowing'; we may want to say it knows more than it is revealing. Derrida and Miller show how Baudelaire's text falls into this category. Another obvious example would be Forster's *Passage to India*, where no amount of detective work will ever reveal what exactly happened—or happens each time we read the novel—in the Marabar Caves. But *no* work of art reveals everything we might want to know, precisely because its secrets have no depth to which we could penetrate in pursuit of that knowledge—much as we're tempted to speculate on characters' inner lives and motives. I return to my point about the work of art as event and act: though the work may stage the search for knowledge, and the reader or viewer may feel thoroughly involved in this staged search, there is no knowledge as such waiting to be uncovered. Every work is a knowing work, every work smiles enigmatically, because there is no way we, or it, can satisfy the thirst for knowledge that it generates.

Of course there is another way of understanding my title: as raising the question: 'Is it possible to know works of art?' In a trivial sense, we can; we can recall colours, shapes, tones, phrases; some of us can recite poems and play sonatas. In a deeper sense, though, as I've been suggesting, the work of art *resists* knowing, refuses to convey knowledge and refuses to be known as a cognitive entity. As Derrida says in his brilliant essay on the poem as hedgehog, 'Che cos'è la poesia?', '[The poem's] event always interrupts or derails absolute knowledge' (235). Not only absolute knowledge, we might add, but everyday

[13] Besides the Mona Lisa, Miller is perhaps remembering, consciously or unconsciously, Arnold's sonnet entitled 'Shakespeare': 'Others abide our question. Thou art free. / We ask and ask—Thou smilest and art still, / Out-topping knowledge.'

knowledge as well. Wilkinson's poem and Kentridge's animations defy our attempts to know in an obvious way; but if I'm correct in my claim that every work of art has its being as an event, not an object, we can't be said to know novels, or symphonies, or paintings. We can re-experience a work with which we're already familiar with a sense of recognition, but when we do it's never quite the same as it was last time, and there is a sense in which every reading or hearing or viewing starts from scratch.

Knowing works of art—or works that we're inclined to call 'knowing', or to which we find ourselves tempted to ascribe the capacity to think or to know—may be relatively few; but every work of art, coming into being as a performed event, engages with our epistemological desires. We act out our knowing, our wanting to know, our wanting to know what it's like to know or not to know; or rather these things are acted out in the experience that is the event of the artwork. If we are different after this experience, it's not because we've added to our store of knowledge, it's because, in gaining access to the work's alterity, singularity, and inventiveness, we've discovered new ways of knowing (and perhaps new ways of not-knowing). Ascribing to works of art the capacity to think or to know (or to smile) is one way of registering metaphorically that process of discovery—or rather of continual discover*ing*, since we don't have any treasure to show when we stop listening or looking or reading. And that, of course, is why we go on doing it.

CHAPTER 9

Affect

Literary affect: McCarthy's *Blood Meridian*

I start this chapter with an example: a passage from Cormac McCarthy's 1985 novel *Blood Meridian, or, The Evening Redness in the West*. The band of mid-19th century American scalp-hunters on which the narrative focuses have camped on a Mexican plain, and the brewing animosity between two of them, both named Jackson, one of whom is white, the other black, is reaching its climax. The white Jackson is sitting with a companion, an ex-priest named Tobin, at a campfire, having earlier insulted his black namesake:

> Jackson sat with his legs crossed. One hand lay in his lap and the other was outstretched on his knee holding a slender black cigarillo. The nearest man to him was Tobin and when the black stepped out of the darkness bearing the bowieknife in both hands like some instrument of ceremony Tobin started to rise. The white man looked up drunkenly and the black stepped forward and with a single stroke swapt off his head.
>
> Two thick ropes of dark blood and two slender rose like snakes from the stump of his neck and arched hissing into the fire. The head rolled to the left and came to rest at the expriest's foot where it lay with eyes aghast. Tobin jerked his foot away and rose and stepped back. The fire steamed and blackened and a gray cloud of smoke rose and the columnar arches of blood slowly subsided until just the neck bubbled gently like a stew and then that too was stilled. He was sat as before save headless, drenched in blood, the cigarillo still between his fingers, leaning toward the dark and smoking grotto in the flames where his life had gone. (107)

Anyone reading or hearing this passage is bound to have a strong response, a response that one could not call simply cognitive. At the same time as apprehending the meanings of these sentences, the reader or hearer is highly likely to experience a feeling.[1] It's not easy to fix on an appropriate name for this feeling—repulsion? disgust? repugnance? horror? Something like this, no doubt, but also perhaps fascination? awe? astonishment? Perhaps even an urge to laugh, albeit uncomfortably. The fact that we can't name the feeling—or perhaps 'complex of feelings' would be a better expression—is significant: it reflects not only the paucity of our vocabulary in dealing with affective experience, itself a reflection of the poverty of our understanding of this domain of our lives, but also the capacity of literature to engage powerfully and subtly with the extraordinary complexity of emotional responses, in which the psychic and the somatic are so inextricably entwined.

McCarthy's account of this horrifying event produces not just some mental simulacrum of affect, but a real feeling that is quite likely to register on the skin or in the pit of the stomach. We may not be able to label the combination of emotions we feel, and of course readers will differ as to the precise composition of the mixture (just as they will differ as to the exact semantic implications of the passage), but there would probably be considerable similarity in the effect the words have on a variety of readers' minds and bodies. Anyone familiar with this and other novels by McCarthy will know that this passage is not untypical in its ability to evoke strong feelings, but however recognizable the style, the exact tenor of the emotional complex in this particular case—as in most of the other passages by McCarthy it might call to mind—is unique.

[1] It's perhaps necessary to emphasize the phrase 'at the same time', in view of the recent emergence of a body of theory, Deleuzian in origin, which regards affective response as pre-semantic and pre-subjective (see, for instance, Marco Abel's *Violent Affect*). Whatever affective response occurs before the reader apprehends the meaning of McCarthy's sentences (a response, presumably, to shapes on the page and the sounds they represent) is likely to be negligible in comparison to what happens once he grasps what is being conveyed—responds to it, in other words, *as language*.

The question I want to explore is the following: what is the relation between the feelings evoked by the work of literature, or more generally the representational work of art, and the feelings we experience directly in response to events and objects in our lives? I should make it clear at the outset that I'm not relying on any principled distinction among the terms 'emotion', 'feeling', and 'affect'. Many attempts have been made to distinguish them, but there is no agreement on how this should be done, and since each term functions differently in different grammatical contexts it's probably wise not to be too dogmatic about their meanings.[2] Ordinary usage would suggest that 'feeling' slides easily from the mental to the sensory and somatic, since one can feel just as legitimately with one's fingers as with one's mind, but suffers from the disadvantage of having no adjectival form. 'Emotion' is a narrower term, and carries with it the potential for more negative connotations, which are brought out when we accuse someone of 'emoting'; while 'affect' and 'affective', although they have a more scientific ring, have no verbal equivalent (since 'to affect' carries a much broader signification). It seems best to employ the terms with some sense of these connotations and limitations, but otherwise not to be too particular about the distinctions one might make among them.

In the tradition of analytic aesthetics, the question I've posed has prompted much discussion. Two recent engagements with the issue—which are also engagements with many of the earlier grapplings with it—are the chapter on 'Emotion and Imagination' in Berys Gaut's *Art,*

[2] For a discussion of attempts to distinguish between 'emotion' and 'affect', see Sianne Ngai's *Ugly Feelings*, 24–7. Ngai takes the difference to be one of degree—the latter being less structured and less fixed—but uses the terms, she says, 'more or less interchangeably' (27); while she employs the term 'feeling' to cover both. Rei Terada, in *Feeling in Theory*, 4–5, and Charles Altieri, in *The Particulars of Rapture*, 2 and 47–8, to take two other examples of the increasing interest in emotion, discriminate among the terms quite differently. The most strenuous attempt to keep 'affect' and 'emotion' separate is that of the Deleuzian affect theorists mentioned in the previous note, for whom the former is a pre-cognitive and pre-representational intensity and the latter the result of converting affect into a subjective experience. See, for example, chapter 1, 'The Autonomy of Affect', of Brian Massumi's *Parables for the Virtual*.

Emotion and Ethics (2007) and the section entitled 'Fiction and Emotion' in Peter Lamarque's 2009 overview *The Philosophy of Literature*.[3] Gaut's chapter is a defence of what he calls 'emotional realism': the view that the emotions one feels in response to fictional works are real, and that, contrary to the arguments of the so-called 'emotional irrealists', there is nothing irrational about feeling them. Lamarque is more even-handed in his survey, but he favours the view that emotional responses to fictional representations and to real events are indistinguishable; fiction, he argues, provokes vivid *imaginings*, and that it is to these that we respond emotionally just as we do to the things themselves.

Literary critics, by contrast, have usually emphasized the importance of distinguishing between the feelings provoked by works of literature and extra-literary feelings. Thus T. S. Eliot, discussing the place of emotion in art in 'Tradition and the Individual Talent' (1919), insists that 'The effect of a work of art upon the person who enjoys it is an experience different in kind from any experience not of art' (*Selected Essays*, 8). William K. Wimsatt and Monroe Beardsley begin a section of their Epilogue to *Literary Criticism: A Short History* with the question: 'What is the relation of the poetic or aesthetic emotion to the emotions of real or ordinary life?'; their answer is that 'poetry works some distinctive change in real-life emotions, and that is why we like it' (740). They elaborate as follows:

> It may be that the poetic way of dealing with these emotions will not be any kind of intensification, compounding, or magnification, or any direct assault upon the affections at all. Something indirect, mixed, reconciling, tensional, might well be the stratagem, the devious technique by which a poet indulged in all kinds of talk about love and anger and even in something like 'expressions' of these emotions, without aiming at their incitement or even uttering anything that essentially involves their incitement. (p. 741)

[3] Other works in this tradition include Matravers, *Art and Emotion*, and Robinson, *Deeper than Reason*. Stephen Davies surveys the immense literature on the topic in 'Responding Emotionally to Fictions', concluding that different emotions need to be treated differently.

Wimsatt and Beardsley here put their fingers on the problem I'm addressing in this chapter, their 'it may be' and (repeated) 'something' conveying the challenge it poses.

Affect and form

In tackling this question, I would like to go back to an argument about the role of emotion in literary responses I sketched very briefly in *The Singularity of Literature*. The context of that sketch was my contention, repeated in this book, that the artwork is not an object but an event, and that it comes into existence, again and again, always differently, each time a reader, listener or viewer experiences the arrangement of sounds or images as a work of art. This, of course, is not a new idea, but the consequences have not always been followed through by those who have embraced it, and in our discussions of works of art we frequently use a language that implies that they are self-sufficient objects, remaining unchanged from response to response.

What kind of event is the work of art? To reiterate my argument in very general terms, it's one that brings the other into the field of the same, in the experience of the reader, listener or viewer (and, multiplied—with variations—across multiple readers, listeners, and viewers, may be said to have a similar effect upon the culture more widely). That is, the complex of habits, associations, proclivities, norms, and so on that gives us, day by day, the world we live in encounters something, however slight, that can't be apprehended without some adjustment, some re-evaluation, some clarification. A responsible reading of a literary work, as I argued in chapter 2, is one that is open to this otherness, and that is willing to put settled modes of thinking and feeling at risk in engaging with it. One element in such a response therefore, however minimal, is a feeling of strangeness, surprise, or wonder—even when we encounter a work for the fifth or twenty-fifth time.[4] The work that is

[4] In *The Pleasure of the Text*, Roland Barthes refers to this quality of response by the untranslatable word *jouissance*, contrasting it with pleasure, a '*comfortable* practice of

completely familiar, that slots comfortably into, and confirms, pre-existing habits and expectations, is one that has lost, or has never had, the singular power of art. (It will be evident that I'm continuing to use 'art' and 'literature' with a normative implication; I make no apology for this, though of course there can be no objection to using the terms without such an implication, in, for instance, a sociological study of cultural practices.) There is always, therefore, an affective dimension to our responses to works of art, if we're responding to them as art, and not as something else (or not *only* as something else, since we're usually doing more than one thing at the same time when we read, view, or listen).

One element in the complex of feelings generated by the work of art is some kind of pleasure: this is a proposition that commands wide agreement, though it has provoked much discussion among philosophers worrying about the paradox presented by pleasurable experiences of negative emotions such as, classically, pity and fear. What I've called the introduction of the other into the field of the same is itself a potentially pleasurable experience, and if we examine the notion of otherness that is at stake here a little more fully it will become clear why this should be so. Simply to challenge existing norms does not guarantee the creation of an artwork; it's easy enough to write a poem that fails to observe conventions of grammar or meaning, or that affronts our moral sense, or that falsifies history in a way that would shock its readers' sensibilities. If *any* kind of otherness were a guarantee of artistic creativity, works of art would be two a penny, and of course there are many artefacts undeserving of the name 'art'—as I'm using the term—produced on just this principle. The otherness that characterizes the work of art has to have a particular relation both to the culture into which it is being introduced and to the culture within

reading' appropriate to the text that does not break with the culture from which it comes (14). See also the arguments of Philip Fisher in *Wonder, the Rainbow, and the Aesthetics of Rare Experiences*. These authors are less inclined than I am to find a grain of wonder in *any* experience of art as art.

which it is being received. One way of putting this is that the work is not other merely in the sense of being different, but it is other because the dominant culture within which it is produced and received *depends* on its exclusion. The artist is someone who has the ability to discern what is occluded, silenced, marginalized by prevailing ways of thinking and feeling, where it's possible to find tensions and fault-lines in what is treated as merely given, and at what cost the apparent coherence and stability of the cultural fabric, and the social, economic and political system out of which it arises, are maintained. The reader, likewise, is given the opportunity of glimpsing possibilities foreclosed by the frameworks that govern daily living. This experience of being given the capacity to see, if only momentarily, beyond the blinkers we normally wear (without, of course, our being aware of them) is an exhilarating one, even if it can involve discomfort at the same time.[5]

Art is not the only cultural practice which breaches the boundaries of the familiar, however, and we need to press harder on the question of its distinctiveness if we're to understand how it engages with our capacities for feeling. If the work of art is an event, it's an event that occurs in a medium (or more than one medium), and part of the pleasure we experience as participants in the event is a pleasure in the medium itself as it reveals some of its powers and possibilities. In the case of language, those powers are manifold: language can hurt, encourage, teach, dismay, enliven, reveal, obscure—the list could go on almost indefinitely, and includes of course both cognitive and

[5] There are, of course, other ways in which the work of art can arouse emotions directly besides producing pleasure through the expanding of mental horizons: I can find myself experiencing anger at the excessive length of a novel, or disappointment at the quality of a poetic line, or regret that a superb play is about to end—but responses of this kind are equally possible when I'm reading a work of history or journalism. Narrative form itself (whether fictional or nonfictional) can provoke emotion: Meir Steinberg usefully identifies three emotions aroused by the three possible relations between *histoire* and *récit*—suspense, curiosity and surprise (see Emma Kafalenos, 'Emotions Induced by Narratives'). Non-programmatic music also relies on formal properties to induce emotions in a direct manner: suspense, tension, surprise, satisfaction all play their part. Rhythm in poetry may work in a similar way.

affective capacities. A literary work shows off the power of the language to do some of these things, but—and this is the important, distinctive point—*without actually doing them.*[6] Or, to be more precise, to the extent that the language of the work does actually hurt or encourage or teach it is not behaving as a work of literature. As literature, it *performs* hurting, encouraging, teaching, and so on, relying on the effectiveness of the *as if* to provide an experience that replicates modes of thinking and feeling in the non-literary domain.[7]

Here we come back to the issue of the multifacetedness of our responses to art. I can read a novel or watch a play and be affected by it in a number of different ways at once. I can glean information from it—about how the other half lives, about the battles of Napoleonic Europe, about unusual sexual practices. I can absorb a moral or theological lesson from it—about how crime doesn't pay, or men are not to be trusted, or God is merciful. Most importantly for the subject of this chapter, I can be disturbed, elated, or terrified by the mere *content* of the artwork—or, to follow Lamarque's argument, by my imagining of its content—just as I can by the content of a historical account or a documentary photograph. But in none of these responses am I treating the work of art *as art.* Something else has to happen—and I do mean *happen*—for this to be the case.

The way the artwork makes this 'something else' happen is through its handling of what we inadequately call *form.*[8] Or to put it differently,

[6] The way Wimsatt and Beardsley convey this insight, in the passage cited above, is that poets do not aim to *incite* the emotions 'expressed'—they rightly put this word in quotation marks—in their work.

[7] For a valuable exploration of the significance of the 'as if' in emotional responses to literature, see Adam Piette, 'Beckett, Affect and the Face'.

[8] A rare example of a discussion of the emotions produced by artworks that recognizes the importance of form is Robinson's *Deeper than Reason.* However, Robinson attributes to form the somewhat limited role of enabling the reader, viewer or listener to cope with threatening material, thus producing pleasure (pp. 195–228). Susanne Langer's once influential theory of the aesthetic articulation of the 'morphology' of feelings (in *Philosophy in a New Key* and *Feeling and Form*) has not worn well. Wimsatt and Beardsley, in the Epilogue from which I quoted earlier, after a discussion of form, observe, 'A close internal relation exists of course between this kind of "form"

it's in responding to the handling of form that the reader of a literary work brings it into being as literature. It's the writer's capacity to *shape* language in a temporal medium that endows it with pleasure-giving power. Any significant feature of language can be shaped in this way, from the sounds of individual phonemes to the collocation of words to the flow of paragraphs and the structuring of chapters or whole novels. And it's through formed language that we're invited to participate in its emotion-arousing capacities; this means we feel the emotions, but always as performances of language's powers.[9] (In a similar way, we understand the events in a novel *as if* they were events in the world we live in.) If art produced the emotions it enacts directly, in a completely unmediated manner, we would be very tentative about exposing ourselves to it. We certainly wouldn't queue to see *King Lear* or let our children read *The Lord of the Rings*. To explore these matters further, let us return to our example from McCarthy.

I invite the reader to try to imagine being present at the scene described in the passage. It's impossible to do so, of course, since the images you conjure up are fictions themselves, unless you have led a very unusual life. But even the effort to conjure up a real event of this nature is enough, I think, to show that although there is a clear connection between the feelings aroused by the passage and the feelings that might be aroused if we were actually sitting by that campfire, there is a crucial difference. A viewer of the scene who was not already hardened by similar sights would be likely to be psychically damaged for life: it would be a traumatic experience to which the body would react violently and by which the mind would probably be overwhelmed.

and the tension of values and emotions' (*Literary Criticism*, 748–9). I discuss the importance of form in *The Singularity of Literature*, 107–21.

[9] This pleasurable experience of the power of language is an aspect of what Jakobson identifies as marking the poetic function of language; he terms it the 'set (*Einstellung*) toward the MESSAGE as such' ('Closing Statement', 356).

Now imagine a historian recounting the scene, as a real event for which there is reliable documentation:

> The quarrel came to a head one night around the campfire when the black man used his knife to decapitate the white man. For some time the severed neck bled profusely into the fire, while the head came to rest at the feet of one of the men, causing him to jump up.

This description evokes some of the feelings I mentioned as probable responses to the McCarthy passage: discomfort, repugnance, perhaps a bodily twitch at the represented scene. What we're responding to is almost entirely the represented content of the sentences, which it's the job of the historian to put before us as lucidly and accurately as possible. What we *don't* get is the complex of emotions that the literary passage gives us—the extraordinary combination of horror and fascination, repulsion and attraction, dismay and pleasure. It's clear that the unique affective power of the passage is not simply the product of the events being represented.

What would it be like to read a more formulaic novelist than McCarthy dealing with the same scene? Let us just take the bleeding neck: we might find ourselves encountering something like this:

> From the gory tubes of the severed neck fountains of crimson blood gushed into the air, falling back into the fire and causing it to hiss and sputter and spew out acrid grey smoke. The man's head rolled horribly on the ground for several feet before coming to rest next to Tobin's foot, its sightless eyes staring into vacancy, making him jump abruptly to his feet in a frenzy of horror and dismay.

The content of the scene is virtually the same, and we may respond to this represented content as we do in reading the historian's account—or we may not, since the bare account of the facts may carry more weight than this overwritten version, especially if we believe in the former case that we're reading a description of a real event. My invented literary passage is in fictional mode, which rids it of its documentary power, but, because of its reliance on cliché and awkward sentence structures, it does not make the most of its freedom to invent. There's not a great deal of pleasure to be had, as we don't sense the power of language through the flaccid and uninventive phrasing.

Returning now to McCarthy's passage, let us look at the beginning of the second paragraph, remembering that a work of literature is something we experience temporally as an event. The claim I'm making is that McCarthy's management of the formal properties of language and of narrative adds to and complicates the direct emotional effect of the represented scene, and that the pleasure of the reader arises from an apprehension—which need not be conscious, though I'm about to force it into consciousness—of that controlled performance, whereby the power of language to elicit emotion, stimulate the imagination, and provoke thought is communicated. (As before, I will use the first person, offering my own responses in the hope that they will be shared by many other readers.)

> Two thick ropes of dark blood and two slender rose like snakes from the stump of his neck and arched hissing into the fire.

'Two thick ropes . . .': my first response is primarily one of puzzlement: I've just read a minimally expressive account of a head being sliced off—the archaic word 'swapt' has struck me by its swiftness and efficiency—and I can't guess why I'm now being told of ropes.

'of dark blood . . .': now the horror of the image hits home as I'm compelled to reinterpret the beginning of the phrase metaphorically. I have to visualize blood issuing from the arteries of the severed neck in such a powerful stream that it keeps its circumference as it rises, like water from a fully open hosepipe. The scene itself, as I imagine it, provokes a powerful affective response, but this is coloured by an acknowledgement (unconscious, in all probability) of the unusualness and precision of the word 'ropes'—a metaphor that now seems so exact that no other word would do. 'Dark', an unexpected adjective, adds to this precision, and echoes 'thick' both in sound and in the suggestion of the repellent quality of the blood. If I shudder at the scene, I also admire the means whereby it is presented to me.

'and two slender...': after the horror a surprising codicil: 'slender' comes from a different aesthetic register, one I associate with attractive rather than repulsive objects, though it hardly palliates the gruesomeness. Again, it's shockingly precise: not thin, or narrow, but slender; and not a medley of arterial spouts but two and two. And the slightly mannered phrasing—we would normally expect a noun after this adjective—adds to the feeling of a chilling detachment, almost an aestheticization, on the part of the narrator. My emotional response is coloured by the verbal event of representation itself.

'rose...': now I get a shocking hint of beauty, very different from the effect of alternatives I can imagine such as 'shot' or 'spurted' or 'jetted': this is language we would expect to describe, say, an attractive garden fountain. Being compelled to see beauty in this hideous spectacle adds to my queasiness, perhaps, but also to my sense that what are being explored are realms of emotion that are usually blocked off.

'like snakes...': a metaphor within a metaphor—the jets of blood are like ropes which are like snakes. As with all the words I'm looking at, this metaphor contributes to the content of the representation, helping me to bring the scene vividly to mind, but its almost excessive literariness continues that feeling of a normally forbidden combination of the aesthetically pleasing and the repellent. It seems at once over-the-top and horribly vivid.

'from the stump of his neck...': if I remained in doubt about these ropes of blood I'm now told, in brutal terms, of their origin. The hint of the aesthetic is gone from the vocabulary, though the echoing monosyllables *thick, dark, snakes*, with *neck* now added, keep alive a subliminal awareness of language as sound; the sentence exploits the potential association, for speakers of English, of the phoneme /k/, and even the shape of the letter *k*, with qualities of harshness.

'and arched hissing into the fire': 'arched' is another precise word (again, something the water in a pretty fountain might do), as is the onomatopoeic 'hissing' (with 'slender', one of only two words of more than one syllable in the sentence). What was already a nightmarish spectacle is made worse by the sound of the blood striking the fire: but again it's important to emphasize that my response is not just to the imagined sound, but to the means whereby it is given to me in words.

I could go on, at great length, to discuss the rest of the paragraph, but I hope the point is clear: this is language displaying its power to horrify, to create acutely felt physical impressions, to blend the aesthetic with the cruelly factual, and doing so by drawing on a range of resources, including diction, metaphor, syntactic shaping, and sound. We take pleasure in that demonstration, and experience something like awe that words, so casual a part of our quotidian experience, can have this capability. There is admiration, too, for the skill of the author, mixed in with our other emotions. If we knew that McCarthy was describing an event that really happened—in other words that he was writing, in part, as a historian (as, indeed, for much of *Blood Meridian* he is, using in particular the recollections of Samuel Chamberlain)—we would still respond to this passage as literary writing. (As I've noted before, there's no reason why something labelled 'history' shouldn't be literary as well, operating as it does through verbal representation, though there's bound to be some tension between the two distinct purposes of the two genres.) There would, however, be some difference in the mixture of emotions in our response, a qualm at the sheer fact of the decapitation.[10]

To clarify the difference that is at stake here, we may imagine a theatrical performance of this scene. A crude representation of the

[10] Dewey gives a clear account of this difference from the point of view of the artist's creation:

> The emotion that was finally wrought out by Tennyson in the composition of 'In Memoriam' was not identical with the emotion of grief that manifests itself in weeping and a downcast frame: the first is an act of expression, the second of discharge. Yet the continuity of the two emotions, the fact that the esthetic emotion is native emotion transformed through the objective material to which it has committed its development and consummation, is evident. (*Art as Experience* 78–9)

decapitation would merely be laughable, providing no pleasure in the performance as art. A representation that was so convincing that for a few moments the audience thought there had been some terrible mistake, and they were witnessing a real decapitation, would, on the other hand, produce sheer horror; the content, in other words, would dominate, and the mode of presentation would be irrelevant. But a skilful production conveying the dreadfulness of the action while making no attempt to hide the artifice of the representation could allow the audience to experience strong emotions in a pleasurably performative mode.[11]

Photography and film raise special issues, since what we see is a material record of some reality (leaving aside all the possibilities of post-shot manipulation, now multiplied a thousandfold with the introduction of digital imaging). The direct impact of the content, what the camera saw, is not itself an aspect of the work's art; the way that content is framed, composed, lit, and so on, is—except, of course, to the degree that the matter recorded is itself a product of art (scriptwriting, make-up, acting, etc.). Responding to a still photograph as a work of art is an event whereby we take in its relevant qualities in a temporal experience, while the temporality of a film is overlaid by the viewer's temporality in enjoying the various ingredients of its art. Because of our willingness to credit photographic images as representations of reality, a scene such as that described by McCarthy would be merely gruesome in a film unless it evinced artistic skill equivalent to that of the author's prose—some of the films of Quentin Tarantino and Michael Haneke come to mind. And if we believed that the decapitation had actually occurred in the shooting, any artistic

[11] The discussion of realism and illusion is, of course, at least as old as Pliny the Elder's story of the contest between the painters Zeuxis and Parrhasius (the former's painted grapes deceiving the birds; the latter's painted curtains deceiving Zeuxis himself). Coleridge's 'willing suspension of disbelief' emphasizes the difference between our responses to the real and to realism. Those performers who injure their own bodies in the course of a performance push at, or beyond, the limits of artistic experience.

qualities would be overwhelmed by the content.[12] Similarly, the debate about the depiction of genital violence in Lars von Trier's film *Antichrist* (2009) would be even more intense if audiences believed that Charlotte Gainsbourg had actually cut off her clitoris with a pair of scissors—though the realism of the scene is such that viewers may have to consciously reassure themselves that it was staged for the camera.

Pleasure in reading

I've claimed that the pleasure produced by an engagement with the successful work of art is, in part at least, a pleasure we feel as our familiar horizons open up to an otherness that we, as products of our culture, had excluded from consciousness. Does this happen in our sample of McCarthy's writing? To answer this question, we need to ask what strikes us as inventive about it. What does it succeed in articulating that we might have thought inarticulable?

The answer doesn't have to involve a massive challenge to our expectations; it can be the familiar presented in a slightly unfamiliar light, the ordinary in an exceptional context. And the expectations challenged can be formal—the way we assume sentences should be shaped or narratives rehearsed—or can range much more widely across any of our habitual modes of response to people, objects and events. McCarthy's choices of diction, use of metaphor, and management of syntax all contribute, as we've seen, to the affective power of the passage, as does the precision of his account of physical details. Through these means, the event of the passage, as we perform it,

[12] J. M. Coetzee points out that, in John Huston's film *The Misfits* (1961), the horses fighting with the men attempting to tame them were real horses experiencing real pain, and implies that we can't respond to these scenes as we usually do to the story-telling of film (*Inner Workings*, 226–7). The way in which our knowledge of the fictionality of what we're watching renders it acceptable is perhaps related to Kant's assertion that we can experience the dynamical sublime only if we're in a position of safety (*Critique of Judgment*, 120).

produces an acknowledgement—involving feelings of repulsion and horror—of the sheer substantiality of the human body and of its consequent vulnerability to physical violence. Our works of art, and our culture more generally, depend on our *not* regarding the body in this light, on a degree of derealization of the perpetual goings-on inside our skins that, we're made to feel by the passage, can be exposed with alarming ease. This is not to say that the book advocates an emphasis on the materiality of the body in our approach to other people; just that it enables us to apprehend the dimension that has to remain out of sight if we're to pursue our normal paths through life—and that there is some value in achieving this apprehension. The strange mixture of beauty and gruesomeness in the sentence we looked at, and our equally unusual mixture of emotions in response, testify to the complexity of this mode of apprehension. Other works of art may arouse in the reader or viewer something like this emotional response, but each is characterized by a singular purchase on the subject, and evokes a singular mix of emotions.

We've identified several ways in which feelings of pleasure are implicated in the experience of the artwork as event: delight in the revelation of the power of the medium produced by the skilful handling of form; admiration for the creator; enjoyment of the opening up of hitherto occluded ways of thinking and feeling. The emotions aroused by the images depicted are not directly experienced as the reality they represent would be, but are staged and controlled by the subtle arrangements of language. For a contrast to the gruesomeness of the passage by McCarthy, we can look briefly at a poem which operates in a very different emotional landscape. It's one of Thomas Hardy's extraordinary 'Poems of 1912–13', written after the death of his wife:

At Castle Boterel

As I drive to the junction of lane and highway,
  And the drizzle bedrenches the waggonette,
I look behind at the fading byway,
  And see on its slope, now glistening wet,
    Distinctly yet

Myself and a girlish form benighted
  In dry March weather. We climb the road
Beside a chaise. We had just alighted
  To ease the sturdy pony's load
    When he sighed and slowed.

What we did as we climbed, and what we talked of
  Matters not much, nor to what it led,—
Something that life will not be balked of
  Without rude reason till hope is dead,
    And feeling fled.

It filled but a minute. But was there ever
  A time of such quality, since or before,
In that hill's story? To one mind never,
  Though it has been climbed, foot-swift, foot-sore,
    By thousands more.

Primaeval rocks form the road's steep border,
  And much have they faced there, first and last,
Of the transitory in Earth's long order;
  But what they record in colour and cast
    Is—that we two passed.

And to me, though Time's unflinching rigour,
  In mindless rote, has ruled from sight
The substance now, one phantom figure
  Remains on the slope, as when that night
    Saw us alight.

I look and see it there, shrinking, shrinking,
  I look back at it amid the rain
For the very last time; for my sand is sinking,
  And I shall traverse old love's domain
    Never again.

It's much harder to say with this poem what alterity it engages with, what exactly its demand for hospitality to the other consists in. And this is because its inventiveness and singularity are in large part a matter of emotion, and we lack, as I've suggested, a vocabulary of sufficient refinement and richness to talk properly about emotional subtleties. Once again, what the writing does with feeling can't be separated from what it does with meaning or with form (and these two aren't separate, either). The telescoping of time and place, so that the speaker looks back through the drizzle and sees himself in the same place at an earlier point of his life, contributes to the paradoxical combination—at least until the last stanza—of a sense of loss with a sense of restitution. In another paradox, the emphasis on the triviality of the remembered occasion united with a sense of its momentousness in the speaker's life contributes to the delicately complicated emotion. And the claim that the personal significance of the moment can be measured against the aeons of terrestrial history is at once boldly confident and ironically accepting of human littleness.

An important part of the poem's inventiveness is constituted by the fusion of these opposed emotions, though once again it's important to note that they are not emotions we feel directly as readers, but emotions enacted in the language of the poem. Since we have a first-person speaker himself reporting on an event that has evoked a strong and complex emotional response, we're exposed to two sets of feelings—those of the speaker, and those the speaker elicits in the imagined listener, whose representative we are. (In the McCarthy example, the emotions *within* the fictional scene are not described, and we have to intuit them—for instance, from Tobin's jerking his foot away.) Hardy's use of the short final line—a two-beat coda after the familiar sequence of four four-beat lines—is rhythmically speaking an afterthought, not necessary to the self-sufficient pattern it succeeds.[13] Its rhyme, too, linking it with the second and fourth lines, gives it something of the quality of an echo. And in the first four stanzas, though it contributes a certain plangency to the movement of the poem, it doesn't add anything of immense important thematically to the four lines before it. In the fifth stanza, however, this little addendum announces the climactic claim of the poem: that the fact of the two lovers walking up this hill next to their chaise is the

[13] Dennis Taylor points out that this stanza form is a descendent of the sapphic stanza, with its final adonic line, a form that Hardy continuously experimented with throughout his career (*Hardy's Metres and Victorian Prosody*, 258–66).

most significant event to have taken place in the millennia of the hill's existence. The claim is bold and brave, but the rhythm of the line, and its relation to what has gone before, is anything but bold, as if that confidence is already ebbing. The final stanza again uses the final short line to reach a climax, but this time to tell us only of loss, grief, and exhaustion.

What analytic aesthetics, in its strenuous engagement with the logic of emotional response, fails to do justice to, I believe, is the multiplicity and variety of art's affective dimension, and in doing so, it fails to pay attention to what is distinctive about the way art deals with emotion. When we read Hardy's poem, we no doubt have an emotional response to the scene depicted—an oldish man imagining he sees the ghost of his dead wife and his younger self through the drizzle on a country road—but in this case this response is not a major ingredient in the feelings we participate in as we read it. It's the speaker's—and behind the speaker, the author's—*words* that arouse, modify, and finally extinguish emotion, and we enjoy participating in their doing so, even as we taste, for a moment, the pain of the bereaved husband. The issue of fiction versus non-fiction, so prominent in those philosophical discussions, is something of a red herring: whether Hardy really had this experience, and is reporting it to us, or whether he imagined the whole thing sitting cosily in his study, or whether—most likely—something that happened provided the germ for the emergence of a poem, which took a life of its own in the writing, is irrelevant to our enjoyment of the affective power of the poem.

* * *

Clearly, the passages I've looked at can't stand for all the manifold works of art that evoke an emotional response; the different arts have different resources and conventions by means of which to create their effects, and within the literary field alone there are numerous possible ways of engaging with readerly affect. *Blood Meridian* does not, for instance, present the reader with a fictional narrator whose emotional responses to the events being related form part of the affective dimension of the work; if that were the case, there would be the added complexity of an empathetic engagement with that narrator. The novel thus usefully demonstrates the inadequacy of expressive theories of emotion in art, largely Romantic in origin but remarkably persistent today. For instance, Robinson, in *Deeper than Reason*, offers an updated version of the Romantic theory, in which it is the artwork rather than the artist that expresses emotion; the reader, viewer, or listener understands the work as the expression of a persona to whose emotions she responds in an emotionally imitative manner.[14] However, the reader's affective response to the passage from *Blood Meridian* under discussion is not primarily a response to the intuited emotions of the narrator or implied author; if this does constitute an ingredient of the complex affectivity of the passage, it's not in mimicking that persona's emotional stance but in reacting against its apparent detachment in the face of such horror.

More often, however, a representational work of art does imply an emotional response to the people, events or objects represented, and is usually taken as an invitation to share that response. A lyric poem would be an obvious example, and most visually and aurally mimetic works—painting, sculpture, music, film—operate by suggesting an affective attitude to what is depicted, though usually this is a quality that is very hard to put into words. But in all these cases, it's the artist's manipulation of the resources of the medium (and this includes both material resources and the habits and expectations of those engaging with the work) that creates the impression of an affective response, and it's that artful manipulation that produces for the reader, listener or viewer what I'm calling a performed emotion.

Blood Meridian is also unusual in being a novel in which empathy with the characters plays very little part; only the unnamed boy, 'the kid', at the centre of the narrative offers the possibility of identificatory involvement, and that involvement is constantly thwarted by the

[14] See, especially, chapter 9, 'A New Romantic Theory of Expression'.

absence of interiority in the descriptions of what he chooses to do and what he witnesses. In most novels, the reader expects a degree of emotional involvement with many characters, as well as emotional responses to their actions, and these two kinds of affective engagement can reinforce or conflict with one another. To take one example of the latter possibility, when the narrator of Aravind Adiga's *The White Tiger* (2008) describes how he brutally murdered his employer, the reader is likely to register both the justifiable anger motivating the young man and revulsion at his act (283–5). And once again, both arise from the skilful handling of language and of the conventions of the novel, and thus have a pleasurable dimension; and these performed emotions are different from the real anger that Adiga's account of poverty and wealth in present-day India may arouse (as a direct response to what is represented in the novel) and the horror that the mere content of the brutal murder provokes.

The emotions experienced by the reader of a work of literature are real; of this there can surely be no doubt. That they are not identical with the emotions that would be felt as a result of direct exposure to the people and events portrayed is also, it seems to me, unquestionable. In arguing that the difference can be explained by regarding the reader's affective responses as performances of the emotions in question, I'm not suggesting that there is a conscious distancing at work: rather, it's a matter of the feelings being coloured by an awareness that they are being prompted by art—and this is a matter not primarily of fiction but of form. It's not enough to say that we respond as we do to McCarthy's depiction of a horrifying event because we know it is fiction; it's McCarthy's superb control of his medium that makes the important difference. We read the novel, that is, as an authored work, and part of the enjoyment that it offers, even in its most macabre passages, lies in the relishing of that authorial achievement. And this is an enjoyment we can experience over and over again, precisely because it's not a response to an object but to an event, or rather the response *is* the event, an event that changes with us as we change.

CHAPTER 10

Hospitality

An inescapably ethical term that links the creative, open kind of literary reading I've been discussing throughout this book with the decisions and actions of the world outside the arts is *hospitality*. Understood in its widest sense, hospitality—which is always hospitality to the other—names an ethical responsibility operative in a huge variety of fields. As Derrida—whose multiple engagements with the topic will be the main substance of the chapter—puts it: '...the questions at once timeless, archaic, modern, current, and future that the single word "hospitality" magnetizes—the historical, ethical, juridical, political, and economic questions of hospitality' (Derrida, 'Hostipitality' 2000, 3).[1] To Derrida's list of questions I would add questions of art and, more specifically for my concern in this study, literature.

The double law of hospitality

When Odysseus emerges naked from the bushes on the shore of the Phaeacian island, the princess Nausicaa doesn't take to her heels like the other girls but instead offers him clothing and, as she says, 'anything else a hard-pressed suppliant deserves from those he meets'. Her father, Alcinous, is no less generous, treating Odysseus royally before he has the slightest inkling of who the stranger is. The guest's story of his wanderings after the fall of Troy, however, includes an

[1] There are two published lectures by Derrida called 'Hostipitality', a seminar published in *Acts of Religion* (ed. Anidjar) and a lecture he gave in Istanbul in 1997, which repeats some of the material from his seminars, published in translation in *Angelaki*. I'll refer to the second as 'Hostipitality' 2000.

episode that reveals a very different way of responding to an unexpected visit: Polyphemus the Cyclops, having discovered Odysseus and some of his men in his cave, promptly polishes off two of them for his supper, and downs another two for breakfast. Only through Odysseus's ingenuity and skill do the others escape. As these contrasting accounts in the *Odyssey* suggest, hospitality has been a significant issue in considerations of interpersonal and intercultural ethics from the beginnings of Western civilization.[2]

How, then, has this ancient notion of hospitality come to be an important concept today? How is it that what John Caputo calls a 'mom-and-apple-pie word'[3] has become a significant node in considerations of both ethical behaviour and even wider domains of human and social action? Our starting point is Emmanuel Levinas, whose philosophy has been so influential on contemporary ethical thought within the continental tradition. Ethics, for Levinas, arises from the encounter between a subject and another being—for Levinas, always a human being. In the paradigmatic ethical event, the other being (or just the Other, usually with a capital letter) demands my attention and care through the sheer fact of his presence before me, and my readiness to attend to the Other's needs, at whatever cost to myself, is, for Levinas, the truly ethical response. This demand of the Other, stemming not from any exercise of power but, on the contrary, from his powerlessness and nakedness, is summed up in Levinas's term *face*—not to be understood as the empirical bodily feature but as the felt force of another's singular presence. *Hospitality* is one possible name for this ethical response to the Other: I open my door to her, no matter how foreign or threatening she seems, I tend to her wants, I take responsibility for her well-being. (A more accurate usage would

[2] See Michael Naas's discussion of these episodes in *Taking on the Tradition*, 155–9, in a lucid chapter on hospitality in Derrida's work, 154–69. See also chapter 1 of Naas's *Derrida from Now On*.

[3] *Deconstruction in a Nutshell*, 109.

be 'it' rather than a personal pronoun, since to categorize the Other as one or other gender is already to limit my responsiveness.)

Nausicaa, faced with a naked, salt-streaked man emerging suddenly from the bushes, is exemplary in offering him succour instead of decamping. Homer tells us that it was Athene who drove fear from her body, and indeed there seems to be something divine in this demonstration of instinctive hospitality towards the alarming stranger. (By the time he encounters Alcinous, Odysseus has been smartened up, again with Athene's aid, so the ruler's generous response to his sudden appearance is perhaps less surprising.) My choice of an epic poem for an illustration of hospitality is somewhat misleading, however: for Levinas, ethical encounters occur constantly, not just in extreme situations. Letting someone go through a doorway before you can be an ethical act.[4]

Levinas does not, in fact, use the term 'hospitality' very often. In his two most important books, *Totality and Infinity* (1961) and *Otherwise than Being* (1974), the word comes up only occasionally, for instance in the discussion of the home that is 'open to the Other' (*Totality and Infinity*, 172–3) or in a description of the subject alienated by the guest who is entrusted to it: 'Hospitality, the one-for-the-other in the ego' (*Otherwise than Being*, 79).[5] Nevertheless, when Derrida, the thinker to whom, above all, we owe the current centrality of this term, calls *Totality and Infinity* 'an immense treatise *on hospitality*' (*Adieu*, 21), it's hard to disagree. Derrida points out that although the word *hospitality* itself is rare in Levinas, the word *welcome* (*l'acceuil*) is everywhere; and Derrida entitles the lecture given a year after Levinas's death in 1995, and

[4] Michael Rosen, in *Dignity*, relates a story about Kant that provides another apt illustration: 'It was nine days before his death and the great man was old and desperately weak. Nevertheless, he refused to sit down before a guest (his doctor) had first taken a seat. When he was finally persuaded to do so, he said: 'Das Gefühl der Humanität hat mich noch nicht verlassen' (The feeling of humanity has not yet left me).

[5] The original reads: 'une incessante aliénation du moi...par l'hôte qui lui est confié—l'hospitalité' (*Autrement qu'être*, 126). Alphonso Lingis's translation, replacing the dash with a full stop, loses the connection between 'hôte' and 'hospitalité'.

from which I've just quoted, 'A Word of Welcome'—or, rather, 'Le mot d'accueil', which is also 'the word *welcome*'.

Derrida cites, from *Totality and Infinity*, one of the uncommon instances of Levinas's use of 'hospitality', occurring in one of the latter's many accounts of the relation of self to Other. In the course of a discussion of intentionality, Levinas states: 'It is attention to speech or welcome of the face, hospitality and not thematization' (22). Derrida continues:

> The word 'hospitality' here translates, brings to the fore, re-produces the two words preceding it, 'attention' and 'welcome'. An internal paraphrase, a sort of periphrasis, a series of metonymies that bespeak hospitality, the face, welcome: tending toward the other, attentive intention, intentional attention, *yes* to the other. Intentionality, attention to speech, welcome of the face, hospitality—all these are the same, but the same as the welcoming of the other, there where the other withdraws from the theme. (22–3)

We'll come back to the importance for Derrida of the opposition between hospitality and thematization; for the moment, I just want to note this very basic understanding of hospitality as the *welcoming of the singular other as an ethical act*, an understanding shared by Levinas and Derrida.

Derrida absorbed a great deal of Levinas's thinking, though he was also one of Levinas's most acute critics.[6] But his admiration for Levinas seems to have grown significantly as the years passed, and by the time of 'A Word of Welcome', in the aftermath of the older man's death, the differences between them emerge not so much in outright critique as in a subtle reworking of Levinas's arguments.[7] Thus Derrida can say, having noted that his language is no longer quite that of Levinas: 'Hospitality is infinite or it is not at all; it is granted upon the welcoming of the idea of infinity, and thus of the

[6] One of the earliest essays Derrida published, 'Violence and Metaphysics', is a lengthy study of Levinas that expresses both strong admiration and sharp disagreement, and in a 1980 essay, 'At This Very Moment in This Work Here I Am', he takes issue with Levinas's mode of argumentation and his privileging of the masculine.

[7] I discuss Derrida's reworking of Levinas's arguments in 'Posthumous Infidelity: Derrida, Levinas and the Third', chapter 7 of *Reading and Responsibility*.

unconditional, and it is on the basis of its opening that one can say, as Levinas will a bit further on, that "ethics is not a branch of philosophy, but first philosophy"' (48). I don't think Levinas would have disagreed with this, but its emphasis is on those aspects of hospitality that are particularly important for Derrida. Hospitality is an opening to the infinite, the unconditional, and this is what makes it prior to any philosophical considerations. Although at this point in his thinking Derrida has embraced the word 'ethics', having at an earlier period of his career been suspicious of it, he is pushing ethics away from the arena of personal responsibility to a more far-reaching consideration of the very foundation of ethics, what he elsewhere calls 'the non-ethical opening of ethics'. And the word *hospitality* occurs frequently in his writing from the mid- 1990s to his death in 2004.

If Levinas's description of the ethical event of hospitality is hard to equate with actual daily meetings with other people, Derrida's is even more so. If a stranger knocks at my door and, seeing that he is tired, I let him come in and sit down, am I participating in the infinite? Could my hospitality be called unconditional? What if he makes his way to my kitchen and starts helping himself to food in the fridge—aren't I likely to impose some conditions at this point? How does Derrida's idea of an infinite hospitality without conditions relate to our dealings with one another in the real world?

Derrida's answer is to split the concept of hospitality—which is not, therefore, a concept—into two, one of which he terms 'unconditional hospitality' and the other 'conditional hospitality'. Alternatively, he refers to 'the *law* of hospitality' and 'the *laws* of hospitality'. The first member of these pairs denotes hospitality that has no limits: as I open my door to the stranger I'm prepared to have my privacy violated, my house trashed, my well-being destroyed. In being hospitable in this sense I'm not even conscious that I *am* hospitable, I don't tell myself that it would be morally correct to be hospitable—or in Levinas's terms, no thematization takes place. There is in fact a reversal of power: the host who extends unconditional hospitality to the guest becomes the subservient one. As Derrida puts it, 'the one inviting becomes almost the hostage of the one invited' ('Hostipitality' 2000, 9).[8] Going beyond literal instances of hospitality to the wider sphere of human relations, I recognize an infinite responsibility for every Other I encounter (and perhaps all those I have not encountered as well). This is, of course, an impossible responsibility, beyond the capacity of any human individual. For Derrida, however, the *impossible* is not synonymous with the *irrelevant* or the *ineffective*.

Conditional hospitality, on the other hand, is the type of hospitality that is possible in the real world. You may come into my house, but please wash your hands before you touch anything. We set limits to our national hospitality as we do to our individual hospitality: we welcome some immigrants and turn away others, we lay down a series of conditions on those who wish to stay. Extending the term to the more general Levinasian situation of responding to any Other, we make practical choices about who we're able to help most effectively, and what sort of help will be most valued. The citizens of a state such as the United Kingdom can and of course often do protest about the conditions imposed on those who are seeking welcome, particularly in the field of immigration and asylum-seeking; but there are few calls for a complete free-for-all.[9]

Now, the difficult question, the question that Derrida raises in many places, is: what is the relation between these two versions of hospitality? And what, in particular, is the status of unconditional hospitality—which Derrida also calls 'pure' and 'absolute' and 'hyperbolical' hospitality, and of which he says at one point, 'if such a thing is thinkable' (*Of Hospitality*, 83,135)? It would be easy to assume that its role is that of an idea or an ideal towards which all hospitality should strive, while accepting that it will always fall short in actual cases.

[8] The fact that the French word 'hôte', like the Latin 'hostis' from which it is derived, can mean both 'host' and 'guest', handily captures this ambiguity—though it can make for difficulties of exposition in theories of hospitality.

[9] As an example of conditional hospitality, Derrida discusses Kant's 'Third Article' in his *Perpetual Peace*, in which Kant proposes a universal right of hospitality, but with strict limits. See 'Hostipitality' 2000, 3–6.

Kant's notion of 'Regulative Ideas' is one version of this view. But Derrida is insistent that this is not how unconditional hospitality enters into the actual hospitality of rules and conditions. Just how it does enter, however, is not easy to say, and he tries a number of different formulations in different texts. Michael Naas, one of Derrida's most acute readers, points out that this constant reformulation is not insignificant: 'The question concerning the link or relation, the articulation, between these two laws, these two regimes of hospitality, must thus be constantly raised, and the language to describe this relation perpetually reinvented' (*Derrida from Now On*, 25).

Three of Derrida's seminars in the series given in 1995–7 and devoted to questions of hospitality have been published, two in the volume *Of Hospitality* and one in the edited collection *Acts of Religion*. In the first of these, given the title 'Question d'étranger' (question of the foreigner or stranger), Derrida associates the pair 'unconditional hospitality/conditional hospitality' with another pair of terms that had become important to him: justice, on the one hand, and law or right on the other. (The French word *droit* refers both to right and to the body of the law.) Justice, too, is unconditional, illimitable—and impossible; law is the limited operation whereby justice may, to some extent at least, be achieved.[10] Thus Derrida asserts:

> Just hospitality [i.e., unconditional hospitality] breaks with hospitality by right [i.e., conditional hospitality]; not that it condemns or is opposed to it, and it can on the contrary set and maintain it in a perpetual progressive movement; but it is as strangely heterogeneous to it as justice is heterogeneous to the law to which it is yet so close, from which in truth it is indissociable. (Derrida and Dufourmantelle, *Of Hospitality*, 25–7)

The paradox is set clearly before us: the two types of hospitality are indissociable, yet heterogeneous; unconditional hospitality breaks with its conditional twin, yet is able to set it in motion and keep it going.

[10] For a thorough study of Derrida's understanding of justice and law, and their relation to hospitality, see de Ville, *Law as Absolute Hospitality*.

The relation is expressed in different words in the next seminar, 'Pas d'hospitalité' ('No hospitality' or 'Step of hospitality'): 'Conditional laws would cease to be laws of hospitality if they were not guided, given inspiration, given aspiration, required, even, by the law of unconditional hospitality' (*Of Hospitality*, 79). Derrida gives us four alternative verbs here to designate the relation between the law of hospitality—he sometimes gives it an upper-case L—and the laws (plural) that govern hospitality on the ground, the fourth of which suggests something new in the picture we're getting: that unconditional hospitality *requires* conditional hospitality. As Derrida explains,

> It wouldn't be effectively unconditional, the law, if it didn't *have to become* effective, concrete, determined.... It would risk being abstract, utopian, illusory, and so turning over into its opposite. In order to be what it is, *the* law thus needs the laws, which, however, deny it, or at any rate threaten it, sometimes corrupt or even pervert it. And must always be able to do this. (*Of Hospitality*, 79).

Conditional hospitality, then, is both necessary to unconditional hospitality and a potential perversion of it; or, in a logic that Derrida explored in many other places as well, conditional hospitality renders unconditional hospitality both possible and impossible.

In the third published seminar, called 'Hostipitality' (a portmanteau that fuses *hospitality* with *hostility*), Derrida sets out another impossible scene of hospitality:

> One must not only not be ready nor prepared to welcome, nor well-disposed to welcome—for if the welcome is the simple manifestation of a natural or acquired disposition, of a generous character or of a hospitable *habitus*, there is no merit in it, no welcome of the other as other. But—supplementary aporia—it is also true that if I welcome the other out of mere duty, unwillingly, against my natural inclination, and therefore without smiling, I am not welcoming him either: One must [*il faut*] therefore welcome without 'one must' [*sans 'il faut'*]: neither naturally nor unnaturally. (361)

Derrida is here invoking the terms of the eighteenth-century debates about true morality: the Kantian argument that only in acting out of duty is one acting morally is set against the belief—propounded, for instance, by the Earl of Shaftesbury—in an innate moral sense, exemplified most endearingly perhaps by the character of Fielding's Tom Jones.[11] But neither of these satisfies Derrida's conception of absolute hospitality: it's an obligation which is not felt as an obligation.

In this seminar, Derrida introduces two new terms for the opposition we're considering, this time seen from the point of view of the host: *visitation* (the arrival of the Other with no input from myself—as Derrida says, 'In visitation there is no door' ['Hostipitality' 2000, 14]) and *invitation* (the welcoming of the Other under pre-ordained conditions):

> It is as if there is a competition or contradiction between two neighboring but incompatible values: *visitation* and *invitation*, and, more gravely, it is as if there were a hidden contradiction between hospitality [i.e., unconditional hospitality] and invitation. Or, more precisely, between hospitality as it exposes itself to the visit, to the visitation, and the hospitality that adorns and prepares itself [*se pare et se prépare*] in invitation. (362)

Derrida goes on to note, in another rejection of a possible way of interpreting the paradox, that these are not two faces, or moments, or dialectical phases, of hospitality; 'Visitor and invited, visitation and invitation, are simultaneously in competition and incompatible' (362).

How, then, does an individual act hospitably, in a way that is informed or energized by absolute hospitality? Levinas frequently describes the ethical event in terms of persecution, being taken hostage, a 'passivity more passive than all passivity', and Derrida's language often takes a similar hue—though one feels the syntax and vocabulary straining as he attempts to explain an event that defies rationality:

[11] For a lively discussion of *Tom Jones* in these terms, see Bernard Harrison, *Henry Fielding's 'Tom Jones'*.

> To be hospitable is to let oneself be overtaken [*surprendre*], *to be ready to not be ready*, if such is possible, to let oneself be overtaken, to not even *let* oneself be overtaken, to be surprised, in a fashion almost violent, violated and raped [*violée*], stolen [*volée*],...precisely where one is not ready to receive—and not only *not yet ready* but *not ready, unprepared* in a mode that is not even that of the 'not yet'. ('Hostipitality', 361).

I'm reminded of the thought processes of the character Dostoevsky in J. M. Coetzee's *Master of Petersburg* as he responds to the howling of a dog during the night, a passage that brilliantly encapsulates both the insistence and the impossibility of the ethics of hospitality to the Other. (I'll come back to the fact that it is a dog, not a human, making an ethical demand.) The dog's wail has entered Dostoevsky's dream in the guise of his dead stepson Pavel's voice, and in due course it wakes him up. Then follows the train of thought that comes very close to Derrida's account of hospitality as violent seizure by something beyond rationality:

> *Because* it is not his son he must not go back to bed but must get dressed and answer the call. If he expects his son to come as a thief in the night, and listen only for the call of the thief, he will never see him. If he expects his son to speak in the voice of the unexpected, he will never hear him. As long as he expects what he does not expect what he does not expect will not come. Therefore—paradox within paradox, darkness swaddled in darkness—he must answer to what he does not expect. (80)[12]

The year 1997 also saw the publication of a short book by Derrida entitled *Cosmopolites de tous les pays, encore un effort!*, translated into English as 'On Cosmopolitanism'. Here Derrida develops the idea of 'cities of refuge' that would welcome refugees, or 'asylum seekers' as we like to call them these days, in contrast the currently prevailing hostility to immigration practised by most economically advanced states in the world; and hospitality lies, of course, at the centre of his

[12] For further discussion, see Attridge, *J. M. Coetzee and the Ethics of Reading*, chapter 5, 'Expecting the Unexpected'.

discussion. In fact, he goes so far as to say that 'ethics is so thoroughly coextensive with the experience of hospitality' that one can say '*ethics is hospitality*' (17). And again we hear of the relationship between unconditional and conditional hospitality; admitting that the practical issues that arise are 'obscure and difficult', he states:

> It is a question of knowing how to transform and improve the law [*droit*], and of knowing if this improvement is possible within an historical space which takes place *between* The Law of an unconditional hospitality, offered *a priori* to every other, to all newcomers, *whoever they may be*, and the conditional laws of a right to hospitality, without which *The* unconditional Law of hospitality would be in danger of remaining a pious and irresponsible desire, without form and without potency, and of even being perverted at any moment. (22–3; translation slightly modified)

Here we have a further development of the idea that it's not only a matter of the necessarily constrained and regulated acts of hospitality being informed by an impulse derived from the pure unconditional variety; the latter also needs the former in order to have any purchase on reality and to avoid being 'perverted'. This form of perversion is different from the form we encountered earlier; there, the conditional laws constituted the potential perversion, here they guard against it—presumably because they reduce the risk that the guest will turn out to be dangerous and destructive.

Derrida continued to worry away at the question of this relationship. In the early 2000s, in an interview with Elisabeth Roudinesco, he moved to this issue from a consideration of the 'sans-papiers', the undocumented immigrants in Paris whose rights he supported during the crisis of 1996:[13]

> Pure hospitality consists in leaving one's house open to the unforeseeable arrival, which can be an intrusion, even a dangerous intrusion, liable

[13] Derrida gave a powerful unscripted speech condemning the French government's policy on immigration at a demonstration in Paris in 1996; a transcription appears in Derrida, Guillaume and Vincent, *Marx en jeu*.

> eventually to cause harm. This pure or unconditional hospitality is not a political or juridical concept. Indeed, ... for a family or for a nation concerned with controlling its practices of hospitality, it is indeed necessary to limit and to condition hospitality. This can be done with the best intentions in the world, since unconditional hospitality can also have perverse effects. (59)

Once again, absolute hospitality can give rise to disastrous consequences. But the relation remains difficult to articulate:

> However, these two modalities of hospitality remain irreducible to one another. ... This pure hospitality, without which there is no concept of hospitality, applies to the crossing of a country's borders, but it also has a role in ordinary life: when someone arrives, when love arrives, for example, one takes a risk, one is exposed. To understand these situations, it is necessary to maintain this horizon without horizon, this unlimitedness of unconditional hospitality, even while knowing that one cannot make it a political or juridical concept. (Derrida and Roudinesco, *For What Tomorrow ...*, 60)

As part of an untranslated seminar, published in 1999 as *Manifeste pour l'hospitalité*, Derrida advances a somewhat different model of the relationship: in a talk entitled 'Hospitality and Responsibility' he speaks of a necessary compromise between the two poles:

> As a French citizen, I have to find a link between, on the one hand, this system of norms constituted by the language, the French constitution, laws and customs, French culture, and, on the other hand, the welcome of the stranger with his or her language, culture, habitus, etc. I have to find a meeting-place, and responsibility consists in inventing this meeting-place as a unique event. (114, my translation)

We are still given very little to help us understand *how* one might find such a link, though it's interesting to note that doing so involves invention and the uniqueness of the *event*—a point we need to come back to. Though there are difficulties in describing how unconditional hospitality enters into an act of hospitality, the *Manifeste* gives at least a clear negative instance: 'If I am sure that the new arrival that I am receiving is perfectly inoffensive and innocent, and will be beneficial to me...this is not hospitality' (137). To the degree that I'm taking a chance in welcoming the other, my action is informed by unconditional hospitality.

In this talk, Derrida asks what our responsibility as potential hosts is, and his answer is quite realistic: it's to offer the greatest hospitality possible. Immediately, however, he raises a problem: both silence and speech towards the guest could be a form of violence, failing to ascertain her needs, or imposing on her my language and norms of conversation (101). (Derrida has speculated before that unconditional hospitality might demand a complete suspension of language [*Of Hospitality*, 135].) And in this work, Derrida gives a slightly different picture of the operation of unconditional hospitality. The passage from pure hospitality to the law and politics is seen, as before, as a perversion, but is then described as a process of both self-perversion and self-perfection whose task is the perpetual improvement of the conditions and definitions of every kind of law (104–5). A similar account is given in an interview entitled 'The Principle of Hospitality', first published in 1997, in which Derrida addresses directly the question of practical politics in the light of his thinking on the topic of unconditional hospitality:

> The two meanings of hospitality remain irreducible to one another, but it is the pure and hyperbolical hospitality in whose name we should always invent the best dispositions, the least bad conditions, the most just legislation, so as to make it as effective as possible.... Calculate the risks, yes, but don't shut the door on what cannot be calculated, meaning the future and the foreigner—that's the double law of hospitality. (*Paper Machine*, 66–7)

After September 11, 2001, Derrida again invoked the distinction between conditional and unconditional hospitality in explaining his resistance to the notion of 'tolerance', and now his emphasis is on the *conceptual* importance of the latter to the former:

> Without at least the thought of this pure and unconditional hospitality, of hospitality *itself*, we would have no concept of hospitality in general and would not even be able to determine any rules for conditional hospitality.... Without this thought of pure hospitality (a thought that is also, in its own way, an experience), we would not even have the idea of the other, of the alterity of the other, that is, of someone who enters into our lives without having been invited. We would not have the idea of love. ('Autoimmunity', 129)

Without the parenthetical comment, we might take this to be about an abstract idea; but it's characteristic of Derrida's understanding of unconditional hospitality that it is also an *experience*.

Hospitality as ethics

The logic—or challenge to logic—that hospitality presents in Derrida's understanding of it is also present in his accounts of many other terms in his favoured lexicon. This problematic relation between an absolute, pure unconditioned and unconditional—what can one call it?—concept? category? impulse? event?—none of these is quite right—and a conditioned and conditional version of the same thing occurs again and again in Derrida's work, increasingly so in the latter part of his career. Several terms with an ethical import are shown to possess an identical duality, what Judith Still, in her book *Derrida and Hospitality*, describes as a relation 'simultaneously... of mutual perversion and mutual need' (15).[14]

Perhaps the earliest of these terms to appear in Derrida's thinking was the *gift*. There is a pure giving, argues Derrida, which occurs without intention to give or acknowledgement by the receiver that giving has occurred, with no gratitude, no reciprocity, no debt, no thanks, no recognition or memory by either party, of the gift. If the gift appears *as* a gift, no giving has taken place.[15] As soon as there is an

[14] Still's book is concerned primarily with conditional hospitality, after an introductory chapter in which she discusses the relation between it and unconditional hospitality.

[15] See Derrida's *Given Time*, especially 7–19.

intention to give, the pure gift is annulled—yet Derrida acknowledges that any actual gift must imply an intention. 'There must be chance', he tells us, 'encounter, the involuntary, even unconsciousness or disorder, and there must be intentional freedom, and these two conditions must—miraculously, graciously—agree with each other' (*Given Time*, 123). He is explicit about the connection between the gift and hospitality:

> In the same way that I have tried to show that the gift supposes a break with reciprocity, exchange, economy and circular movement, I have also tried to demonstrate that hospitality implies such a break; that is, if I inscribe the gesture of hospitality within a circle in which the guest should give back to the host, then it is not hospitality but conditional hospitality. ('Hospitality, Justice and Responsibility', 69)

Derrida is also explicit about the connection between hospitality and *forgiveness*: 'Forgiveness granted to the other is the supreme gift and therefore hospitality par excellence.' He finds a 'scene of forgiveness at the heart of hospitality': 'Whoever asks for hospitality asks, in a way, for forgiveness', but 'the welcoming one must ask for forgiveness from the welcomed one even prior to the former's own having to forgive' ('Hostipitality', 380). And as with hospitality, forgiveness is manifested in two ways:

> It is important to analyse at its base the tension at the heart of the heritage between, *on the one side*, the idea which is also a demand for the *unconditional*, gracious, infinite, aneconomic forgiveness granted *to the guilty as guilty*, without counterpart, even to those who do not repent or ask forgiveness, and *on the other side*, as a great number of texts testify through many semantic refinements and difficulties, a conditional forgiveness proportionate to the recognition of the fault, to repentance, to the transformation of the sinner who then explicitly asks forgiveness. (*Cosmopolitanism and Forgiveness*, 34–5)[16]

[16] For a longer text by Derrida on the question of forgiveness, see 'To Forgive: The Unforgivable and the Imprescriptible'.

Here is exactly the same duality, the same relation without relation. (Derrida later speaks of the 'abyss' between the two instances of forgiveness). Once again, we're told, 'these two poles, *the unconditional and the conditional*, are absolutely heterogeneous, and must remain irreducible to one another' and yet 'they are nonetheless indissociable' (44). He continues, 'If one wants, and it is necessary, forgiveness to become effective, concrete, historic; if one wants it to *arrive*, to happen by changing things, it is necessary that this purity engage itself in a series of conditions of all kinds.... It is between these two poles, *irreconcilable but indissociable*, that decisions and responsibilities are to be taken' (44–5).

A similar relation without relation—Derrida also calls it a 'double-bind'—between the unconditional and the conditional is observable in a number of Derrida's other preoccupations in his later work.[17] *Justice*, as we've seen, is set against *droit* or the operation of laws; *democracy* is understood as always to come, actually existing democracies being all too limited; and there are enough mentions of *love* (as in the interview with Roudinesco I cited earlier) to suggest that it exhibits the same features, although Derrida never, to my knowledge, wrote at length directly on this topic.[18] In every case, the absolute or pure instance is 'impossible': Derrida often inserts the phrase 'if there is such a thing' after a term like 'unconditional hospitality' or 'forgiveness' to signal that its occurrence is not something we could ever observe or be sure of.

[17] In addition to the preoccupations I've considered here, Derrida includes *promise* and *testimony* among 'a whole chain' of topics associated with hospitality ('As If It Were Possible', 357). Thomson usefully traces the similarities between hospitality and friendship (*Deconstruction and Democracy*, 92). Another term in the list would be *responsibility*. We might remember, too, that Derrida describes the fullest possible realization of the university as 'the university without condition' (see the essay of that name).

[18] In the film *Derrida*, directed by Kirby Dick and Amy Ziering Kofman, asked to say whatever he wants about love, he states 'I have nothing to say about love', but goes on to offer a short speech on the subject (79, 81 in the published screenplay). And the question of love, in many forms, permeates his writing, notably in 'Envois' and *The Politics of Friendship*, but in many other places as well. See also Peggy Kamuf, 'Deconstruction and Love'.

But, as I've already said, impossibility for Derrida is not fruitlessness; on the contrary, without the impossible nothing would happen. Every description of the unconditional implies impossibility: impossible hospitality, impossible forgiveness, impossible justice, impossible giving. In *The Gift of Death*, Derrida gives a vivid sketch of the impossibility of ethics as responsibility for the singular other: each time one responds to the needs of some other, one is failing to respond to the needs of uncountable other others. Even in choosing to speak French, says Derrida, he is sacrificing all the other languages he might speak. Yet the impossibility of ethics does not imply that ethical acts cannot happen; on the contrary, they could not be ethical otherwise.

Hospitality, then, is one of a number of terms for the ethical movement from the self, or the other in the self, to the other; or, perhaps more precisely, it's an overarching name for the various manifestations of that movement. 'For hospitality is not some region of ethics,' says Derrida, 'it is ethicity itself, the whole and the principle of ethics' (*Adieu*, 50).

Invention, grace, and life

So far, I've been considering hospitality as an ethical attribute or injunction; Derrida, as we've seen, went so far as to say that hospitality *is* ethics. If ethics is fundamentally a matter of the relation of one person to singular others, as Levinas certainly believed, hospitality is one possible name for that relation, whether conceived as a moral duty or as generosity of spirit (to return to the opposition between Kant and Shaftesbury). The gift, forgiveness, democracy, justice, love: they too all have ethical overtones. But the role of hospitality is not confined to the domain of the ethical. Its wider reach is suggested by the codicil to the following restatement, in a late essay, of the paradoxical relation we are now familiar with: 'Only an unconditional hospitality can give meaning and practical rationality to a concept of hospitality. Unconditional hospitality exceeds juridical, political, or economic calculation. *But nothing and no-one happens or arrives without it*' (*Rogues* 2005, 149; my italics, translation modified).

This last sentence implies a scope of operation well beyond that of hospitality as an ethical good, or even beyond ethics *tout court*. The French word awkwardly translated by 'happens or arrives' in this sentence is *arrive*, a word that combines both these meanings, and can also mean 'come'. In his discussions of hospitality, Derrida often uses the related noun *arrivant*, a term equally resistant to translation; it appears in one quotation above as 'newcomer' and in another as 'arrival'. Its usefulness is manifold. By combining the senses of 'arrival' and 'occurrence', personal reference and impersonality, it generalizes the moment of hospitality: not just the person coming to your door, but the event that unexpectedly takes place. It reminds us, too, that hospitality to the other is also hospitality to the future: it's an openness to whatever will come.[19]

Here is Derrida in *Aporias*, in a passage that sums up much of what I've already said:

> The new *arrivant*, this word can, indeed, mean the neutrality of *that which* arrives, but also the singularity of *who* arrives, he or she who comes, coming to be where s/he was not expected, where one was awaiting him or her without waiting for him or her, without expecting *it* [*s'y attendre*], without knowing what or whom to expect, what or whom I am waiting for—and such is hospitality itself, hospitality toward the event. (33)

In including the possibility that the *arrivant* is not human—'*that which* arrives'—Derrida goes well beyond Levinas: the other to which one is responsible may be an animal, a culture, a language, an idea.[20] And the passage introduces another crucial term: the *event*. For Derrida, the event properly so-called is the unexpected event, the event that is not

[19] See Derrida's discussion of hospitality and the future in 'Hostipitality' 2000, 11.

[20] See, for example, 'Hostipitality' 2000, 4: 'What can be said of, indeed can one speak of, hospitality toward the non-human, the divine, for example, or the animal or vegetable?' See also Derrida's discussion of Lawrence's 'The Snake' in *The Beast and the Sovereign*, 236–49.

part of a predictably unfolding series. Hospitality toward the event is therefore another way of stating openness to the future. And the term *event* is connected by Derrida to the term *invent* (as well as *advent*, coming). An *invention* is an event that, in an unprecedented and unforeseeable way, opens up new ground for thought, feeling, and action. (Invention is, it hardly needs saying, impossible. To remain within the realm of possibility is not to invent, simply to realize what is already implicit in things as they are.)

In 2003 Derrida published *Voyous* (translated as *Rogues* in the posthumous 2005 English version), in which he revisited a number of these questions. He gives a powerful, though still far from transparent, description of the role of the impossible—or, as he names it here, the 'im-possible'—in which he makes clear his resistance to any understanding of the unconditional, including unconditional hospitality, as a merely abstract idea. On the contrary, it is felt, and felt as violence:

> It is not the inaccessible, and it is not what I can indefinitely defer: it announces itself; it precedes me, swoops down upon and seizes me *here and now* in a nonvirtualizable way, in actuality and not potentiality. It comes upon me from on high, in the form of an injunction that does not simply wait on the horizon, that I do not see coming, that never leaves me in peace and never lets me put it off until later. Such an urgency cannot be *idealized* any more than the other as other can. This im-possible is thus not a (regulative) *idea* or *ideal*. (*Rogues*, 84)

But, violent though this movement is, Derrida also associates it with *grace*, a very different conception of an unsolicited gift from elsewhere, and a word we encountered in the Introduction in Coetzee's work. Two of my earlier quotations by Derrida have used the word 'gracious': if the involuntary and the voluntary gift agree, they do so 'miraculously, graciously', and unconditional forgiveness is described as 'gracious'. Derrida doesn't develop this implicit connection between the Christian concept of an unmerited and freely given boon and the unconditional gift of forgiveness or hospitality, but it does provide a counter-image to that of a ravishing power, though both involve being taken by surprise.

To be hospitable, then, is to be *inventive* in one's relation to the Other. Or, to be more precise, to the singular Other, to the Other's singularity, 'the singularity of *who* arrives', as we've just heard Derrida saying. For hospitality doesn't simply require an open door; it requires that the other's *specific* needs be taken care of. Naas points out that unconditional hospitality itself is in a double-bind because of the need to be open to anyone without demanding identification, and the need to address the specificity of the case in front of you—requiring identification (*Taking on the Tradition*, 164–5). The event is always singular, which is to say that it exceeds all possible norms and rules and programmable expectations. To make a just decision—something implicit in the event of hospitality—is, Derrida says in his account of justice, to act not in *defiance* of the accumulated laws and precedents that are relevant in a particular case, but as it were to *reinvent* all those laws and precedents in order to do justice to the singularity of this case. To quote *Of Hospitality* again, 'If I practice hospitality "out of *duty*"..., this hospitality of paying up is no longer an absolute hospitality, it is no longer graciously offered beyond debt and economy [note the idea of *grace* again], offered to the other, a hospitality invented for the singularity of the new arrival, of the unexpected visitor' (83). Many strands come together in this sentence: a rejection of Kant's view of ethics as duty, an association of hospitality with the gift ('offered beyond debt and economy'), the notion of invention, the *arrivant* (translated here as 'new arrival'), visitation as opposed to invitation, and the importance of the singularity of the other.

Derrida stresses the importance of invention in the gesture of hospitality to the other in *Manifeste pour l'hospitalité*, and, surprisingly perhaps, associates it with poetic creation:

> The decision in favour of hospitality requires that I invent my own rule. In this sense, the language of hospitality must be *poetic*: it's necessary that I speak or that I hear the other in a place where, in a certain sense,

> language reinvents itself.... It's necessary that each time I say to the other, 'Come, enter, make yourself at home', my act of welcome should occur as if it were the first time in history; it should be absolutely singular. (113; my emphasis)

This absolute singularity is not just a characterization of the individual stranger; it's what constitutes the *arrivant*, and the event of its arrival, more generally.

There is another important dimension to hospitality to the other we haven't touched on yet: as Derrida says, 'Hospitality implies, for the host receiving and the guest received, being first of all hospitable to the other *in oneself*' (*Manifeste*, 139), and in another place he asks 'Is not hospitality an interruption of the self?', continuing that 'one will not understand anything about hospitality if one does not understand what "interrupting oneself" might mean, the interruption of the self by the self as other' (*Adieu*, 51, 42). In other words, hospitality doesn't issue from a sovereign, self-assured subject, but from a subject already divided; and it's this self-division that makes hospitality possible. Derrida is fond of saying that any decision worthy of the name is taken by 'the other in me', and we see a similar insistence here. Peggy Kamuf relates this insistence to Derrida's challenge to the traditional concept of the possible, which is always what is possible for 'me', 'for whatever poses sameness to itself, returns to itself, and claims sovereignty over its selfsame self as over its own homogeneous, undifferentiated domain' (*To Follow*, 92). Judith Butler's argument in *Giving an Account of Oneself*, that ethics and responsibility presuppose a subject 'opaque to itself, not fully translucent and knowable to itself' (19), runs along similar lines.

Derrida, in effect, proposes two versions of human existence. One is a mechanical succession of occurrences, including the welcoming of strangers, the giving of gifts, the forgiving of criminals, the judging of cases, and the creation of art, in which everything happens according to the rules of rational calculation, everything is predictable, everything travels along the smooth rails of convention and convenience.

The other is a series of unpredictable events, a constant changing of course, a repeated risk-taking that sometimes turns out well, sometimes badly. In this second version, there is also welcoming, giving, forgiving, judging, and creating, but they look very different; in fact, from the perspective of the second version, these activities as they would take place in the context of the first are not worthy of the names attached to them: 'hospitality' is the authoritarian subjection of any arrival to strict rules, 'giving' is merely an economic exchange, 'forgiving' is only granted to the penitent and forgivable, 'judging' is the application of laws that could be carried out by a computer, and the 'literature' produced is merely pastiche and cliché. What all these lack is openness to the future, inventiveness, an affirmative response to the absolute singularity of the other, the acceptance that any opening to the good is also potentially an opening to the bad. The field of activities to which this opposition applies is potentially infinite: any situation in which a decision is required admits of two possibilities—a calculation that points unmistakeably in one direction or a leap into the unknown because the choice is wholly undecidable. For Derrida, only the latter deserves the name of decision, and every decision, although it undertakes the fullest possible exercise of reason and calculation, finally moves beyond the rational and the calculable, and affirms the other.

As we've seen, however, the opposition is not actually so stark: life requires a transaction, a negotiation between the unconditional and the conditional. (We've noted that Derrida on one occasion uses the word 'compromise', but I'm not sure this is a helpful term, suggesting as it does a mid-way position; certainly, his other accounts of the relation are less comforting.) Much of existence is inevitably of the first kind, but in order for life to be life and not a mechanical procession the activities mentioned have to be injected with, or inspired by, or subjected to, the spirit of the unconditional, inventive, risky, open, unpredictable, uncontrollable alternative, foreign to the order of knowledge and calculation, and always open to perversion. One name for this constant negotiation between the unconditional and the conditional, the unconditioned and the conditioned, is 'deconstruction'.

Another way of approaching this knot is to consider the ethical imperatives that have governed Western traditions of thought and behaviour since Ancient Greece (I can't speak of other civilizations). They would include hospitality, justice, responsibility, forgiveness, generosity. In each case, it is as if Derrida has asked, 'What is the most absolute form of these imperatives; what would happen if we followed through these widely acknowledged and enduring values to their purest or most logically complete or fullest imaginable manifestation?' The result is not a series of ideals to be striven for, but rather a much more ambiguous set of demands, which are as liable to be destructive as productive, and which are all, from the beginning, subject to perversion and betrayal. Were they not so liable, they would not be what they are. Hence the need to introduce conditions, laws, limits; and hence the never-ending interaction and negotiation between the unconditional and the conditional.

Hospitality to the other, therefore, can be seen as the motor, the energizing principle, of human life itself—or, indeed, of all existence. One of Derrida's most astute recent commentators, Martin Hägglund, has argued that hospitality and its related terms are not ethical at all, that they don't imply an 'ought'; for Hägglund they are just descriptions of how things happen.[21] Hägglund identifies the unconditional with the fundamental structure of the event: the interdependence of time and space that Derrida calls *différance* or the trace-structure. Nothing is entirely given in itself, in other words, and it's this otherness implicit within any entity that makes change possible, indeed inevitable. Without openness to the coming of the other, nothing would change. For Hägglund, then, terms like 'hospitality', 'justice',

[21] See Hägglund, *Radical Atheism*; and see also my review of Hägglund's book in *Derrida Today* and Hägglund's response, 'The Non-Ethical Opening of Ethics'. Pheng Cheah offers a similar account of unconditional hospitality as 'the structural exposure of any finite being or thing—mineral, vegetable, animal or human and, indeed, any form of presence—to the coming of time as pure event' ('To Open', 72).

and 'gift' have no ethical force, since they arise from the very nature of existence as a series of transformations.

Hägglund's is a strong reading, and has its own logical consistency, but it fails to account for a great deal in Derrida's treatment of these events. For instance, when an interlocutor proposes that the necessary processes of practical life and politics are where the injunction 'we must' arises, Derrida disagrees: 'When I feel that "I must" . . . , of course, I enter a process, but in the name of something that doesn't tolerate the process. It's immediate. For instance, I must answer the call of the other: it's something which has to be absolute, unconditional and immediate, that is, foreign to any process' ('Hospitality, Justice and Responsibility', 72). Now it may be that at moments like this—and I've quoted many others—Derrida has contaminated the purity of his own logic by introducing an ethical dimension; or it may be that it's precisely the operation of the logic identified by Hägglund that makes ethics possible (which is to say, of course, im-possible). My sense is that there is a tension within Derrida's thought that reflects exactly the tension between unconditional and conditional hospitality: that is to say, a tension between deconstruction as an account of what *happens* and deconstruction as an account of what *should* happen. Derrida's language reflects this tension, which is, finally, a productive one: 'Unconditional hospitality, which is neither juridical nor political, is nonetheless the condition of the political and the juridical. For these very reasons, I am not even sure whether it is ethical, insofar as it does not even depend on a decision. But what would "ethics" be without hospitality?' ('Autoimmunity', 129).

Hospitality and literary criticism

What does all this have to do with literary criticism? It will be evident already that this discussion of hospitality has much in common with the account of the work of literature I've been presenting in this book. We've seen that hospitality, as Derrida understands it, requires an inventive response to the singular other, and that he calls this 'poetic'.

In his fullest account of invention, in the essay 'Psyche: Invention of the Other', he turns to poetry, using as an example a short poem by Francis Ponge. The poem introduces a new possibility into the language, and thus requires a new mode of reading; but at the same time this expansion of the field of literary writing and reading allows for institutional inscription and mechanical imitations. Invention, including poetic invention, is a matter of hospitality to the unpredictable other, the undecidable event, the future, the *arrivant*; absolute newness would make no impact, however, and it's the folding of the new into what is already in existence (itself altered in the process) that constitutes the work of invention. The unconditional has to be realized as the conditioned.

The inventive artist is one who is fully in command of the materials and conventions of his art-form, or techne, but rather than simply producing a rearrangement of that material finds a way of making a space for the new, the other, the hitherto unthinkable or unperceivable. The scenario is exactly that of the hospitality of visitation: rather than *inviting* some already known idea or formal arrangement or quality of feeling into the work in progress, the successful artist finds a way of destabilizing the fixed structures of knowledge, habit, and affect, so as to make a *visitation* possible, and seeks to welcome the other, the *arrivant*, in a work that does justice to its singularity. Innumerable accounts by writers, painters, musicians of the way their best achievements happened testify to this process. In 'I Have a Taste for the Secret', Derrida uses the notion of hospitality to talk about the writer's responsibility to future readers—a responsibility not to give the reader something that is wholly and immediately intelligible, but to leave a space open for individual interpretation (31–2). Most philosophers would no doubt disagree, but most writers of literary works would have no difficulty with this idea.

But hospitality isn't relevant only to the creation of the work of art; it pertains also to reception. To do justice to the singularity and alterity of the literary work—that singularity and alterity brought into being thanks to the writer's inventive hospitality to the *arrivant*—is to read with a readiness to welcome the other. If one imposes on the work a fixed set of norms, one can offer only conditional hospitality to the inventive achievement of the author. A reading that operates on the basis of unconditional hospitality, however, if there can be such a thing, approaches the work prepared to reassess and revise all the assumptions and habits brought to it. As in every other instance we've looked at, effective hospitality to the literary work involves informing and energizing one's conscientious, careful, rule-governed reading with the unlimited, unpredictable force of unconditional openness to whatever might arrive. Literary translation, too, which is a peculiarly intensive mode of reading, is a form of hospitality—hospitality to another language, and to a work and its writer in that language—and it too requires the closest attention to the governing protocols of linguistic interpretation together with a constant openness to unforeseen possibilities of inventiveness. In *Manifeste pour l'hospitalité*, Derrida describes what he considers an inadequate translation of the word 'hôte' in Camus—the translator conveys only the meaning 'guest' and not 'host'—and calls this 'a good example of the way in which a translation may be a phenomenon of hospitality…or the refusal of hospitality' (117–18).

* * *

The outcome of hospitable reading, as I've been arguing throughout this book, is a change in the reader, perhaps not only in the way he reads other works but more widely too. Without hospitality to what is new, other, outside the borders of my comprehension and comfort, I will put down the poem or the novel, or leave the theatre, just the same as I was before my engagement with the text. There can be no absolute guarantee that this change will be for the good, but without this risk—minimized, fortunately, by the operation of the norms of conditional hospitality—there would be no genuine openness to the other and no possibility of doing justice to the singular work of literature.

REFERENCES

Abel, Marco. *Violent Affect: Literature, Cinema and Critique after Representation*. Lincoln, NE: University of Nebraska Press, 2008.

Adams, Lorraine. 'Those Who Dwell Therein'. *New York Times Sunday Book Review*. August 27, 2006. <http://www.nytimes.com/2006/08/27/books/review/Adams.t.html>.

Adiga, Aravind. *The White Tiger*. London: Atlantic Books, 2008.

Adil, Alev. 'Home Truths in Egypt's Multi-story Saga'. Review of al-Aswany, *The Yacoubian Building*. *Independent*, February 16, 2007. <http://www.independent.co.uk/arts-entertainment/books/reviews/the-yacoubian-building-by-alaa-al-aswany-trans-humphrey-davies-436484.html>.

Adorno, Theodor. *Aesthetic Theory*. Trans. Christian Lenhardt. London and Boston: Routledge and Kegan Paul, 1984.

Adorno, Theodore. *Aesthetic Theory*. Trans. Robert Hullot-Kentor. London: Athlone Press, 1997.

Agamben, Giorgio. *The Coming Community*. Trans. Michael Hardt. Minneapolis: University of Minnesota Press, 1993.

Al-Aswany, Alaa. 'Egypt Is in a State of Reserve and Backwardness'. <http://en.qantara.de/Egypt-Is-In-a-State-of-Reserve-and-Backwardness/8833c174/index.html>.

Al-Aswany, Alaa. 'Like Being in Love: Literary Reflections on the Revolution'. <http://www.independent.co.uk/news/people/profiles/alaa-al-aswany-like-being-in-love-literary-reflections-on-the-revolution-2201506.html>.

Al-Aswany, Alaa. *The Yacoubian Building*. Trans. Humphrey Davies. London: Harper Perennial, 2007.

Altieri, Charles. *The Particulars of Rapture: An Aesthetics of Affect*. Ithaca: Cornell University Press, 2003.

Arnold, Matthew. 'The Function of Criticism at the Present Time' (1864). In *'Culture and Anarchy' and Other Writings*. Ed. Stefan Collini. Cambridge: Cambridge University Press, 1993. 26–52.

Aspden, Rachel. 'Sex and the City, Egyptian-style'. Review of al-Aswany, *The Yacoubian Building*. *Observer*, February 18, 2007. <http://www.guardian.co.uk/books/2007/feb/18/fiction.features/print>.

Attridge, Derek. 'Don Paterson's *Ars Poetica*'. In *Don Paterson: Contemporary Critical Essays*. Ed. Natalie Pollard. Edinburgh: Edinburgh University Press, 2014. 21–33.

Attridge, Derek. *J. M. Coetzee and the Ethics of Reading: Literature in the Event*. Chicago: University of Chicago Press, 2004.

Attridge, Derek. *Peculiar Language: Literature as Difference from the Renaissance to James Joyce*. 2nd edn., Abingdon: Routledge, 2004.

Attridge, Derek. *Reading and Responsibility: Deconstruction's Traces*. Edinburgh: Edinburgh University Press, 2010.

Attridge, Derek. Review of Martin Hägglund, *Radical Atheism*. *Derrida Today* 2 (2009): 271–81.

Attridge, Derek. *The Rhythms of English Poetry*. London: Longman, 1982.

Attridge, Derek. *The Singularity of Literature*. Abingdon: Routledge, 2004.

Attridge, Derek, and David Jonathan Y. Bayot, *Derek Attridge in Conversation*. Manila: De La Salle University Publishing House, 2014.

Attridge, Derek, and Henry Staten, *The Craft of Poetry: Dialogues on Minimal Interpretation*. Abingdon: Routledge, 2015.

Aw, Tash. 'Upstairs, Downstairs'. Review of al-Aswany, *The Yacoubian Building*. *Daily Telegraph*, January 28, 2007. <http://www.telegraph.co.uk/culture/books/3662789/Upstairs-downstairs.html>.

Badiou, Alain. *Logics of Worlds. Being and Event II*. Trans. Alberto Toscana. London: Continuum, 2013.

Badiou, Alain. 'Que pense le poème?' In *L'art est-il une connaissance?* Ed. Roger-Pol Droit. Paris: Le Monde Éditions, 1993. 214–24.

Badiou, Alain. 'Qu'est-ce que la littérature pense?' In *The Idea of the Literary*. Ed. Nicholas Harrison. Special issue of *Paragraph* 28.2 (July, 2005): 35–40.

Badiou, Alain. *Saint Paul: The Foundation of Universalism*. Trans. Ray Brassier. Stanford: Stanford University Press, 2003.

Badiou, Alain. *Theoretical Writings*. Ed. and trans. Ray Brassier and Alberto Toscano. London: Continuum, 2006.

Barthes, Roland. 'From Work to Text'. In *Image Music Text*. Ed. Stephen Heath. New York: Hill and Wang, 1977. 155–64.

Barthes, Roland. *The Pleasure of the Text*. Trans. Richard Miller. New York: Hill and Wang, 1975.

Barthes, Roland. *The Preparation of the Novel*. Trans. Kate Briggs. New York: Columbia University Press, 2011.

Bateson, F. W. 'The Responsible Critic: Reply' and 'Postscript'. In Leavis, ed., *A Selection from 'Scrutiny'*, 303–8, 315–16.

Bennington, Geoffrey. *Lyotard: Writing the Event*. Manchester: Manchester University Press, 1988.

Best, Stephen, and Sharon Marcus. 'Surface Reading: An Introduction'. *Representations* 108 (2009): 1–21.

Blanchot, Maurice. *The Space of Literature*. Trans. Ann Smock. Lincoln: University of Nebraska Press, 1982.

Boden, Margaret A. 'What is Creativity?' In *Dimensions of Creativity*. Ed. Margaret A. Boden. Cambridge: MIT Press, 1996. 75–117.

Bourdieu, Pierre. *Distinction: A Social Critique of the Judgement of Taste*. Trans. Richard Nice. London: Routledge and Kegan Paul, 1984.

Bourdieu, Pierre. *The Logic of Practice*. Trans. Richard Nice. Cambridge: Polity Press, 1990.

Bourdieu, Pierre. *Pascalian Meditations*. Trans. Richard Nice. Cambridge: Polity Press, 2000.

Bourdieu, Pierre. *The Rules of Art: Genesis and Structure of the Literary Field*. Trans. Susan Emanuel. Stanford: Stanford University Press, 1995.

Boyd, William. *Any Human Heart*. London: Hamish Hamilton, 2002.

Bradley, A. C. 'Poetry for Poetry's Sake'. In Bradley, *Oxford Lectures on Poetry*, 2nd edn. London: Macmillan, 1959. 3–36.

Brooks, Cleanth. 'Criticism and Literary History: Marvell's Horation Ode'. *Sewanee Review* 55 (1947): 199–222.

Brooks, Cleanth. 'A Note on the Limits of "History" and the Limits of "Criticism"'. *Sewanee Review* 61 (1953): 129–35.

Bush, Douglas. 'Marvell's Horatian Ode'. *Sewanee Review* 60 (1952): 363–76.

Butler, Judith. *Giving an Account of Oneself*. New York: Fordham University Press, 2005.

Cameron, Dan, Carolyn Christov-Bakargiev, and J. M. Coetzee. *William Kentridge*. London: Phaidon, 1999.

Caputo, John D. *Deconstruction in a Nutshell: Conversations with Jacques Derrida*. New York: Fordham University Press, 1997.

Carter, Ronald. *Language and Creativity: The Art of Common Talk*. London: Routledge, 2004.

Cassin, Barbara, ed. *Dictionary of Untranslatables: A Philosophical Lexicon*. Translation edited by Emily Apter, Jacques Lezra, and Michael Wood. Princeton: Princeton University Press, 2014.

Chaouli, Michel. 'Criticism and Style'. *New Literary History* 44 (2013): 323–44.

Cheah, Pheng. 'To Open: Hospitality and Alienation'. In *The Conditions of Hospitality: Ethics, Politics, and Aesthetics on the Threshold of the Possible*. Ed. Thomas Claviez. New York: Fordham University Press, 2013. 57–80.

Clark, Timothy. *Derrida, Heidegger, Blanchot: Sources of Derrida's Notion and Practice of Literature*. Cambridge: Cambridge University Press, 1992.

Clark, Timothy. *The Poetics of Singularity: The Counter-Culturalist Turn in Heidegger, Derrida, Blanchot and the Later Gadamer*. Edinburgh: Edinburgh University Press, 2005.

Clark, Timothy. 'Singularity in Criticism', review of Attridge, *The Singularity of Literature*. *The Cambridge Quarterly* 33 (2004): 395–8.

Clark, Timothy. *The Theory of Inspiration: Composition as a Crisis of Subjectivity in Romantic and Post-Romantic Writing*. Manchester: Manchester University Press, 1997.

Coetzee, J. M. 'As a Woman Grows Older'. *New York Review of Books*, Jan 15, 2004. <http://www.nybooks.com/articles/archives/2004/jan/15/as-a-woman-grows-older/>.

Coetzee, J. M.. *Diary of a Bad Year*. London: Harvill Secker, 2007.

Coetzee, J. M.. *Disgrace*. London: Secker and Warburg, 1999.

Coetzee, J. M.. *Elizabeth Costello: Eight Lessons*. London: Secker and Warburg, 2003.

Coetzee, J. M.. *Inner Workings: Literary Essays 2000–2005*. London: Harvill Secker, 2007.

Coetzee, J. M.. *The Master of Petersburg*. London: Secker and Warburg, 1994.

Coleridge, S. T. *Collected Letters*. Ed. E. L. Griggs. 6 vols. Oxford: Oxford University Press, 1956–71.

Collini, Stefan, ed. *Interpretation and Overinterpretation*. Cambridge: Cambridge University Press, 1992.

Connor, Steven. 'Modernism and the Writing Hand' [1999] <http://www.bbk.ac.uk/english/skc/modhand.htm>.

Culler, Jonathan. 'Derrida and the Singularity of Literature', *Cardozo Law Review* 27 (2005–6): 869–75.

Danto, Arthur. 'The Artworld'. *Journal of Philosophy* 61 (1964): 571–84.

Davidson, Donald. *Inquiries into Truth and Interpretation*. Oxford: Oxford University Press, 1984.

Davidson, Donald. 'Locating Literary Language'. In *Literary Theory after Davidson*. Ed. Reed W. Dasenbrock. University Park: Pennsylvania State University Press, 1993. 295–308.

Davidson, Donald. 'What Metaphors Mean'. In *On Metaphor*. Ed. Sheldon Sacks. Chicago: University of Chicago Press, 1979. 29–45.

Davies, Peter Maxwell. *Mr Emmet Takes a Walk*. London: Boosey & Hawkes, 1999.

Davies, Stephen. 'Responding Emotionally to Fictions'. *Journal of Aesthetics and Art Criticism* 67 (2009): 269–84.

De Bolla, Peter. *Art Matters*. Cambridge: Harvard University Press, 2001.

De Man, Paul. *Allegories of Reading: Figural Language in Rousseau, Nietzsche, Rilke, and Proust*. New Haven: Yale University Press, 1979.

De Ville, Jacques. *Law as Absolute Hospitality*. London: Routledge, 2011.

Deleuze, Gilles. *The Logic of Sense*. Ed. Constantin V. Boundas, trans. Mark Lester with Charles Stivale. New York: Columbia University Press, 2004.

Deleuze, Gilles. 'On Leibniz'. *Lectures by Gilles Deleuze*. <http://deleuzelectures.blogspot.co.uk/2007/02/on-leibniz.html>.

Derrida, Jacques. *Acts of Literature*. Ed. Derek Attridge. New York: Routledge, 1992.

Derrida, Jacques. *Aporias*. Trans. Thomas Dutoit. Stanford: Stanford University Press, 1993.

Derrida, Jacques. 'As If It Were Possible: "Within Such Limits"...' In Derrida, *Negotiations*. Ed. and trans. Elizabeth Rottenberg. Stanford: Stanford University Press, 2002. 343–70.

Derrida, Jacques. 'At This Very Moment in This Work Here I Am'. In *Re-Reading Levinas*. Ed. Robert Bernasconi and Simon Critchley. Bloomington: Indiana University Press, 1991. 11–48.

Derrida, Jacques. 'Autoimmunity: Real and Symbolic Suicides'. In Giovanni Borradori, *Philosophy in a Time of Terror: Dialogues with Jürgen Habermas and Jacques Derrida*. Chicago: University of Chicago Press, 2003. 85–136.

Derrida, Jacques. *The Beast and the Sovereign*, vol. 1. Trans. Geoffrey Bennington. Chicago: University of Chicago Press, 2009.

Derrida, Jacques. '"Cette étrange institution qu'on appelle la littérature"'. In *Derrida d'ici, Derrida de la*. Ed. Thomas Dutoit et Philippe Romanski. Paris: Galilée, 2009. 253–92.

Derrida, Jacques. 'Che cos'è la poesia?' In *A Derrida Reader: Between the Blinds*. Ed. Peggy Kamuf. New York: Columbia University Press, 1991. 221–37.

Derrida, Jacques. *Cosmopolitanism and Forgiveness*. Trans. Mark Dooley and Michael Hughes. London: Routledge, 2001.

Derrida, Jacques. 'Envois'. In Derrida, *The Post Card: From Socrates to Freud and Beyond*. Trans. Alan Bass. Chicago: University of Chicago Press, 1987. 1–256.

Derrida, Jacques. 'Force of Law: The "Mystical Foundation of Authority"'. In *Deconstruction and the Possibility of Justice*. Ed. Drucilla Cornell, Michel Rosenfeld, and David Gray Carlson. New York: Routledge, 1992. 3–67.

Derrida, Jacques. *The Gift of Death & Literature in Secret*. Trans. David Wills. Chicago: The University of Chicago Press, 2008.

Derrida, Jacques. *Given Time: I. Counterfeit Money*. Trans. Peggy Kamuf. Chicago: University of Chicago Press, 1992.

Derrida, Jacques. 'Hospitality, Justice and Responsibility: A Dialogue with Jacques Derrida'. In *Questioning Ethics: Contemporary Debates in Philosophy*. Ed. Richard Kearney and Mark Dooley. London: Routledge, 1999. 65–83.

Derrida, Jacques. 'Hostipitality'. *Angelaki* 5.3 (2000): 3–18.

Derrida, Jacques. 'Hostipitality'. In *Acts of Religion*. Ed. Gil Anidjar. New York: Routledge, 2002. 356–420.

Derrida, Jacques. 'I Have a Taste for the Secret'. In Jacques Derrida and Maurizio Ferraris, *A Taste for the Secret*. Trans. Giacomo Donis. Ed. Giacomo Donis and David Webb. Malden, MA: Blackwell, 2001. 1–92.

Derrida, Jacques. 'Literature in Secret: An Impossible Filiation'. In Derrida, *The Gift of Death*. Trans. 117–58.

Derrida, Jacques. *Manifeste pour l'hospitalité*. Ed. Mohammed Seffahi. Grigny: Éditions Paroles d'Aube, 1999.

Derrida, Jacques. *Paper Machine*. Trans. Rachel Bowlby. Stanford: Stanford University Press, 2005.

Derrida, Jacques. 'Passions: "An Oblique Offering"'. In *Derrida: A Critical Reader*. Ed. David Wood. Oxford: Blackwell, 1992. 5–35.

Derrida, Jacques. *Politics of Friendship*. Trans. George Collins. London: Verso, 1997.

Derrida, Jacques. 'Psyche: Invention of the Other'. In Derrida, *Psyche: Inventions of the Other*, volume 1. Ed. Peggy Kamuf and Elizabeth Rottenberg. Stanford: Stanford University Press, 2007, 1–47.

Derrida, Jacques. *Rogues: Two Essays on Reason*. Trans. Pascale-Anne Brault and Michael Naas. Stanford: Stanford University Press, 2005.

Derrida, Jacques. 'Signature Event Context'. In Derrida, *Limited Inc*. Ed. Gerald Graff. Evanston: Northwestern University Press, 1977. 1–23.

Derrida, Jacques. *Signéponge/Signsponge*. Trans. Richard Rand. New York: Columbia University Press, 1974.

Derrida, Jacques. '"This Strange Institution Called Literature": An Interview with Jacques Derrida'. *Acts of Literature*. 33–75.

Derrida, Jacques. 'To Forgive: The Unforgivable and the Imprescriptible'. In *Questioning God*. Ed. John D. Caputo, Mark Dooley, and Michael J. Scanlon. Bloomington: University of Indiana Press, 2001. 21–51.

Derrida, Jacques. 'The University without Condition'. In Derrida, *Without Alibi*. Ed. Peggy Kamuf. Stanford: Stanford University Press, 2002. 202–37.

Derrida, Jacques. 'Violence and Metaphysics: An Essay on the Thought of Emmanuel Levinas'. In Derrida, *Writing and Difference*. Trans. Alan Bass. London: Routledge and Kegan Paul, 1978. 79–153.

Derrida, Jacques. 'White Mythology: Metaphor in the Text of Philosophy'. In Derrida, *Margins of Philosophy*. Trans. Alan Bass. Chicago: University of Chicago Press, 1982. 207–72.

Derrida, Jacques, and Anne Dufourmantelle. *Of Hospitality*. Trans. Rachel Bowlby. Stanford: Stanford University Press, 2000.

Derrida, Jacques, Marc Guillaume, and Jean-Pierre Vincent. *Marx en jeu*. Paris: Descartes & Cie, 1997.

Derrida, Jacques, and Elisabeth Roudinesco. *For What Tomorrow…A Dialogue*. Stanford: Stanford University Press, 2004.

Dewey, John. *Art as Experience*. New York: G. P. Putnam's Sons, 1958.

Dick, Kirby, and Amy Ziering Kofman. *Derrida: Screenplay and Essays on the Film*. Manchester: Manchester University Press, 2005.

Dickie, George. *The Art Circle: A Theory of Art*. New York: Haven, 1984.

Dickinson, Emily. *Poems: Reading Edition*. Ed. R. W. Franklin. Cambridge: Harvard University Press, 1998.

Dimock, Wai-Chee. 'A Theory of Resonance'. *PMLA* 112 (1997): 1060–71.

Donoghue, Emma. *Room*. London: Picador, 2010.

Dryden, John. *Poems 1685–1692*; *Works*, vol. 3. Ed. Earl Miner and Vinton A. Dearing. Berkeley: University of California Press, 1969.

Dufrenne, Mikel. *The Phenomenology of Aesthetic Experience*. Trans. Edward S. Casey et al. Evanston: Northwestern University Press, 1973.

Dutton, Denis, ed. *The Forger's Art: Forgery and the Philosophy of Art*. Berkeley: University of California Press, 1987.

Eliot, T. S. *Selected Essays*. New York: Harcourt Brace Jovanovich, 1950.

Emerson, Ralph Waldo. 'Shakspeare; or, the Poet.' In Emerson, *Representative Men* (1850). <http://www.bartleby.com/90/0405.html>

Empson, William. *Seven Types of Ambiguity.* Third Edition. New York: New Directions, 1966.

Felski, Rita. '"Context Stinks"'. *New Literary History* 42 (2011): 573–91.

Felski, Rita. *Uses of Literature.* Malden, MA: Blackwell, 2008.

Fish, Stanley. 'How to Recognize a Poem When You See One'. In Fish, *Is There a Text in this Class?: The Authority of Interpretive Communities.* Cambridge: Harvard University Press, 1980. 322–37.

Fisher, Philip. *Wonder, the Rainbow, and the Aesthetics of Rare Experiences.* Cambridge: Harvard University Press, 1998.

Freeman, John. 'A Window into Rich Life of Cairo Apartments'. *San Francisco Chronicle,* August 13. <http://www.sfgate.com/cgi-bin/article.cgi?f=/c/a/2006/08/13/RVGROK9TJ91.DTL>.

Freeman, Lisa A. 'Why We Argue about The Way We Read: Introduction'. *Eighteenth Century* 54 (2013): 121–4.

Gasché, Rodolphe. *Inventions of Difference: On Jacques Derrida.* Cambridge: Harvard University Press, 1994.

Gasché, Rodolphe. *Of Minimal Things: Studies on the Notion of Relation.* Stanford: Stanford University Press, 1999.

Gasché, Rodolphe. *The Wild Card of Reading: On Paul de Man.* Cambridge: Harvard University Press, 1998.

Gaut, Berys. *Art, Emotion and Ethics.* Oxford: Oxford University Press, 2007.

Genette, Gérard. *The Aesthetic Relation.* Trans. G. M. Goshgarian. Ithaca: Cornell University Press, 1999.

Genette, Gérard. *The Work of Art: Immanence and Transcendence.* Trans. G. M. Goshgarian. Ithaca: Cornell University Press, 1997.

Gibbs, Jr, Raymond W. *The Poetics of Mind: Figurative Thought, Language, and Understanding.* Cambridge: Cambridge University Press, 1994.

Goodman, Nelson. *Languages of Art: An Approach to a Theory of Symbols.* 2nd edition. Indianapolis: Hackett, 1976.

Gourgouris, Stathis. *Does Literature Think? Literature as Theory for an Antimythical Era.* Stanford: Stanford University Press, 2003.

Graves, Robert. *Collected Poems 1965.* London: Cassell, 1965.

Greenberg, Clement. *Collected Essays and Criticism,* vol. 4: 'Modernism with a Vengeance, 1957–1969'. Chicago: University of Chicago Press, 1995.

Grenville, Kate. *Sarah Thornhill.* New York: Grove Press, 2012.

Guibbory, Achsah, ed. *The Cambridge Companion to John Donne.* Cambridge: Cambridge University Press, 2006.

Hägglund, Martin. 'The Non-Ethical Opening of Ethics: A Response to Derek Attridge'. *Derrida Today* 3 (2010): 295–305.

Hägglund, Martin. *Radical Atheism: Derrida and the Time of Life.* Stanford: Stanford University Press, 2008.

Hale, Dorothy J. 'Fiction as Restriction: Self-Binding in New Ethical Theory of the Novel'. *Narrative* 15 (2007): 187–206.

Hallward, Peter. *Absolutely Postcolonial: Writing between the Singular and the Specific.* Manchester: Manchester University Press, 2001.

Hallward, Peter. *Badiou: A Subject to Truth.* Minneapolis: University of Minnesota Press, 2003.

Halter, Ed. Review of William Kentridge, '9 Drawings for Projection'. *The Village Voice,* February 14th, 2006. <http://www.villagevoice.com/film/0607,halter,%2072199,20.html>

Hardy, Thomas. *Complete Poems.* Ed. James Gibson. London: Macmillan, 1976.

Harrison, Bernard. *Henry Fielding's 'Tom Jones': The Novelist as Moral Philosopher.* Brighton: Sussex University Press, 1975.

Heidegger, Martin. 'What Calls for Thinking?' In Heidegger, *Basic Writings.* Ed. David Farrell Krell. New York: Harper & Row, 1977. 341–68.

Heidegger, Martin. *What is Called Thinking?* Trans. J. Glenn Gray. New York: Harper & Row, 1968.

Housman, A. E. *The Name and Nature of Poetry.* Cambridge: Cambridge University Press, 1933.

Hughes, Ted. *Collected Poems.* Ed. Paul Keegan. London: Faber and Faber, 2003.

Hume, David. *A Treatise of Human Nature.* London: J. M. Dent, 1911.

Hurley, Michael D. 'How Philosophers Trivialize Art: *Bleak House, Oedipus Rex,* "Leda and the Swan"'. *Philosophy and Literature,* 33 (2009): 107–25.

Ingarden, Roman. *The Literary Work of Art: An Investigation of the Borderlines of Ontology, Logic and the Theory of Language.* Evanston: Northwestern University Press, 1973.

Iser, Wolfgang. *The Act of Reading: A Theory of Aesthetic Response.* Baltimore: John Hopkins University Press, 1978.

Jakobson, Roman. 'Closing Statement, from the Viewpoint of Linguistics: Linguistics and Poetics'. In *Style in Language.* Ed. Thomas A. Sebeok. Cambridge: M.I.T. Press, 1960. 350–77.

James, Henry. *What Maisie Knew.* Ed. Douglas Jefferson. Oxford: Oxford University Press, 1966.

Jarvis, Simon. 'What Does Art Know?' In *Aesthetics and the Work of Art: Adorno, Kafka, Richter.* Ed. Peter de Bolla and Stefan H. Uhlig. London: Palgrave Macmillan, 2009. 57–70.

Johnson, Thomas H., and Theodora Ward, eds. *The Letters of Emily Dickinson.* 3 vols. Cambridge: Harvard University Press, 1958.

Kafalenos, Emma. 'Emotions Induced by Narratives'. *Poetics Today,* 29 (2008): 377–84.

Kamuf, Peggy. 'Deconstruction and Love'. In *Deconstructions: A User's Guide.* Ed. Nicholas Royle. London: Palgrave, 2000. 151–70.

Kamuf, Peggy. *To Follow: The Wake of Jacques Derrida.* Edinburgh: Edinburgh University Press, 2010.

Kant, Immanuel. *Critique of Judgment*. Trans. Werner S. Pluhar. Indianapolis: Hackett Publishing Company, 1987.

Keats, John. *Selected Letters*. Ed. Grant F. Scott. Revised edition. Cambridge: Harvard University Press, 2002.

Kenner, Hugh. *A Homemade World*. New York: Alfred A. Knopf, 1975.

Kittler, Friedrich. *Discourse Networks, 1800/1900*. Trans. Michael Metteer with Chris Cullens. Stanford: Stanford University Press, 1990.

Kittler, Friedrich. *Gramophone, Film, Typewriter*. Trans. Geoffrey Winthrop-Young and Michael Wutz. Stanford: Stanford University Press, 1999.

Kronick, Joseph. 'Between Act and Archive: Literature in the Nuclear Age'. In *Future Crossings: Literature between Philosophy and Cultural Studies*. Ed. Krzysztof Ziarek and Seamus Deane. Evanston: Northwestern University Press, 2000. 52–75.

Lakoff, George, and Mark Johnson. *Metaphors We Live By*. Chicago, University of Chicago Press, 1980.

Lamarque, Peter. *The Philosophy of Literature*. Malden, MA: Blackwell, 2009.

Lamarque, Peter, et al. Symposium on Lamarque, *The Philosophy of Literature*, *British Journal of Aesthetics* 50:1 (2010): 77–106.

Langer, Susanne. *Feeling and Form*. New York: Charles Scribner's Sons, 1953.

Langer, Susanne. *Philosophy in a New Key*. Cambridge: Harvard University Press, 1942.

Lawlor, Leonard. 'Jacques Derrida'. *Stanford Encyclopedia of Philosophy*. <http://plato.stanford.edu/entries/derrida/>.

Leavis, F. R. *The Common Pursuit*. London: Chatto and Windus, 1952.

Leavis, F. R. *New Bearings in English Poetry: A Study of the Contemporary Situation* (1932). Harmondsworth: Penguin, 1972.

Leavis, F. R. 'The Responsible Critic, or the Function of Criticism at Any Time' and 'Rejoinder'. In *A Selection from 'Scrutiny'*, vol. 2, 280–303, 308–15.

Leavis, F. R. *Revaluation: Tradition and Development in English Poetry*. Harmondsworth: Penguin, 1964.

Leavis, F. R., ed. *A Selection from Scrutiny*, 2 vols. Cambridge: Cambridge University Press, 1968.

Leighton, Angela. *On Form: Poetry, Aestheticism, and the Legacy of a Word*. Oxford: Oxford University Press, 2007.

Levinas, Emmanuel. *Autrement qu'être ou au-dela de l'essence*. Paris: Kluwer Academic, 1996.

Levinas, Emmanuel. 'Entretien.' In *Lire Levinas*. Ed. Salomon Malka. Paris: Cerf, 1989. 103–14.

Levinas, Emmanuel. *Otherwise than Being, or Beyond Essence*. Trans. Alphonso Lingis. Pittsburgh: Duquesne University Press, 1998.

Levinas, Emmanuel. *Totality and Infinity: An Essay on Exteriority*. Trans. Alphonso Lingis. Pittsburgh: Duquesne University Press, 1969.

Love, Heather. 'Close but not Deep: Literary Ethics and the Descriptive Turn'. *New Literary History* 41 (2010): 71–91.

Macherey, Pierre. *A quoi pense la littérature?* Paris: PUF, 1990.

Macherey, Pierre. *The Object of Literature*. Trans. David Macey. Cambridge: Cambridge University Press, 1995.

Mack, Michael. *How Literature Changes the Way We Think*. London: Continuum, 2012.

Marcus, Sharon. *Between Women: Friendship, Desire, and Marriage in Victorian England*. Princeton: Princeton University Press, 2009.

Massumi, Brian. *Parables for the Virtual: Movement, Affect, Sensation*. Durham, NC: Duke University Press, 2002.

Matravers, Derek. *Art and Emotion*. Oxford: Oxford University Press, 1998.

McCarthy, Cormac. *Blood Meridian, or, The Evening Redness in the West*. London: Picador, 1989.

Mehrez, Samia. *Egypt's Culture Wars: Politics and Practice*. London: Routledge, 2008.

Miller, Andrew H. 'Implicative Criticism, or the Display of Thinking'. *New Literary History* 44 (2013): 345–60.

Miller, J. Hillis. 'Derrida's Topographies'. In Miller, *Topographies*. Stanford: Stanford University Press, 1995. 291–315.

Muldoon, Paul. *The End of the Poem: Oxford Lectures in Poetry*. London: Faber and Faber, 2009.

Muldoon, Paul. *General Admission*. Oldcastle: Gallery Books, 2006.

Muldoon, Paul. *Moy Sand and Gravel*. London: Faber and Faber, 2010.

Muldoon, Paul. *To Ireland, I*. London: Faber and Faber, 2011.

Naas, Michael. *Derrida from Now On*. New York: Fordham University Press, 2008.

Naas, Michael. *Taking on the Tradition: Jacques Derrida and the Legacies of Deconstruction*. Stanford: Stanford University Press, 2003.

Nancy, Jean-Luc. *Being Singular Plural*. Trans. Robert D. Richardson and Anne E. O'Byrne. Stanford: Stanford University Press, 2000.

Nancy, Jean-Luc. *The Inoperative Community*. Ed. Peter Connor. Trans. Peter Connor et al. Minneapolis: University of Minnesota Press, 1991.

Ngai, Sianne. *Ugly Feelings*. Cambridge, MA: Harvard University Press, 2005.

Nice, Pamela. 'A Conversation with Alaa al-Aswany on *The Yacoubian Building*'. *Al Jadid* 12.56/57. <http://www.aljadid.com/interviews/Alaa-al-Aswany-interview.html>.

North, Christopher. 'Noctes Ambrosianae LVI'. *Blackwood's Magazine* 29 (April, 1831), 688–720.

North, Michael. *Novelty: A History of the New*. Chicago: University of Chicago Press, 2013.

Pater, Walter. *The Renaissance: Studies in Art and Poetry* (1893), ed. Adam Phillips. Oxford: Oxford University Press, 1986.

Paterson, Don. 'The Domain of the Poem,' *Poetry Review* 100.4 (Winter 2010): 81–100, and 101.1 (Spring 2011): 71–95.

Piette, Adam. 'Beckett, Affect and the Face'. In *Affects, Texts, and Performativity*. Ed. Alex Houen. Special issue of *Textual Practice*, 25. 2 (2011): 281–95.

Plotnitsky, Arkady. 'Thinking Singularity with Kant and Paul de Man: Aesthetics, Epistemology, History, and Politics'. In *Legacies of Paul de Man*. Ed. Marc Redfield. New York: Fordham University Press, 2007. 129–61.

Quayson, Ato, Debjani Ganguly, and Neil ten Kortenaar. 'Editorial: New Topographies'. *Cambridge Journal of Postcolonial Literary Inquiry* 1 (2014): 1–10.

Rancière, Jacques. *Aesthetics and Its Discontents*. Trans. Steven Corcoran. Cambridge: Polity Press, 2009.

Rancière, Jacques. *The Politics of Aesthetics*. Trans. Gabriel Rockhill. London: Continuum, 2004.

Reynolds, Joshua. *Discourses on Art*. Ed. Robert R. Wark. New Haven: Yale University Press, 1997.

Ricks, Christopher. *Allusion to the Poets*. Oxford: Oxford University Press, 2002.

Ricks, Christopher. *Dylan's Visions of Sin*. New York: Viking, 2003.

Ricks, Christopher. *Essays in Appreciation*. Oxford: Oxford University Press, 1996.

Ricks, Christopher. *The Force of Poetry*. Oxford: Oxford University Press, 1984.

Ricks, Christopher. *Keats and Embarrassment*. Oxford: Oxford University Press, 1974.

Ricoeur, Paul. *The Rule of Metaphor*. Trans. Robert Czerny. Toronto, University of Toronto Press, 1977.

Robinson, Jenefer. *Deeper than Reason: Emotion and Its Role in Literature, Music, and Art*. Oxford: Oxford University Press, 2005.

Rodenbeck, Max. 'The Long Wait: A Special Report on Egypt'. *The Economist*, July 17, 2010.

Rosen, Michael. *Dignity: Its History and Meaning*. Cambridge: Harvard University Press, 2012. Kindle edition.

Rosenblatt, Louise. *The Reader, the Text, the Poem: The Transactional Theory of the Literary Work*. Carbondale: Southern Illinois University Press, 1978.

Ruthven, K. K. *Faking Literature*. Cambridge: Cambridge University Press, 2001.

Salama, Vivan. 'As *Yacoubian Building* Sets to Head West, The Author Discusses the Story's Message'. *Daily News Egypt*, December 8, 2005. <http://archive.today/HRTzr>.

Shusterman, Richard. *The Object of Literary Criticism*. Amsterdam: Rodopi, 1984.

Shusterman, Richard. *Pragmatist Aesthetics: Living Beauty, Rethinking Art*. 2nd edn. Lanham, MD: Rowman & Lirttlefield, 2000.

Sperber, Dan, and Deirdre Wilson. *Relevance: Communication and Cognition*. Cambridge: Harvard University Press, 1988.

Staten, Henry. 'The Origin of the Work of Art in Material Practice'. *New Literary History* 43 (2012): 43–64.

Staten, Henry. 'The Wrong Turn of Aesthetics'. In *Theory after 'Theory'*. Ed. Jane Elliott and Derek Attridge. Abingdon: Routledge, 2011. 223–36.

Still, Judith. *Derrida and Hospitality: Theory and Practice*. Oxford: Oxford University Press, 2010.

Szafraniec, Asja. *Beckett, Derrida, and the Event of Literature*. Stanford: Stanford University Press, 2007.

Taine, Hyppolite. *History of English Literature*. Trans. H. van Laun, vol. I. New York: Holt & Williams, 1871.

Taylor, Dennis. *Hardy's Metres and Victorian Prosody*. Oxford: Oxford University Press, 1988.

Terada, Rei. *Feeling in Theory: Emotion after the 'Death of the Subject'*. Cambridge: Harvard University Press, 2001.

Thomson, Alex. *Deconstruction and Democracy: Derrida's Politics of Friendship*. London: Continuum, 2005.

Turner, Mark. *The Literary Mind*. New York: Oxford University Press, 1996.

Wershler-Henry, Darren. *The Iron Whim: A Fragmented History of Typewriting*. Ithaca, NY: Cornell University Press, 2007.

Wicomb, Zoë. 'The Challenge is to Capture Marginal Stories'. *2 Paragraphs*, Dec. 19, 2013. <http://2paragraphs.com/2013/12/13404/>.

Wicomb, Zoë. *David's Story*. New York: Feminist Press, 2001.

Wilde, Oscar. *The Soul of Man Under Socialism*. <http://www.gutenberg.org/dirs/etext97/slman10h.htm>.

Williams, Raymond. Foreword to L. J. Jordanova, *Languages of Nature: Critical Essays on Science and Literature*. London: Free Association Books, 1986.

Wimsatt, William K., and Monroe Beardsley. *Literary Criticism: A Short History*. London: Routledge & Kegan Paul, 1957.

Wood, Michael. *Literature and the Taste of Knowledge*. Cambridge: Cambridge University Press, 2005.

Ziarek, Krzyzstof. *The Force of Art*. Stanford: Stanford University Press, 2004.

Ziarek, Krzyzstof. *The Historicity of Experience: Modernity, the Avant-Garde, and the Event*. Evanston: Northwestern University Press, 2001.

INDEX